BEYOND POSITIVISM

BEYOND POSITIVISM

Critical Reflections on
International Relations

edited by
Claire Turenne Sjolander
and Wayne S. Cox

Lynne Rienner Publishers ■ Boulder and London

Published in the United States of America in 1994 by
Lynne Rienner Publishers, Inc.
1800 30th Street, Boulder, Colorado 80301

and in the United Kingdom by
Lynne Rienner Publishers, Inc.
3 Henrietta Street, Covent Garden, London WC2E 8LU

Library of Congress Cataloging-in-Publication Data
Beyond positivism : critical reflections on international relations /
    editors, Claire Turenne Sjolander and Wayne S. Cox.
        p. cm.
    Includes bibliographical references and index.
    ISBN 1-55587-483-5 (alk. paper)
        1. International relations—Philosophy. 2. Positivism.
I. Sjolander, Claire Turenne, 1959–   . II. Cox, Wayne S., 1962–
IN PROCESS
327'.01—dc20   93-33324
                                                            CIP

British Cataloguing in Publication Data
A Cataloguing in Publication record for this book
is available from the British Library.

Printed and bound in the United States of America

∞   The paper used in this publication meets the requirements
     of the American National Standard for Permanence of
     Paper for Printed Library Materials Z39.48-1984.

To Pauline Jewett,
whose commitment, ideals,
and radicalism inspired a generation

Contents

Preface

In November 1989, a group of senior graduate students in political science at Carleton University came together out of a mutual desire to explore the metatheoretical debates that were brewing in international relations. In part, this was occasioned by the publication of Yosef Lapid's article "The Third Debate: On the Prospects of International Theory in a Post-Positivist Era" in *International Studies Quarterly*. Lapid was at that time a visiting scholar in the Department of Political Science at Carleton, and his presence spurred us to debate with him the nature and consequences of the "Third Debate" for research in international relations. We believed that his text had captured the movement toward an understanding of the discipline of international relations in metatheoretical terms, yet we also believed that his critics revealed the extent to which the Third Debate, if indeed it had ever really taken place, offered no clear direction to scholarship in the field. It became evident that our sympathy for Lapid's work, as well as for that of his critics, was not simply the result of our rejection of realism, but was in fact the result of a more fundamental rejection of positivism as a theory of knowledge.

This book was engendered by this critical reexamination of the meaning of the Third Debate. The project flourished, however, not only with the support of our authors, but with the assistance of many colleagues and friends. For their financial support as we began the project, we would like to express our gratitude to the deans of the Faculty of Social Sciences and the Faculty of Graduate Studies and Research at Carleton University, as well as to Carleton's Department of Political Science and to the Graduate Students' Association. The Centre for International Relations of Queen's University is to be equally thanked for its financial support. We are most grateful to Michael Dolan and John Sigler for their confidence in the significance and merit of this endeavor. For their helpful comments on key aspects of the project, we are indebted to Brian David Mussington, Jean-François Rioux, Max Cameron, D. Keith Heintzman, Lynn Krieger Mytelka, David Haglund, and Charles Pentland. Fuyuki Kurasawa assisted us in a number of tasks related to the final editing of the manuscript and has our thanks and appreciation. Gail Mordecai has offered constant moral support and has been a wonderful ally in the management of the financial and administrative affairs of this project. The task of editing the manuscript was eased considerably by the support of the wonderful staff at Lynne Rienner Publishers. In particular, we owe our thanks to Michelle Welsh, who was always there to answer our questions about the editing process, and whose helpfulness and patience we deeply appreciate. All of the authors are grateful to Sandra Rush; the entire manuscript benefited from her considerable editorial skills. In addition, we owe a special debt of gratitude to Lynne Rienner, who has been an important help to us and a constant source of encouragement. We would also each like to thank our colleagues at our respective universities for the supportive intellectual environment they have provided us with.

We would be remiss if we did not thank the people in our lives who have had to endure the trauma of the editing of this volume. In particular, we owe a debt to Claire's husband, John, for listening to countless hours of what must have appeared to be incomprehensible debate about the Third Debate, for making innumerable trips between Ottawa and Kingston, Ontario, and yet for always believing that the enterprise had an important purpose. Viggo and Vibeke Sjolander of Kingston, Ontario, have opened their home to us many times during this project. We also would like to express our gratitude to Eleanor Cox, Don and Carole Cox, Robert and Evelyn Turenne, Larry and Marion Rentler, Maureen and David Lees, and Graham Stebbings and Bride Farrell. Their kindness and generosity made the task at hand a little easier.

Finally, we would like to thank each other. As young scholars with little experience in editing, we were quite unaware of the task we had set for ourselves when we accepted the job of project editors. So equal has this partnership been that it seems unfair that one name has to precede the other on the cover or as authors of the introduction. Heads won.

C.T.S.
W.S.C.

1

Critical Reflections on International Relations

Wayne S. Cox & Claire Turenne Sjolander

Fields, of course, are made. They require coherence and integrity in time because scholars devote themselves in different ways to what seems to be a commonly agreed-upon subject matter. Yet it goes without saying that a field of study is rarely as simply defined as even its most committed partisans—usually scholars, professors, experts, and the like—claim it is. Besides, a field can change so entirely, in even the most traditional disciplines like philology, history, or theology, as to make an all-purpose definition of the subject matter almost impossible.

—*Edward Said* (1979)

Fields are made, and nowhere does this seem to be more the case than in the evolution of theory in the study of international relations; for international relations is a field that has developed around a series of explosive, discipline-defining debates. Between World War I and World War II, the "First Debate" of international relations centered around idealist and realist conceptions of global politics. In the 1960s, the "Second Debate" flourished, pitting historical and interpretive methods against behavioralist science. During the 1980s, international relations scholars were confronted by contending interpretations of their field at the level of metatheory, a development some have characterized as the "Third Debate." *Beyond Positivism: Critical Reflections on International Relations* seeks to move beyond the metatheoretical stalemate of the Third Debate, and in so doing, to reopen some of the conclusions of the first and second.

Born of the upheavals of World Wars I and II, the First Debate asked questions as to the subject matter of international relations. Was international relations to be the study of a global, unified society, focusing upon international and supranational mechanisms to manage global conflict (Wilsonian idealism), or was it to be about the international relations of states (realism)? By the 1950s, the study of international relations as defined in North America had come to eschew the voluntarist basis of idealism, and had adopted instead the statist, power-centered conceptions of global politics found in realism. Tempered by two world wars, realism became the dominant theoretical approach in a discipline increasingly oriented by problem-solving research projects with subfields defined around such issues as foreign policy studies, conflict analysis, and war studies.

During the 1960s, international relations' Second Debate asked questions as to which method was most appropriate in the search for knowledge in the field. A reflection of the larger "behavioral revolution" that was burning throughout the social sciences, the Second Debate focused upon the choice between the scientific method, with its implied capacity for value-free research, and historicism, often accused of ransacking history in the interests of (normative) theoretical objectives. The outcome of this Second Debate was found in the imperfect dominance of behavioralist methods and of an underlying positivist scholarship in international relations. In part, the dominance of behavioralism was attributable to its success in defining the research agenda of related social science disciplines—in particular, economics and psychology. As well, the rationalist basis of the scientific method in disciplinary terms coincided well with the rationalism of postwar Western society, particularly in its emphasis on science as the potential solution to all problems. Finally, the behavioral revolution was successful insofar as it appeared to proffer the tools that would further the research-problem orientation of realism; war studies, for example, could now depend on huge data bases that detailed the occurrence and mortality of wars throughout the ages.

By the early 1970s, an uncomfortable relationship had developed between the conclusions derived by behavioralist-realist scholarship and changing international realities. This lack of congruence was particularly worrisome for the research-problem-driven field that international relations had become. The oil crises of the 1970s challenged the realist assumption that large, industrialized states were the only crucial actors in global politics and suggested that a preeminent focus on military and war studies might not capture the major sources of potential international conflict. At the same time, the Vietnam War seemed to challenge many of realism's state-power assumptions, and the activities of multinational corporations along with the dependency relationship between the First and Third Worlds raised questions as to the realist assumption that war and peace were the most important problems faced by the international system. The shifting grounds of international politics also led to charges that the method of international relations scholarship had driven the field to trivialize that which could not be quantified, and had thus further limited the discipline's ability to respond to international changes.

The initial response to these challenges was to be found in one simple idea—greater intellectual pluralism. Although the study of international relations remained basically a realist and, more fundamentally, a positivist pursuit, the margins of the discipline became open to new scholarship that redefined both its content and method. The pluralist "moment" of the 1970s created its own confusions, however—confusions that were particularly frustrating to a discipline long used to defining its contributions to knowledge in terms of specific research agendas. By the late 1970s, therefore, international relations set about redefining itself yet again, this time as neorealism.

The neorealist project expanded the boundaries of the field as it had been defined under realism (legitimizing the study of nonmilitary issues, for example) while it reasserted the primacy of positivist "science" (although not insisting on the quantitative bent of the behavioralist revolution). Not surprisingly, the strongest critics of neorealism emerged largely, although not exclusively, from outside the U.S. international relations community. These critiques were in great part heightened by neorealism's claim not to have a political project, a position consistent with the positivist claims of value neutrality inherent in neorealism's orientation to science. By further marginalizing the critics who had been allowed, if only to a limited extent, to flourish under the pluralist moment, neorealism almost necessarily led to a questioning of the political premises of its agenda. The clash between critics and neorealists crystallized in the interparadigm debate of the 1980s. For the first time in the evolution of international relations, metatheoretical distinctions between paradigms became important, at least for some.

Throughout the decade of the 1980s, therefore, the discipline of international relations found a new subject for evaluation—itself. Motivating this introspection, the boundaries of the discipline appeared increasingly unclear and at times even contradictory. Although this clash between critics and neorealists has been labeled as the third of the discipline-defining debates in international relations, a decade of paradigm definition did not enable the field to move beyond the level of metatheoretical distinctions. Critics, united in their desire to reveal the political agenda behind neorealist scholarship, nevertheless were unable to put forward a consistent definition of the basis of paradigm division. The Third Debate, therefore, became characterized by the elaboration of typologies of international relations paradigms, variously emphasizing method-ological, value, subject, and epistemological distinctions.

In the face of a proliferation of metatheoretical typologies, soci-ologists of the Third Debate (Lapid, 1989, or Holsti, 1985, for exam-ple) called for a renewed pluralism—the construction of a new plu-ralist moment in international relations. In contradistinction to the pluralism of the 1970s, the pluralism of the Third Debate would be tied to metatheoretical concerns rather than to specific research pro-grams or projects. Cast in such a light, however, the Third Debate at the close of the 1980s looked a lot like the interventions against the redefinition of realism present at the outset of the decade. As a result, even sympathetic scholars were led to trivialize the Third Debate, limiting its contribution as "yet another preface to a major project . . . another call to a new beginning, another metatheoretical debate for the consumers of international relations theory" (Biersteker, 1989:266).

The dawn of the 1990s has found the interparadigm, or Third Debate, at an impasse. Although it revealed the existence and importance of political projects and related metatheoretical presup-positions, unlike its predecessors the Third Debate could not offer a clear path to choice. The first two debates posed themselves as choices permitting the construction of better theory; realism was preferable to idealism, and positivism to historicism, because these routes were deemed to offer better avenues to scholarship. In this context, the Third Debate was never a true debate precisely because it avoided advancing criteria that would permit a choice between paradigms.

In its wake, the Third Debate has left open two broad avenues for research in international relations. The first has seen scholars return to more traditional research projects and research agendas, many similar to those that have defined international relations scholarship since its inception. The second avenue has been marked by a critical turn, with scholars preoccupied by the more fundamen-tal implications of the metatheoretical distinctions suggested by the Third Debate. In particular, this questioning has highlighted episte-mology as one of the key remaining issues international relations has failed to examine. Whereas the First Debate, with its preoccupa-tion with the subject of international relations, suggested a theory of being, and the Second Debate around methodological considerations proposed a theory of doing, international relations has only skirted the essence of a real third debate, one that would preoccupy itself with a theory of knowing. As the critics of neorealism variously sought to uncover the political project underlying realism's reconstruction, scholarship of necessity became more sensitive to the fact that fields of study are politically constructed—that, in Edward Said's words, fields are made. This sensitivity becomes the criterion of reflexivity: "the capacity of a perspective to reflect on its own origins and conditions of existence" (Gill and Law, 1988:23). How we approach theory becomes the central question, and the central dichotomy becomes one between positivist and postpositivist, or theoretically reflexive, avenues. This, we argue, becomes the true legacy of the Third Debate, the distinction between those for whom knowledge is socially constructed and theory is therefore inherently reflexive, and those for whom it is not. As international relations learns to self-consciously reflect upon itself, the construction of the choices of the First and Second Debates become more apparent, and new avenues for research are opened.

While this critical project has thus begun to expose the limits of traditional theoretical constructs in the discipline, the insights of these critical perspectives have only occasionally been used as a basis upon which alternative understandings of international relations can be developed. This has meant, in effect, that the full implications of theoretical reflexivity within the field remain largely unexplored. *Beyond Positivism: Critical Reflections on International Relations* accepts as a starting point the value of critical perspectives and celebrates the resulting potential toward theoretical reflexivity in the discipline. In order to build upon this critical foundation, however, we must move well beyond the Third Debate and seek to redefine a field that concerns itself intrinsically not only with being and with doing, but also with knowing. The lessons of reflexivity must become paramount, leaving open the reconstruction of international relations as a discipline without the limitations of the choices advanced by the First and Second Debates.

This book evaluates the merits of a critical approach to international relations theory and displays the virtues of reflexivity in addressing the contemporary concerns of the discipline. The chapters share in common a critical perspective on the traditional development of international relations theory. As such, they all seriously question the state-centric realist, as well as the positivist assumptions that have guided so much of the scholarship in the study of international relations. Their shared commitment to reflexive theory leads them to eschew the subject/object distinction inherent in positivism, and thus to accept the centrality of the political or normative content of international relations theory. The chapters, therefore, are motivated by a concern with the fact that theorizing about "empirical reality" helps to construct that very reality, an orientation that permits both theoretical and empirical explorations beyond the central concerns as defined by mainstream international relations theory. These chapters do not, however, aspire to the creation of a new counterhegemony, but rather seek to bring reflexive concerns into the subject matter at the mainstream of the field. The book raises theoretical issues stemming from critical perspectives on the discipline and proposes paths to research suggested by these critical avenues.

In the text's opening chapter, "Reflexivity and International Relations Theory," Mark Neufeld establishes a context in which we can evaluate the contribution of the Third Debate and proposes ways by which the study of international relations can move in a direction genuinely marked by reflexive research. He argues that the Third Debate in itself has not enhanced the prospects for the growth of a theoretically reflexive discipline and questions the utility of the paradigmatic conceptualizations of the discipline that were at the heart of this interparadigm debate. To move beyond the stalemate of the Third Debate, scholarship must reconceptualize the discipline and abandon the positivist tenet of truth as correspondence and its implied assumption of the separation of subject and object, which has inhibited theoretical reflexivity. Applying the insights of political and social theory, Neufeld proposes the concept of stances as a means to evaluate the possibilities for theoretical reflexivity. This concept of stances serves as a useful epistemological tool that lends focus to the remaining chapters in the volume, all the while elaborating the bases of the critical project in international relations.

Following this introductory chapter, which raises the critical metatheoretical issues left unanswered by the Third Debate, the volume turns its attention to the application of this postpositivist, critical base in the construction of theoretical alternatives through an examination of a series of cases. In response to the concerns raised by Biersteker and others as to the utility of the Third Debate in the development of international relations, the next three chapters help to answer the more general question of what postpositivist scholarship might look like. Each of these chapters examines an issue of current concern to the discipline: U.S. hegemony and international trade, the new world order and the Gulf War, and the role of multinational corporations in defining the international energy regime. Each does so, however, through the adoption of an orientation to research that is decidedly neither realist nor positivist, founded on the assumption that all theory is inherently political.

Claire Turenne Sjolander's chapter, "The Discourse of Multilateralism: U.S. Hegemony and the Management of International Trade," examines the apparently contradictory free trade/fair trade manifestations of the discourse of U.S. trade policy. In particular, the chapter focuses on the U.S. negotiating position with respect to "new issues" in the Uruguay Round of GATT negotiations. Turenne Sjolander argues that the free trade focus on multilateralism characteristic of the postwar era in fact helped to conceal an agenda defined narrowly by the hegemonic interests inherent in Pax Americana. In contrast, the current fair trade derogations from this rhetoric respond not so much to a decline in the hegemonic order per se, but rather to a change in the role of the United States within that order. The consequences of this derogation, however, are to be found not only in a need to retheorize the foundation of the role of the state in international trade itself, but also in a fundamental weakening of the basis of the multilateral trade structure, with important implications for the other participants within it. Trade policy analyses that do not ask who theory is for and why all too often fail to identify the normative basis of the structure of international trade and of the discourse of the leading players within it.

Moving from this discussion of U.S. hegemony in the realm of international trade, Wayne Cox launches an analysis of the role of hegemonic social relations in the use of violence by both state institutions and civil societies. In his chapter "The Politics of Violence: Global Relations, Social Structures, and the Middle East," Cox addresses the theoretical inadequacy of state-centric realist and neorealist conceptions of the war and peace *problematique*, which has been central to the discipline of international relations. He argues that the theorizing of state agency alone is a wholly inadequate means by which to conceive of the social basis of violence, and he calls into question the apolitical nature of such theorizing. In an overview of the Iran-Iraq War and its links to the Gulf War, Cox addresses the nature of relationships of dominant and subordinate groups and theorizes social violence within a framework that integrates both the state and civil society. A sociostructural conceptualization of violence allows us to analyze long-term social relations within both domestic and international societies, understanding, for example, that the domestic upheavals of the Iranian revolution were an important factor in the Iraqi decision to launch a transboundary war, and laid the ground for Iraqi aggression against Kuwait. This new conceptualization of international relations theory's central *problematique* defies the traditional compartmentalization of mainstream conceptualizations and offers a more holistic appreciation of the global environment as a result.

In affirmation of the argument of previous chapters that non-state actors are significant in global politics, the third case chapter addresses the predominant role of multinational corporations in shaping international economic regimes. In a chapter entitled "Neo-

8   *Wayne S. Cox & Claire Turenne Sjolander*

realism or Hegemony? The Seven Sisters' Energy Regime," Gregg J. Legare undertakes an analysis of international energy relations over the last fifty years to evaluate the claims of regime theorists and neo-realists that state power and hegemonic stability are the key factors in explaining the international system and the prevalence of order or disorder within it. The chapter argues that the development of the international energy economy directly contradicts one of the key assertions of neorealist regime theory—that state power sets the conditions for societal power and brings order to international relations. In particular, rather than states being "naturally in a state of anarchy," this chapter argues that state intervention around the axis of North-South conflict actually created anarchy and volatility in the international political economy. Far from being a force for order and cooperation, states were drawn into energy politics by the collapse of a private (corporate) hegemonic regime and were a force for conflict and discord as a result. Legare contends that only through reflexive theorizing can this become apparent.

The case chapters answer some of the "how" when we ask about the enterprise of postpositivist critical international relations. If we are to be theoretically reflexive, however, it is incumbent upon us to problematize the critical theoretical enterprise itself. The final three chapters of the volume address some of the questions arising from the case chapters and speak to some of the issues left unquestioned. Tony Porter begins to address this task in his chapter "Postmodern Political Realism and International Relations Theory's Third Debate." This chapter examines a variant of postmodern critical scholarship that has entered international relations theory as a response to the impasse of the Third Debate. In particular, Porter argues that despite beneficial insights, that aspect of postmodernism reflected in international relations has failed to resolve the problems encountered by positivism that the Third Debate aimed to overcome. Because positivism privileges the referent of texts and postmodernism privileges the text, both fail to deal adequately with the constructed interrelationship of the two. Porter offers structuration theory as a means of reconciling, or providing a theoretical link between, referent and text in the study of international relations.

Although a focus upon epistemology creates the potential for reflexive international relations theory, the discipline still fails to grapple with some of the fundamental biases intrinsic to itself. Susan Judith Ship, in her chapter "And What About Gender? Feminism and International Relations Theory's Third Debate," argues that the most significant unaddressed bias is the androcentric presuppositions of positivist as well as postpositivist scholarship. The failure to confront the significance of gender in the social construction of knowledge, Ship argues, has weakened the "critical" cutting edge of the new critical international relations theory.

Ship's chapter reviews the treatment of gender in contemporary international relations theory from a variety of perspectives, bringing to light literature and arguments that have been systematically marginalized in the discipline. This review leads her to question the emancipatory nature of consequent political projects, which fail to challenge the interrelated hierarchies of privilege that condition women's diverse experiences and their political concerns. Ship responds to this failure by calling for a revised perspective that explores the changing relationships among ideas, social discourses, social conditions, and social relations, and consequently opens up space for practical empowerment strategies for disadvantaged social groups. In calling for the forging of closer links between academics and social movements, Ship argues that research *on* women may finally become research *for* women.

In order to confront this lacuna of international relations theory—its failure to address the participation of women as well as other marginalized social groups—and to translate this into possibilities for concrete political action, international relations theory must create the intellectual space into which such action can be directed. There follows, therefore, a real political necessity to reconceptualize international relations' key actor—the state. E. Fuat Keyman offers an assessment of one attempt at this enterprise in his chapter "Problematizing the State in International Relations Theory."

Keyman posits that international relations theory has reached an impasse derived from its unquestioned acceptance of the state as an ontologically given central actor. His chapter provides an evaluation of the potential contribution to the resolution of this impasse of the state-as-actor literature, drawing from key contemporary debates in political and historical sociology. Reviewing the work of such important scholars as Theda Skocpol, Fred Halliday, Anthony Giddens, and Michael Mann, Keyman suggests that this perspective is an important corrective to mainstream international relations theory (largely political realism) in that it points out the significance of "domestic" or internal politics for an analysis of the interstate system. He argues, however, that whatever their advantages, the state-as-agency approaches operate with a statist image of international relations and an essentialist conception of the state. In the end, Keyman holds that if the state-as-agency model is to be used to overcome any impasse, it is not the impasse of international relations theory that will be overcome, but the impasse of the realist paradigm, for the state-as-agency model provides for realism a thorough historical and theoretical account of the state and of the interstate system. In advancing his critique, Keyman lays the foundations for the development of a new conception of the state, one focused upon the complex interrelationship between state and society, yet one that privileges neither.

The varying epistemological and theoretical perspectives that make up this volume illustrate the promise that a movement beyond the Third Debate holds for meaningful theoretical development in international relations as a discipline. By eschewing doctrinaire notions of science and by enunciating an ethic of holism and epistemological self-consciousness, this project aims to open a measure of space for alternate articulations of the political, and thus of the possible. This possibility of alternate political projects is founded on a shared commitment to reflexive international relations theory, which accepts that theory is as much a reflection of the world as it is, as a construction of the world as it might be. In international relations theory, such a perspective may help integrate the discipline into the more critical debates proceeding within other areas of political and social theory, and may also expand the purview of theoretical enquiry beyond perfunctory calls for a postpositivist synthesis.

Beyond Positivism: Critical Reflections on International Relations provides an essential link between the reflexive turn in the discipline, which has been marginalized by its narrowly metatheoretical discourse, and alternative theoretical understandings of the traditionally central concerns of the field. Rather than ignoring the valuable insights that theoretical reflexivity can offer the discipline, this volume integrates critical tools of reflexivity into the mainstream, thereby pushing the study of international relations beyond its narrow positivist confines.

2

Reflexivity and International Relations Theory

MARK NEUFELD

In the context of recent discussions of (meta)-theoretical restructuring in the discipline of international relations, the question of reflexivity has achieved prominence. Specifically, it has been argued that enhanced reflexivity in international relations theory is a central contribution of the current postpositivist theoretical restructuring associated with the Third Debate (Lapid, 1989:235–254).

If true, this is certainly a welcome development, especially given that "for many years the international relations discipline has had the dubious honor of being among the least self-reflexive of the Western social sciences" (Lapid, 1989:249–250). Unfortunately, there is good reason to question this optimistic assessment. Specifically, there is good reason to question whether the so-called Third Debate really has coincided with a fundamental break with positivist conceptions of theory and knowledge, and, by extension, with the beginning of an era of reflexive theorizing in the discipline. Rather, one could argue that the Third Debate represents at best a limited move in the direction of reflexive theorizing.

This chapter has three main objectives. First, the core elements of reflexivity are detailed. Attention is given to the sense in which reflexivity involves an important break with positivist notions of theory. Second, the contributions of a sampling of international relations scholars to the Third Debate are examined to determine to

A previous version of this chapter appeared in *Millennium: Journal of International Studies*, Vol. 22, No. 1 (Spring 1993).

what extent the elements of reflexivity are in evidence. It is argued that the break with positivist conceptions of theory and knowledge is at best partial, and that the contribution of the Third Debate to reflexivity is, consequently, a limited one. Finally, the contributions of two variants of critical international relations theory are examined to determine if theorizing at the margins of the discipline offers more evidence of reflexivity than mainstream contributions. Here it is argued that although the answer is affirmative, it is important to note that some critical theoretical traditions are more reflexive than others.

Before proceeding to a development of the main argument, however, it is useful to note the specificity of the exercise represented here. This is an exercise in international metatheory. Perhaps the best way to clarify the meaning of metatheory is by analogy. Consider, for example, the discipline's treatment of empirical evidence. Although the discipline is concerned with incorporating facts into explanatory accounts, it has generally not subscribed to what some have labeled the position of "barefoot empiricism." That is to say, international relations scholars have generally not subscribed to the view that facts speak for themselves. On the contrary, it is generally held that facts require interpretation in order to have meaning—interpretation that is the product of the application of theory to facts. In short, the meaning of facts is not a factual question, but a theoretical one. Consequently, given that explanation is one's goal, "there is nothing so practical as a good theory."

The insufficiency of this widely held position is that it leaves unanswered a very important question: What constitutes good theory? And just as answering the question "What do these facts mean?" requires a move to a higher level of abstraction than that of the empirical—namely, the theoretical—so does the question "What constitutes good theory?" In short, just as the meaning of facts is not a factual but a theoretical question, so the nature of good theory is not a theoretical question but a metatheoretical one.

International metatheory, then, is that subfield of international relations that seeks an answer to the question "What constitutes good theory?" As such, it is a vital part of the quest for explanatory accounts of the subject matter of the discipline. Indeed, if it is true that facts are dependent upon theory for their meaning, and that theory, in turn, is dependent on metatheoretical reflection to ensure its adequacy, then the general assessment of the place of metatheory may be in need of significant revision. Metatheory is not an unproductive distraction from the real substance of the discipline, the theoretically informed analysis of empirical evidence. Rather, metatheory is the indispensable foundation of competent scholarly activity, and it is vital for ensuring the adequacy of the explanatory accounts developed. Indeed, the relative neglect of metatheoretical questions may go some way in accounting for some of the serious limitations to which the discipline of international relations has been subject, and of which the traditional lack of reflexivity is but one example.

Defining Theoretical Reflexivity

> That we disavow reflection is positivism.
> —*Jürgen Habermas* (1971)

In a very general sense, theoretical reflexivity can be defined as reflection on the process of theorizing. More specifically, reflexivity in terms of international relations theory can be understood to entail three core elements: (1) self-awareness regarding underlying premises; (2) the recognition of the inherently politico-normative dimension of paradigms and the normal science tradition they sustain; and (3) the affirmation that reasoned judgments about the merits of contending paradigms are possible in the absence of a neutral observation language. These three elements are treated in turn. Furthermore, each element is related to the dominant conception of theory and knowledge in the discipline—that of positivism.

Being aware of the underlying premises of one's theorizing is the first core element of theoretical reflexivity. That is, theoretical reflexivity is understood to involve attention to, and disclosure of, the too often unstated presuppositions upon which theoretical edifices are erected. If reflexivity were limited to this first element, then the positivist forms of theorizing that have dominated the discipline of international relations would qualify with little difficulty as reflexive forms of theory; positivist notions of theory require that the sum total of generalizations be derived axiomatically from clearly identified starting assumptions (Olson and Onuf, 1985:1–25). The two additional core elements, however, are incompatible with—and indeed, they emerged from challenges to—positivist forms of theory, and their presence makes reflexivity a virtual antonym of positivism.

The second element of reflexivity is recognition of the inherently politico-normative content of paradigms and the normal science traditions they generate. To understand the sense in which this element of reflexivity stands in opposition to positivist theorizing, it is useful to discuss, albeit briefly, some of the defining characteristics of the positivist approach to knowledge.

To begin, it is important to note the centrality of the identitarian-inspired tenet of truth as correspondence. This tenet has stood as one of the core elements of the positivist tradition throughout its history—from Auguste Comte to the Vienna Circle to the contemporary variations of positivism offered by Karl Popper and, most recently, by Imre Lakatos. That is, positivism stipulates that theoretical explanations will be true to the extent that they accurately reflect empirical reality, to the extent that they correspond to the facts.

The tenet of truth as correspondence rests upon a particular assumption: that of the separation of subject and object, of observer and observed. In other words, the tenet of truth as correspondence assumes that through the proper application of research design and techniques, the researcher(s) can be factored out, leaving behind a description of the world "as it truly is." In short, the tenet of truth as correspondence is the expression of the goal of rendering science a process without a subject.

The consequence of this tenet and of this assumption is that a number of problematic issues are swept aside. In making the separation of subject and object a defining condition of science, the positivist approach ignores the active and vital role played by the community of researchers in the production and validation of knowledge. Truth as correspondence ignores the fact that the standards that define reliable knowledge are dependent upon their acceptance and application by a research community.[1]

As a result, a number of important questions not only go unanswered, they are never raised. These include questions of the historical origin and nature of the community-based standards that define what counts as reliable knowledge, as well as questions of the merits of those standards in the light of possible alternatives. These questions do not arise in positivist-inspired theorizing because the central standard of scientific truth—that of truth as correspondence—is seen to belong not to a time-bound human community of scientific investigators, but to an extrahistorical natural realm. In short, the knowledge-defining standards of positivism are understood to be "nature's own" (Rorty, 1979:xxvi).

In contrast, a theoretically reflexive orientation is one in which the starting point stands in radical opposition to that of positivism in that it rejects the notion of objective standards existing independently of human thought and practice. Reflexively oriented theorists draw philosophical sustenance from the efforts to develop a post-positivist philosophy of science associated with the work of Thomas Kuhn and Paul Feyerabend, as well as the linguistic turn in social and political theory manifest in the Wittgensteinian analysis of language games, neopragmatist renditions of Gadamerian philosophical hermeneutics, and Michel Foucault's analysis of power-knowledge discourses.[2] As different as these approaches are, all serve to undermine the assumption that it is ever possible to separate subject (the knower) and object (the known) in the manner postulated by positivism. Simply put, if the paradigm (language game/ tradition/ discourse) not only tells us how to interpret evidence, but determines what will count as valid evidence in the first place, the tenet of truth as correspondence to the facts can no longer be sustained.

The notion of reflexivity directs us beyond merely identifying the underlying assumptions of our theorizing to recognizing that the very existence of objective standards for assessing competing knowledge claims must be questioned. Furthermore, it moves us to understand that the standards that determine what is to count as reliable knowledge are not nature's, but rather always *human* standards— standards that are not given but made, not imposed by nature but adopted by convention by the members of a specific community.

In so doing, we are compelled to acknowledge the politico-normative content of scholarly investigation. Seeing knowledge-defining standards as community-created conventions in specific contexts moves us to see that

> evolving descriptions and ever-changing versions of objects, things, and the world issue forth from various communities as *responses to certain problems, as attempts to overcome specific situations, and as means to satisfy particular needs and interests.* (West, 1989:201; emphasis added)

In short, ideas, words, and language are not mirrors that copy the "real" or "objective" world—as positivist conceptions of theory and knowledge would have it—but rather tools with which we cope with "our" world (West, 1989:201). Consequently, there is a fundamental link between epistemology—the question of what counts as reliable knowledge—and politics—the problems, needs, and interests deemed important and legitimate by a given community.[3]

The inextricably politico-normative aspect of scholarship has an important consequence for the social sciences in terms of the incommensurability thesis (i.e., that contending paradigms are not only incompatible but actually have no common measure). In the case of the natural sciences, one may reasonably contest the thesis that contending paradigms are incommensurable, given their shared politico-normative goal of instrumental control of nature. In the case of the social sciences, however, different paradigms not only have different terminologies, but are often constructed in terms of quite different values and oriented to serving quite different political projects. Consequently, the thesis of the radical incommensurability of contending paradigms in a social science such as international relations is much more difficult to dispute.

We arrive now at the third core element of a fully reflexive orientation: the affirmation of the possibility of reasoned judgments in the absence of objective standards. Once again, this element of reflexivity can best be understood in relation to positivism. As was noted above, positivism strives, by means of the separation of subject and object, to derive a neutral observation language that will allow for a point-by-point comparison of rival paradigms. In this context, it is important to note that the possibility of a neutral observation language is at the very core of the positivist notion of reasoned assessment of empirical claims. Indeed, it is not going too far to assert that for positivists this assumption is at the core of reason itself.

The faith in the possibility of a neutral observation language and the accompanying conviction that such a language is a necessary condition for reasoned assessment explain much of the distress exhibited by positivists in the face of the assertions about incommensurability. To accept incommensurability is, for positivists, to promote what Popper termed the "myth of the framework" according to which "we are prisoners caught in the framework of our theories; our expectations; our past experiences; our language;" and thus to accept that we cannot communicate with or judge those working in terms of a different paradigm (Popper, 1970:56).

In contrast, reflexive theorists accept incommensurability as the necessary consequence of the fact that paradigm-specific knowledge-defining standards are themselves intimately connected to and embedded in competing social and political agendas, the politico-normative contents of which are not amenable to any neutral observation language. At the same time, however, reflexive theorists do not accept that recognizing contending paradigms as incommensurable means reasoned assessments are impossible. Rather, a reflexive orientation sees how both the positivist insistence on truth as correspondence and Popper's notion of the myth of the framework are expressions of a common philosophical apprehension. They are both expressions of what Bernstein has termed the "Cartesian anxiety"— the notion, central to identitarian thinking from René Descartes to the present, that should we prove unsuccessful in our search for the Archimedean point of indubitable knowledge that can serve as the foundation for human reason, then rationality must give way to irrationality, and reliable knowledge to madness.[4] As the driving force of modern philosophy, the Cartesian anxiety—which is reflected in positivism's insistence on the ahistorical, extrasocial standard of truth as correspondence—is bound up with the conception of knowledge that Aristotle called *episteme*: apodictic knowledge of the order and nature of the cosmos. Furthermore, the peculiarly modern fear that the undermining of the viability of *episteme* must lead inexorably to irrationality and chaos is the result of the limiting of the modern conception of knowledge and rationality to *episteme*.

This limiting of reason, moreover, has resulted in the marginalization and impoverishment of normative discourse. Given the positivist emphasis on the centrality of a neutral observation language, the treatment of normative issues in mainstream social science has typically taken the form of descriptive accounts of individual value preferences. One might, of course, engage in crude utilitarian calculation to determine the course offering the most in terms of human happiness. Foreclosed, however, is the reasoned adjudication of the inherent value of competing normative claims. Indeed, in the realm of normative discourse the hold of the positivist model of social science has been so powerful that it made us "quite incapable of seeing how reason does and can really function in the domain" (Taylor, 1985:230).[5]

Consequently, the means of exorcising the Cartesian anxiety lies in elucidating a conception of reason that is not limited to *episteme*, and does not depend on a fixed Archimedean point outside of history or the existence of a neutral observation language. It is worth noting, moreover, that just such an effort has been under way in contemporary social and political theory. It is evident in Charles Taylor's privileging of Hegel's interpretive or hermeneutical dialectics—a form of reasoning that, in contrast to the claim of strict dialectics (which makes claims to an undeniable starting point), posits no such foundation and yet still aims to convince us by the overall plausibility of the interpretation it gives (Taylor, 1979:64). It is evident in Hans-Georg Gadamer's linguistically based reappropriation of the Aristotelian notion of *phronesis*, which, in contrast to *episteme*, is oriented to the exercise of reasoned judgment in the context not of the timeless and unchanging, but of the variable and contingent. It is also evident in Jürgen Habermas's contribution to the theory of communicative action, in particular the discursive validation of truth claims. Perhaps most strikingly, given the predominance achieved by the notion of "paradigm" in contemporary international relations theory, it is evident in Richard Bernstein's reevaluation of Kuhn as someone whose work does not lead us to the myth of the framework—as was charged by Popper—but rather evidences a movement toward a form of practical reason having great affinity to Gadamer's reconceptualization of *phronesis*.[6] In all of these efforts and more, the emphasis is upon the elucidation of a dialogic form of reason that refuses to limit our conception of human rationality to a mechanical application of an eternal, unchanging standard; that affirms that a broader and more subtle conception of reason is possible than that which underlies both the positivist tenet of truth as correspondence and that of radical relativism as the logical consequence of incommensurability; that experiences no self-contradiction when employing a "language of qualitative worth,"[7] and is thus as suited to a consideration of normative claims as it is to empirical ones.

Expanding the conception of reason beyond positivistic *episteme* is vital to a reflexive orientation; for having reclaimed normative discourse as a domain in which reason can and does function, reflexive theorists argue that what makes paradigms incommensurable—the politico-normative content of the normal science they generate—also makes reasoned assessments of them possible. In short, judgments about contending paradigms are possible by means of reasoned assessments of the politico-normative content of the projects they serve, of the ways of life to which they correspond.[8]

Having established what reflexivity is, perhaps it would be useful, by way of conclusion, to state briefly what it is not. Reflexivity is not a research program designed to provide cumulative knowledge about the world of empirical facts or about the world of theory. Nor can reflexivity be reduced to the idea that although agreement on facts is possible, value disagreements will continue to plague scholars in their quest for disciplinary consensus. Finally, reflexivity does not provide specific, a priori standards or criteria for assessing the merits of contending paradigms.

Reflexivity is a metatheoretical stance involving (1) a recognition of the interrelationship of the conception of facts and values on the one hand, and a community-specific social and political agenda on the other, and (2) an openness to engaging in reasoned dialogue to assess the merits of contending paradigms. Whether such a stance is in evidence in recent theorizing within the discipline of international relations is the question we shall now address.

The Third Debate Reconsidered

We move now to a consideration of reflexivity in terms of international relations theory. First, a consideration will be given to the issue of reflexivity in terms of a recently arisen metatheoretical debate in the discipline—international relations theory's Third Debate. This contemporary debate, which dates from the late 1980s, can be seen as the third in a series of discipline-defining debates in the twentieth century; the first being that between idealism and realism in the 1940s and 1950s, and the second centering around the 1960s' confrontation between history and science.

On the one hand, one can understand the Third Debate in the same general terms as the First and Second Debates: namely, as an expression of the ongoing quest for better theory.[9] At the same time, one should also see the Third Debate in terms of contemporary developments in the realm of social and political theory. It has been suggested that the claim that "international relations is a discrete area of action and discourse, separate from social and political theory," can no longer be sustained (Hoffman, 1987:231). In fact, nowhere is there better evidence for this position than in international relations theory's Third Debate.

To reiterate, the Third Debate is part of the search for better theory, like the debates that preceded it. In the case of this debate, however, and in line with the emphasis of contemporary social and political theory, this search is being conducted not in terms of individual propositions or hypotheses but in terms of larger conceptual schemes. The Third Debate is a discourse about choice of analytic frameworks. It involves a focus on metascientific units (i.e., on paradigms), in which particular attention is directed to examining the underlying premises and assumptions of the paradigms in contention.

A good example of this approach to the ongoing quest for better theory is the work of Michael Banks. In an important contribution to the Third Debate, Banks has conceptualized the present state of the discipline in terms of three contending paradigms: realism, pluralism, and structuralism.

> Each of the three starts with a wholly different basic image. For realists, the world society is a system of "billiard-ball" states in intermittent collision. For pluralists, it is a "cobweb," a network of numerous criss-crossing relationships. For structuralists, it is a "multi-headed octopus," with powerful tentacles constantly sucking wealth from the weakened peripheries towards the powerful centres. (Banks, 1985a:12)

These contrasting images, notes Banks, serve as the foundation for the erection of theoretical structures. These structures, while internally coherent, contradict one another in terms of major theoretical categories including (1) actors, (2) dynamics, (3) dependent variables, (4) subject boundaries, and (5) specific concepts.

With regard to actors, Banks has argued, "realists see only states; pluralists see states in combination with a great variety of others; and structuralists see classes." With regard to dynamics, "realists see force as primary; pluralists see complex social movements; structuralists see economics." Finally, as concerns dependent variables,

> realists see the task of IR [international relations] as simply to explain what states do; pluralists see it more grandly as an effort to explain all major world events; and structuralists see its function as showing why the world contains such appalling contrasts between rich and poor. (Banks, 1985a:12–13)

With regard to subject boundaries,

> Realists define the boundaries of their subject in a narrow, state-centric fashion, often preferring the term "international politics" to describe it. Pluralists widen the boundaries by including multinational companies, markets, ethnic groups and nationalism as well as state behaviour, and call their subject IR or world society. Structuralists have the widest boundaries of all, stressing the unity of the whole world system at all levels, focusing on modes of production and treating inter-state politics as merely a surface phenomenon. (Banks, 1985a:13)

And finally, as regards specific concepts, Banks notes:

> Some concepts are found only in one paradigm, because they are of crucial importance to it: deterrence and alliances in realism, ethnicity and interdependence in pluralism, exploitation and dependency in structuralism. Others, however, are used with broadly similar meanings in all three: power, sovereignty, and law, for example. Yet others, like imperialism, the state, and hegemony, are used in all three but with sharply different interpretations. (Banks, 1985a:13)

It is clear that there is much room for disagreement with the specifics of Banks's intervention. His conceptualization of the contending paradigms—from their basic images through to their contrasting notions of actors, dynamics, and so on—can be challenged as to its accuracy and adequacy. Indeed, disagreements may extend all the way to the labels used to designate contending paradigms. In contrast to Banks's (1985a) use of the terms realism, pluralism, and structuralism, for example, Holsti (1985) prefers classical tradition, global society, and neo-Marxism; Viotti and Kauppi (1987) employ realism, pluralism, and globalism; and McKinlay and Little (1986) identify their paradigms by the labels of realist, liberal, and socialist.[10] The point remains, however, that Banks's work serves as an excellent example of how the emphases of contemporary philosophy of science have spilled over into the discipline of international relations and influenced the form that interventions have taken in the Third Debate.

The Third Debate has special significance in terms of the concerns of this chapter. Beyond the immediate arguments about the number, identifying characteristics, and appropriate labels for the paradigms in international relations theory, the Third Debate affords a valuable opportunity for exploring the issue of theoretical reflexivity in the discipline.

It has been argued that international relations theory's Third Debate not only reflects the influence of contemporary social and political theory (i.e., the focus on metatheoretical units), but it is a direct expression of post/antipositivist currents. In the words of Yosef Lapid, the Third Debate is "linked, historically and intellectually, to the confluence of diverse antipositivistic philosophical and sociological trends" (Lapid, 1989:237). Indeed, it is because the Third Debate has been understood as marking international relations theory's break with positivist orthodoxy that it has been associated with an important increase in theoretical reflexivity within the discipline of international relations.

Later sections of this chapter challenge this interpretation of the Third Debate. It is argued that to see the Third Debate as marking a conclusive break with the positivist legacy and an opening to theoretical reflexivity would be a mistake. Rather, it is suggested that for two important reasons the Third Debate's contribution to increased reflexivity in the discipline has been limited. First, a significant number of interventions in the Third Debate continue to be structured in terms of positivism's tenet of truth as correspondence. Second, of the interventions that do evidence an attempt to break with the notion of truth as correspondence, the vast majority remain trapped within positivist-derived conceptions of reasoned assessment. In both cases, reflexivity remains foreclosed.

Interventions in the Third Debate

On the basis of our discussions of positivism and reflexivity, three possible stances with regard to contending paradigms can be distinguished. The first stance, corresponding to the positivist tradition's tenet of truth as correspondence, is that of "commensurable and therefore comparable." Rival paradigms are comparable, asserts this position, because ultimately they can be assessed according to a common standard—that of correspondence to the real world. This stance, it will be remembered, is incompatible with the notion of reflexivity in that it sees the standard for what constitutes reliable knowledge as nature's own, and thus beyond criticism.

A second stance with regard to contending paradigms corresponds to the Popperian notion of the myth of the framework. According to this stance, rival paradigms are "incommensurable and therefore incomparable." This stance breaks with positivism to the degree that it recognizes that standards for what constitute reliable knowledge are human constructs and social conventions. However, it remains firmly attached to the positivist conception of reasoned assessment—in particular, the idea that the acceptance of incommensurability means that rival standards cannot be compared and assessed. This stance embodies the first two elements of reflexivity, but nonetheless fails in incorporating the third.

Finally, a third stance can be identified. According to this stance—a stance associated with efforts to elucidate dialogic, nonfoundationalist conceptions of reason—rival paradigms are "incommensurable yet still comparable." This stance recognizes the context-dependent nature of the standards for what constitutes reliable knowledge and of the coping vocabularies devised by different communities. It also affirms that these conventions and vocabularies can be compared and assessed by means of reasoned deliberation about their politico-normative content. This stance—and this stance alone—qualifies as fully reflexive.

With these three stances in mind, we can now move to an examination of the Third Debate. Interventions in the Third Debate can be classified and assessed in terms of their break with positivism and their contribution to reflexivity. We begin with the first stance: commensurable and therefore comparable.

Stance I: Commensurable and Therefore Comparable

One of the best examples of Stance I, commensurable and therefore comparable, in the Third Debate is found in the writings of Holsti (1985, 1989). To begin, there is no question that Holsti is most comfortable within the realist—or in his terms, "classical"—tradition. Indeed, *The Dividing Discipline* can be seen as a spirited defense of the realist approach to the study of international politics at a time when calls are being heard for its replacement.

What is even more important in terms of the present discussion, however, is Holsti's adherence to a Lakatosian version of positivism, including the positivist tenet of truth as correspondence. Holsti's allegiance to positivism is clearly evidenced in his statements concerning the purpose of theory and the nature of knowledge accumulation. According to Holsti,

> the ultimate purpose of theoretical activity is to enhance our understanding of the world of international politics; [it is to] increase our knowledge of the *real world* by helping to guide research and interpret data. . . . We add to knowledge primarily when we render reality more intelligible by seeking generalizations of empirical validity. (Holsti, 1989:255–256; emphasis added)

It is out of the understanding that theory is a reflection of the real world that Holsti has explained the origins of the contending paradigms that constitute the Third Debate. "A plethora of . . . 'paradigms,'" Holsti has noted, "is an expression of greater international complexity." And because "our world is complex and growing more so," he has asserted, "it is . . . unlikely that any single theory or perspective . . . could adequately explain all of its essential characteristics." Thus, he concludes, "theoretical pluralism is the only possible response to the multiple realities of a complex world" (Holsti, 1989:255–256).

It should be noted, however, that for Holsti, paradigmatic pluralism is more than just an inevitable condition of theorizing that tries to comprehend a complex reality. In addition, pluralism is an important principle that, when respected, serves some very beneficial functions. Clearly echoing Lakatos's rejection of the Popperian notion of strict falsification, Holsti has affirmed that

> pluralism . . . guards against the hazards of "intellectual knockouts," those attempts to disown past methodologies and theories on the assumption that they are entirely wrong. . . . This was a major shortcoming of the most extreme behaviourism and of some recent efforts to demolish realism and its variants. (Holsti, 1989:255–256)

In addition to guarding against straightforward falsification of paradigms that, despite anomalies, have proven their worth as interpretive tools, the principle of pluralism also serves to insure that the discipline keeps progressing in its quest for ever-truer descriptions of reality. Thus, Holsti has noted, if the dominant realist tradition shows itself to be inadequate as a description of reality, "then new departures may help us redirect inquiry into the proper channels." If realism is lacking, he has argued, it can be refurbished by grafting new theoretical formulations onto it (Holsti, 1985:viii).

It is important to note that despite his support for paradigmatic pluralism, Holsti was not arguing that all paradigms are of equal

value. In keeping with the positivist tenet of truth as correspondence, paradigms may be evaluated according to the accuracy of
their description of the facts. As Holsti has noted,

> progress is thus not measured by unlimited accumulation of per-
> spectives, paradigms, models, or methodologies any more than it is
> by the replacement of "units of knowledge". Some perspectives,
> models, and the like should and do have higher intellectual claims
> than others. The ultimate test is how elegantly and comprehensibly
> they describe and explain the *important* persisting, new, and devel-
> oping realities. (Holsti, 1989:258; emphasis added)

Thus, early in *The Dividing Discipline*, Holsti affirmed that "isomor-
phism" and "correspondence with the observed facts of international politics" are the standards by which rival paradigms must be
assessed (Holsti, 1985:vii).

Indeed, it is on the basis of its transhistorical correspondence
with the facts that Holsti has continued to promote the realist paradigm over its rivals. In an interesting reversal of the traditional infe-
riority ascribed to social scientists in comparison with their natural
science counterparts, Holsti has affirmed:

> We cannot throw away paradigms (or what passes for them) as
> natural scientists do, à la Kuhn, because the anomalies between
> reality and its theoretical characterization are never so severe in
> international relations as they are in the natural sciences. None of
> the thinkers of the past portrayed the world of international (or
> world) politics in so distorted a manner as did the analysts of the
> physical or astronomical universe prior to the Copernican revolu-
> tion. (Holsti, 1989:257)[11]

From his affirmations that competing paradigms may be "syn-
thesized" ("grafted" one onto the other), and that realists have been
more successful than many physicists in approximating reality—not
to mention his assertion that "correspondence with the observed
facts of international politics" is the basis upon which rival paradigms must be assessed—it is clear that Holsti has not accepted the
incommensurability thesis. The theory-ladenness of all facts, as well
as the politico-normative content of all theorizing, is something he
cannot embrace. As Holsti has noted, "I remain skeptical of the 'liberation of theory from data,' or, as Halliday has put it, a 'rejection of
empiricism in favor of a theoretical approach that accepts the place
of data in a subordinate position'" (Holsti, 1989:259).

The implications of Holsti's rejection of the notion of incommensurability for increased theoretical reflexivity are clear. In the continued affirmation of the notion that nature's own standards—specifically truth as correspondence—must be applied in the knowledge

validation process, the possibility of critical reflection on the social origins and politico-normative content of the conventions that define what is to count as reliable knowledge remains remote. Theoretical reflexivity, to the degree that it figures at all, is reduced to the much more limited notion of "careful examination of assumptions and premises" (Holsti, 1989:255).

In conclusion, it should be noted that a significant number of interventions in the Third Debate—of which Holsti's stands out only because of its clarity—are consistent with the positivist-inspired stance of commensurable and therefore comparable. As a consequence, the interpretation of the Third Debate as marking a disciplinary shift toward postpositivist theoretical reflexivity bears being reconsidered.

Stance II: Incommensurable and Therefore Incomparable

Although the majority of the interventions in international relations theory's Third Debate reflect Stance I, it should be noted that there are important exceptions. Noteworthy among these are those of theorists who have adopted Stance II: incommensurable and therefore incomparable.

An important intervention by McKinlay and Little (1986) is a good example of this stance in the Third Debate. McKinlay and Little's starting point is that the source of the paradigms found in the literature—in their terms, realism, liberalism, and socialism—is not to be found in international complexity. Rather, contending paradigms are expressions of radically different politico-normative orders embedded in competing ideological frameworks.

Highlighting the links between paradigms and specific social-political agendas is one of the ways in which Stance II adherents demonstrate a clear advance over those of Stance I in terms of reflexivity. The treatment of the realist paradigm in international relations theory serves as a good example. As Smith has argued, because international relations theory, as primarily an "American discipline," has been

> so closely identified with the foreign policy concerns of the country, it is not surprising that the assumptions of Realism have proven to be so difficult to overcome. This is because the focus of Realism, namely how to maximize power so as to manage international events, fits extraordinarily well with the needs of a hegemonic power. The three key elements of Realism's account of world politics, the national interest, power maximization and the balance of power, are particularly well-suited to the requirements of a foreign policy for the U.S. (Smith, 1987:198–199)

In short, from the perspective of Stance II, realism is understood not as a neutral description of the world as it truly is, but rather as a coping vocabulary of a specific community (e.g., U.S. state managers) designed to address certain problems or to satisfy particular needs and interests. Furthermore, the assessment of realism as a coping vocabulary can be undertaken only in relation to the problems defined and the needs and interests identified. Consequently, the success of realism has, with due respect to Holsti, had less to do with its alleged accuracy in grasping the facts of international politics than with its demonstrated utility for guiding state managers in their activities of state- and nation-building. That is to say, the realist paradigm has validated its truth claims by demonstrating its ability to guide state policymaking.

If the success of the realist paradigm cannot be understood apart from particular social actors and their political projects—specifically U.S. state managers dedicated to the maintenance of American hegemony—then a similar relationship must hold for other paradigms. As Smith has noted:

> just as it has been argued . . . that the U.S. policy agenda dominated the study of international relations by dominating Realism within the U.S., so we should expect different paradigms [i.e., pluralism and structuralism] to appeal to persons in different settings. (Smith, 1987:202)[12]

In their discussion of rival paradigms in international relations theory, Alker and Biersteker (1984) have adopted a similar tack. It is noteworthy that their stated aim is to evidence a "broader and deeper kind of political and epistemological self-consciousness" than that found within the positivist tradition—a self-consciousness that recognizes "the deep connections between the social and political contexts of particular theoretical enterprises and the kind of work actually done" (Alker and Biersteker, 1984:138). Thus, in a manner similar to Smith, they have affirmed:

> Two global superpowers both able to destroy each other, but likely to self-destruct in the same process, are likely to have scholars especially interested in "global interdependence" or "peaceful coexistence." . . . Anti-colonial revolutionaries in relatively underdeveloped countries are driven by other practical imperatives. (Alker and Biersteker, 1984:138–139)

In sum, unlike Stance I, Stance II accepts that contending paradigms in international relations theory are incommensurable, and that the hope of paradigm synthesis held out by the adherents of Stance I is thus a pipe dream. The consequence of incommensurability, McKinlay and Little have noted, is that "even when the models [i.e., paradigms] look to the same topics, the general framework within which the topic is processed leads to systematic variation in problem explication" (McKinlay and Little, 1986:267).

With their rejection of the notion of a theory-independent realm of facts by which one can assess the merits of competing paradigms, and a recognition of the politico-normative content of the normal science traditions, adherents of Stance II appear to be on the post-positivist path to theoretical reflexivity. Unfortunately, this is not the case. It is not the case because the adherents of Stance II remain trapped by a notion of reason limited to *episteme*. Consequently, they equate the incommensurability of paradigms with that of the incomparability of paradigms.

Again, McKinlay and Little serve as a useful example. The ability to assess the merits of competing paradigms, they have argued, "presupposes some form of comparatively valid evaluation procedure, entailing some decision rule which would stipulate which model was to be retained." Given that any evaluation procedure that might be proposed would be no more than a social convention, and hence inherently contestable, comparative assessments are virtually impossible. The "only comparatively valid test procedure," they have concluded, "is to enquire whether each model is internally consistent." They have judged this criterion to be met in each case (McKinlay and Little, 1986:269–270).

Indeed, not only is comparative assessment virtually impossible, McKinlay and Little have argued, but the very idea of meaningful communication between the adherents of rival paradigms—and the learning that is a product of that communication—is out of the question.

> [The] sophistication and internal coherence of each model, combined with their very different goals, structural arrangements and belief systems, make meaningful inter-model debate well-nigh impossible. . . . Compromise and constructive debate can largely only be conducted within the confines and parameters of a single model. (McKinlay and Little, 1986:272–273)

Given the assumption of the essential incomparability of paradigms, how is one to account for paradigm choice by members of the research community? The position of James Rosenau on this issue is a good example of how Stance II adherents respond to this question. In accordance with the core assumptions of the stance of incommensurable and therefore incomparable, Rosenau has affirmed that "the way in which analysts become adherents of one or another approach is not necessarily based on intellectual or rational calculation." What then is the explanation for paradigm choice? By definition, the explanation must be found outside the realm of reason and argumentation. Rosenau's answer is consistent, if disconcerting: "Our temperaments," he affirms, "are the central determinants of which approach we will find more suitable" (Rosenau, 1982:4–5).

To conclude, then, the second stance of incommensurable and therefore incomparable, having broken with positivism in important respects, remains trapped within the positivist-reinforced limitation of reason to *episteme*. Neither reasoned assessment nor even communication between paradigms is possible. By definition, they are condemned to "pass like ships in the night" (McKinlay and Little, 1986:273). As a consequence, and despite some important progress beyond Stance I, for Stance II reflexivity remains foreclosed.

Beyond the Third Debate

We have examined the two stances to which the interventions in mainstream international relations theory's Third Debate correspond. In each case, we have seen that the possibilities for the development of theoretical reflexivity—to the degree that they exist at all—remain limited. At the same time, Stance III, "incommensurable yet still comparable"—the only stance that represents a fully reflexive orientation—is not represented. This raises an important question: Beyond the Third Debate, is there any evidence of this third stance in contemporary theorizing in the discipline?

For examples of Stance III it is necessary to move outside the mainstream to the margins of the discipline. Here two distinct traditions of "critical" international relations theory will be examined: (1) Gramscian-inspired neo-Marxist international relations theory and (2) postmodern international relations theory.

In a contribution that predates the Third Debate by several years, Robert Cox (1986) has evidenced a clear awareness of the core elements of theoretical reflexivity. Beyond attention to basic assumptions, Cox also has shown a clear awareness of the politico-normative content of any theoretical enterprise. Specifically, he has argued that it is necessary to recognize that "theory is always *for* someone and *for* some purpose" and that theory is shaped by a *problematique* rooted in the "human experience that gives rise to the need for theory" (Cox, 1986:207, 217–218). Accordingly, there is "no such thing as theory in itself, divorced from a standpoint in time and space." As a consequence, Cox has argued, "when any theory so represents itself, it is more important to examine it as ideology, and to lay bare its concealed perspective" (Cox, 1986:207–208). In short, paradigms and theories are expressions of diverse perspectives linked to disparate social and political projects. It is therefore a central task of the theorist to achieve "a perspective on perspectives" by becoming "more reflective upon the process of theorizing itself," by becoming "clearly aware of the perspective which gives rise to theorizing, and its relation to other perspectives" (Cox, 1986:208).

As such, Cox's position represents a clear break with the positivist notion of truth as correspondence and distinguishes itself clearly from the stance of commensurable and therefore comparable. At the same time, it is important to note that Cox broke as well with the position of Stance II. Refusing to equate incommensurability with incomparability, Cox has affirmed that achieving a perspective on perspectives is oriented to a specific goal: "to open up the possibility of *choosing a different valid perspective*" (Cox, 1986:207–208; emphasis added).

The perspective on perspectives that Cox has presented involves a distinction between two types of theorizing—two distinct, rival, and incommensurable paradigms. The first Cox has labeled "problem-solving theory," an approach distinguished by the fact that it "takes the world as it finds it, with the prevailing social and power relationships and the institutions into which they are organized, as the given framework for action" (Cox, 1986:208). In contrast to problem-solving theory, the second approach, that of critical theory, is distinguished by the fact that it "stands apart from the prevailing order of the world and asks how that order came about"; that is, it "does not take institutions and power relations for granted but calls them into question by concerning itself with their origins and how and whether they might be in the process of changing" (Cox, 1986:208).

Despite the recognition of the incommensurability of these two approaches, Cox has shown himself quite ready to engage in a reasoned comparison of them by means of a critical examination of their politico-normative content.

> The strength of the problem-solving approach lies in its ability to fix limits or parameters to a problem area and to reduce the statement of a particular problem to a limited number of variables which are amenable to relatively close and precise examination. The *ceteris paribus* assumption, upon which such theorizing is based, makes it possible to arrive at statements of laws or regularities which appear to have general validity but which imply, of course, the institutional and relational parameters assumed in the problem-solving approach. (Cox, 1986:208)

However, Cox has insisted, problem-solving theory's assumption of a fixed order

> is not merely a convenience of method, but also an ideological bias. Problem-solving theories can be represented . . . as serving particular national, sectional, or class interests, which are comfortable within the given order. Indeed, the purpose served by problem-solving theory is conservative, since it aims to solve the problem arising in various parts of the complex whole in order to smooth the functioning of the whole. (Cox, 1986:208)

While acknowledging problem-solving theory's strengths, Cox nonetheless has judged critical theory superior on the basis of its emancipatory politico-normative content, as shown by three basic attributes. First, critical theory recognizes that it stems from a perspective. Second, "critical theory contains problem-solving theories within itself, but contains them in the form of identifiable ideologies, thereby pointing to their conservative consequences." And third, critical theory, having as a principal objective the clarification of the "range of possible alternatives," "allows for a normative choice in favor of a social and political order different from the prevailing order" (Cox, 1986:209–210).

It is, of course, possible to raise reasoned objections to Cox's conclusion regarding the relative merits of the two approaches. But the contestability of his conclusions should not distract us from the significance of Cox's intervention in terms of reflexivity: namely, that reasoned comparison of incommensurable approaches is not only necessary, but possible, and that it is possible once one extends the grounds of assessment to include the politico-normative dimensions of rival theoretical enterprises.

Happily, it would appear that Cox's concern with promoting a reflexive brand of theorizing has been taken up by others within the tradition of Gramscian-inspired critical international relations.[13] Beyond this tradition, however, is there any possibility that new developments in the area of critical international relations theory (in particular, the rise of postmodern international relations) hold out a hope for an expansion of reflexive theorizing within the discipline?

At best, the potential for postmodern international relations to contribute to reflexivity is mixed. On the one hand, postmodern contributions clearly break with the positivist notion of truth as correspondence. As one commentator correctly has noted, for postmodernists, "knowledge is grounded in language and language does not reflect 'reality.' Rather it creates and reproduces a world which is never definitive but always in transformation" (P. Rosenau, 1990:6). Indeed, drawing out the hidden politico-normative content of ostensibly neutral, apolitical knowledge discourses has been a major focus of postmodern contributions. Postmodernists have insisted that all theorizing is done from some perspective, that the goal of "apocalyptic objectivity"—that is, "a totalizing standpoint outside of time and capable of enclosing all history within a singular narrative, a law of development, or a vision of progress toward a certain end of humankind" (Ashley, 1987:408)—is untenable.

There is, however, a problem, for while insisting on the politico-normative content of dominant knowledge discourses in the discipline—for example, neorealism—postmodernists have been strangely reluctant to spell out, or even acknowledge, the politico-normative content of their own approach. In short, it is not at all clear what can be meant by the statement that "poststructuralism [postmodernism] . . . is an emphatically political perspective" but one "which refuses to privilege any partisan political line" (George and Campbell, 1990:281). What is politics without partisanship? What is a political perspective that denies having a project (political line)? And if postmodernism accepts that "all theory is for someone and for something," then what and whom is postmodernist theory for? There are hints in recent postmodern contributions—for example, for persons occupying "marginal sites"; for aiding them to

> proceed in a register of freedom to explore and test institutional limitations in a way that sustains and expands the cultural spaces and resources enabling one to conduct one's labours of self-making in just this register of freedom, further exploring and testing limitations. (Ashley and Walker, 1990:391)

However, the designated audience and political-practice implications of postmodern theorizing should be spelled out in a more direct and developed fashion.

Demonstrating that postmodernism satisfies the third requirement of reflexivity—that it affirms that reasoned judgments are possible even in the face of incommensurability—is also difficult. Some commentators have concluded that postmodernism's claim that "knowledge is essentially narrative, provisional and 'groundless'" should be taken to imply that "it is meaningless to seek the one 'best interpretation' (to establish the superiority of one interpretation over another)" (P. Rosenau, 1990:86); that postmodernism maintains that each paradigm "creates its own categories and none are superior to any other"; that "classification, because it involves judgement, is arbitrary" (P. Rosenau, 1990:85). If this is an accurate assessment of postmodernism, then it would have to be concluded that in spite of all of its criticism of logocentric modes of thought, postmodern international relations will remain trapped within the positivist-derived stance of incommensurable and thus incomparable, and that as a consequence its contribution to the development of reflexivity in the discipline will remain minimal.

Establishing the accuracy of this negative assessment of post-modernism is not a simple matter. On the one hand, there are a number of recent interventions by those associated with the tradition that lend some credence to the idea that this assessment of post-modernism is more the result of the hold of positivist categories regarding the nature of reason on postmodernist international relations' critics than in the approach itself. It is significant, for example, that George and Campbell (1990), authors of one of the central contributions to a special issue on postmodernist international relations, have attempted to demarcate their work from those that remain entrapped within Bernstein's notion of the "Cartesian anxiety": "the modernist proposition . . . asserts that either we have some sort of ultimate 'foundation' for our knowledge or we are plunged into the void of the relative, the irrational, the arbitrary, the nihilistic" (George and Campbell, 1990:289)—a demarcation that would place postmodern international relations firmly on the path to the reflexive stance of incommensurable yet still comparable. In a similar fashion, Ashley and Walker's defense of a postmodern "ethics of freedom" against the charge that it sanctions "a sort of licentious activity whose credo might be 'Anything goes!'" can be read as an affirmation of the possibility of the reasoned adjudication of rival politico-normative claims, which is central to comparing the incommensurable (Ashley and Walker, 1990:389).

On the other hand, simple assertions are not sufficient on their own to establish postmodernism's suitability for conducting reasoned discourse about incommensurable projects and knowledge frameworks. For even if postmodernists do not make the mistake of equating reason with *episteme*, it is still difficult to see how they can reconcile their proclaimed desire to contribute to reasoned debates with the totalizing critique of reason that has marked much post-modernist work. Indeed, in light of the latter, one might reasonably conclude that postmodernism is better suited to undermining the role of reason in toto than to expanding the notion of reason beyond the confines of positivist *episteme* in a way consistent with reflexivity.

Conclusion

It may be useful to conclude by reflecting on some of the implications of a fully reflexive orientation for the members of the international relations scholarly community on a personal, self-definitional level. As was noted, a reflexive orientation leads us to view rival paradigms as incommensurable coping vocabularies linked to contending social agendas and political projects. It was also noted that recognizing such a link greatly facilitates rationally comparing incommensurable paradigms. Simply put, once the link between coping vocabulary and political project is recognized, the question "Which paradigm is superior?" can be restated as "Which general social agenda/political project is most appropriate in terms of the needs of the planet?" Likewise, the question of "What is reliable knowledge?" can be reformulated as "How should we live?"

This recognition is imperative in the discipline of international relations. Given that paradigms validate themselves in terms of both social actors and specific purposes, the question of social identity and political purpose can no longer be avoided by those who comprise the community of international relations scholars. If it is true that at the level of scholarship, paradigms "compete by virtue of the accounts they provide in explaining *what we as scholars . . . define as central to our purpose, enquiry, ideology*" (Smith, 1987:202; emphasis added), then reflexivity directs us to a broader debate about which purposes, which enquiries, and which ideologies merit the support and energy of international relations scholars. If it is true that, in the words of Fichte, "the choice between comprehensive theories rests on one's interests entirely" (cited in Feyerabend, 1975:128), then the nature of the interests with which international relations scholars identify themselves must be considered.

To adopt a fully reflexive stance is to recognize that participating in the "normal science" tradition of any paradigm means, consciously or not, lending support to a specific political project; it is to accept that to engage in paradigm-directed puzzle solving is, intentionally or not, to direct one's energies to the establishment and maintenance of a specific global order. As a consequence, it becomes vital to engage in a critical examination of the relative merits of rival political projects and of contending global orders. Once it is recognized that the knowledge-defining standards that we adopt are not neutral but have an undeniable politico-normative content, then it becomes imperative that we make a reasoned assessment of that content a central component of our deliberations about international politics.

Of course, the notion that all scholarship has a politico-normative content may well provoke significant resistance in the members of a community who have labored hard to achieve for the discipline the title of "science." Such a notion runs counter to the self-image of impartial, unbiased observer of international reality. Indeed, it may even prompt the charge that reflexivity is but a veiled attempt to "politicize the discipline." If it does so, this would indeed be ironic. The point of reflexivity is, after all, that the study of world politics always has been informed by political agendas and that it is time that the content of those agendas be brought out into the open and critically assessed.

Notes

1. It is true, of course, that neopositivists such as Karl Popper implicitly acknowledged the theory-dependent nature of empirical evidence, a recognition that would seem to pose considerable problems for the notion of truth as correspondence. Despite this recognition, however, truth as correspondence remained the regulative ideal of positivist social science, whereas the difficulties posed by theory-dependence were addressed in the efforts to specify rules of correspondence.

2. For a useful introduction to these traditions, see George and Campbell (1990).

3. It is important not to confuse the notion of the inherently politico-normative content of paradigms with the considerably less radical argument (in that it remained consistent with the regulative ideal of truth as correspondence) advanced by postbehavioralists—that scholars needed to become more aware of their personal "value biases" and the way these could distort the accuracy of empirical findings. In contrast, the argument from theoretical reflexivity is that (1) the (politico)-normative dimension of scholarship is not the property of individual scholars but adheres to the process of scholarly inquiry itself, and (2) the politico-normative content of scholarship is not a "contamination" of empirical research, but, in fact, constitutive of all such research (e.g., in determining what will count as a fact). For a clear statement of the postbehavioralist position on values and social science, see David Easton (1971).

4. As Bernstein has noted:

> With a chilling clarity Descartes leads us with an apparent and ineluctable necessity to a grand and seductive Either/Or. *Either* there is some support for our being, a fixed foundation for our knowledge, *or* we cannot escape the forces of darkness that envelop us with madness, with intellectual and moral chaos. (Bernstein, 1985:86)

5. It is true, of course, that only the logical positivists advocated the extreme position that normative claims were just so much nonsense, and that others in the positivist tradition—Popper, for example—were more sympathetic to the idea that normative theorizing could produce knowledge. So strong is the notion of truth as correspondence in the positivist tradition, however, that even the most sympathetic have been hard pressed to explain how reason could serve in assessing the truth value of normative claims.

6. See Taylor (1979), Gadamer (1988), Habermas (1984), and Bernstein (1985).

7. The term is Charles Taylor's.

8. An example of how a judgment about contending paradigms may be made on the basis of their politico-normative content is provided by Connolly (1974). He has argued that where evidence is insufficient to dictate the choice between competing theories in social science (as is the case when incommensurability obtains), a certain presumption should operate in favor of the theory that is more optimistic. See Connolly (1974:63–64).

9. See Chapter 1 by Cox and Turenne Sjolander for a more detailed discussion of this subject.

10. Similarly, in his overview of the subfield of international political economy, Gilpin (1987) speaks in terms of the nationalist, liberal, and Marxist perspectives.

11. With these remarks, Holsti also has demonstrated a misunderstanding of Kuhn's position. Kuhn has never suggested that one theory or paradigm (e.g., pre-Copernican astronomy) is replaced by a succeeding paradigm because its successor provides a more accurate description of reality. Indeed, Kuhn's notion of the incommensurability of succeeding paradigms is designed to counter exactly this conception of linear progress toward an ever more accurate description of the real world. It should be noted, however, that Holsti's adherence to the "linear progress" school of thought is thoroughly consistent with the Lakatosian reformulation of the positivist tradition.

12. "After all," Smith has noted, "if you are not a great power, in Morgenthau's use of the term, what foreign policy options do you have?" (Smith, 1987:201).

13. One sees the concern with reflexivity in the work of Stephen Gill (1991), for example.

3

The Discourse of Multilateralism: U.S. Hegemony and the Management of International Trade

CLAIRE TURENNE SJOLANDER

America is by no means the worst trade policy offender—but it is no longer the world's most enthusiastic champion of free trade either. If the Uruguay round fails, the lack of such a powerful champion may plunge the world into a ruinous series of protectionist battles which existing GATT rules will do little to restrain. Even if the round succeeds, as it probably will, the victory may prove Pyrrhic. Treaties and institutions are no substitute for conviction. Sadly, America has lost its conviction that free trade—not "fair" trade—is best.

—*The Economist*, April 11, 1992, p. 66

The free trade/fair trade rhetoric that has characterized the politicization of trade in the United States since the 1970s has been attributed to a variety of sources. On the one hand, as Jagdish Bhagwati has argued in numerous reviews of U.S. trade policy,[1] the turn to the discourse of fair trade is a manifestation of the "diminished giant" syndrome. As a declining hegemon faced with costly and painful domestic economic restructuring, the U.S. commitment to free trade, which had characterized the heyday of its hegemony, would inevitably decline as well. Under this interpretation, U.S. derogations from the spirit of the multilateral trading structure risk undermining its foundations, working to ensure that "fair trade [becomes] an enemy of free trade, not its ally" (Bhagwati and Irwin, 1987:127).

The contrary argument, on the other hand, portrays the United States as an earnest *defender* of trade liberalization, and suggests that in its pursuit of (ever narrower) alternatives to multilateral trade, the United States might actually be *advancing* the cause of free trade. As U.S. senator Max Baucus has argued in presenting the case for bilateral trade negotiations:

37

> Pursuing bilateral agreements actually increases the chances that the United States will be able to achieve its trade objectives in the Uruguay Round. Rather than draining interest from multilateral negotiations, active bilateral negotiations will actually increase other nations' interest in the GATT. . . . [This seemingly contradictory scenario will come about because] potential foot-draggers will realize that if they are unwilling to negotiate through the GATT, the United States will conclude bilateral agreements with other trade partners. Thus, active bilateral negotiations increase the cost of stalling in the GATT and improve chances for an eventual GATT agreement. (Baucus, 1989:21)

This chapter presents an analysis of U.S. trade policy in the new issues negotiations of the Uruguay Round of the General Agreement on Tariffs and Trade (GATT), up to the failure to meet its original December 1990 deadline. Given the acknowledged and central role of the United States in shaping the postwar multilateral trading order and its lead in pushing for the ambitious and highly inclusive Uruguay Round of negotiations, this case would appear to present a useful benchmark from which to assess the changing nature of the global order. Given their central importance to the international trade structure, the Uruguay Round negotiations also permit us to address the questions around U.S. hegemony that underline the fair trade/free trade debate. In so doing, this chapter focuses most specifically upon those issues that have first been introduced as part of the GATT negotiations in the Uruguay Round—trade in services, trade-related investment measures (TRIMs), and trade-related intellectual property rights or restrictions (TRIPs).

In part, the negotiation of these new issues is instructive because it marks the most significant potential extension of the GATT system since its creation in the immediate postwar era. As such, it is possible to argue that the multilateral trading structure and the rhetoric of trade liberalization that surrounds it is dynamic and healthy—despite, and perhaps even because of[2] the slow progress of the Uruguay Round negotiations. At the same time as the multilateral option appeared to be strengthened, however, the Uruguay Round witnessed the passing into law of what many have viewed as one of the most ubiquitous symbols of state unilateralism—the strengthened Section 301 provisions of the U.S. Omnibus Trade and Competitiveness Act of 1988. This trend to derogation was also evident in a general increase in quasi-protectionist actions, particularly on the part of the Group of Seven industrial countries (the G7), running the gamut from the "negotiation" of Voluntary Export Restraints (VERs) and Orderly Marketing Arrangements (OMAs), through to the more consistent adoption of antidumping and countervailing duty actions. Equally, the negotiation and strengthening of bilateral and regional trade agreements has also raised questions as to the health of multilateralism. More specifically, therefore, this chapter focuses upon the apparent contradictions between the discourse of U.S. derogations from multilateralism (the language of fair trade), and its espoused rhetoric of liberalized, multilateralized, or "free" trade in the context of the GATT negotiations.

At first glance, debates over U.S. trade policy might not seem a particularly fertile ground for analysis characterized by reflexivity. As *Harper's Magazine* reported in its "exposé" of the objectives of U.S. trade policy, "The average reader sees the acronym GATT, followed, say, by a reference to the European Community or the Group of Seven industrial nations, and soon the eyes begin to glaze and a hand reaches mechanically to turn the page" (Mead, 1992:37). Yet, it is precisely *because* the eyes begin to glaze—*because* trade remains politicized only at the margins—that a critical analysis marked by reflexivity is most useful. As Neufeld has argued in Chapter 2, reflexivity is characterized by three elements: (1) self-awareness regarding underlying premises; (2) awareness regarding the specifically political or normative content of any theoretical enterprise (an awareness based in part on a rejection of the subject/object distinction inherent in positivism); and (3) despite the consequent absence of value-free or objective criteria, a commitment to the possibility of reasoned discussion and evaluation of normative projects. It is precisely *because* the explicitly political or normative content of trade policy and of the structure of the international trading system has so consistently, and yet so functionally, been marginalized that an examination of the discourse of trade policy and the assumptions that underline it hold out the greatest potential for critical analysis.

In seeking to examine the discourse of trade policy, and more specifically of U.S. policy in the Uruguay Round of GATT negotiations, the goal of this research is not restricted to the advancement of an alternative reading of contemporary trade issues. Critical analysis also defines its objectives in underlining the political nature of the theoretical enterprise itself. Once the state, the domestic and international context in which it finds itself, and the discourse it advances are defined, and once the interrelationships between them are established, international relations theory opens itself to the possibility of becoming, more explicitly, a theory of politics. If the state itself can be made to be political, the possibilities for political change become more apparent. Specifying the political, particularly in the realm of the "depoliticized" field of trade policy, begins to address the need to open space in international relations theory so that, in the words of Jim George, "voices otherwise marginalized can be heard;

... questions otherwise suppressed can be asked, . . . [and] points of analytical closure can be opened for debate" (George, 1989:273). Understanding how the discourse of trade policy creates potentialities for the advancement of particular political agendas permits us to conceptualize openings for alternate agendas. Given that trade is often conceived as the lifeblood for most of the world's states, understanding its discourse and uncovering its political objectives have profound potential implications for much of the world's population.

Internationalization, the State, and the Politicization of Trade

The advent of markedly different, and potentially contradictory, trade policies has taken place within a context loosely characterized by the crisis of U.S. hegemony and the supersession of Pax Americana, that hegemonic structure defined in the postwar era. As Robert Cox has argued, Pax Americana as an international economic order has been defined by the internationalization of production, supported and encouraged by the institutional structures created around the Bretton Woods agreements. Through this process of internationalization, the economy has moved from an international one based on exchange to a world economy focused on production (Cox, 1987:244).[3] In this new international division of labor, increasingly mobile capital and technology, largely controlled by transnational (rather than national) corporations and financial interests, have become the privileged actors structuring the transboundary or transnational economy.

In tandem with the internationalization of production, Cox has identified a parallel process, which he terms the internationalization of the state, defined as:

> The global process whereby national policies and practices have been adjusted to the exigencies of the world economy of international production. Through this process the nation state becomes part of a larger and more complex political structure that is the counterpart to international production. (Cox, 1987:253)

This process has implied an important change in the role of the state in the management of its integration into the international economy. Under the international economy model of exchange, the state acts as a buffer between the international and domestic realms, and defends the latter economy when necessary. Through this defense, the state derives its political legitimacy. As the state becomes "internationalized," however, it is placed in a halfway position, increasingly driven (or constrained) to facilitate the internationalization of production and the consequent restructuring of the national economy. This occurs in part because the state finds itself accountable not only to its domestic constituency, but increasingly to the multilateral institutional structures that facilitate the fashioning of the world economy through the internationalization of production. Focusing on the processes underlying the structuring of a multilateral economic order in the postwar era, Cox is able to identify the *interests* clearly implicated in its institutionalization—in essence, he is able to answer the question of "theory for whom?"

In contrast to the structuring principles of the prewar order, the postwar tenets of the neoliberal economy, coupled with a profound suspicion of political isolationism, were to give a central place to multilateralism as a shaping feature of the emerging institutional structures and political practice in the postwar world. Although this structuring principle of the world political economy loosely emerged from the experiences of the industrialized powers throughout the depression and two world wars, the concrete foundations of this multilateralism were found in a wartime compromise between the United States and Great Britain (Ikenberry, 1992). The United States was able to use its economic leverage to pressure Britain to abandon the preferential trade and payments system, which had defined the Commonwealth trading bloc—in essence, to abandon protectionism within economic blocs as a privileged vehicle to promote enhanced trade. Out of this compromise, multilateralism came to define the structure of Pax Americana, that is, the structure of the U.S.-centered hegemonic world order. More simply,

> economic multilateralism meant the structure of world economy *most conducive to capital expansion on a world scale*; and political multilateralism meant the institutionalized arrangements made at that time and in those conditions for inter-state cooperation on common problems. There was, for some people, an implicit compatibility, even identity between economic and political aspects of multilateralism: political multilateralism had as a primary goal the security and maintenance of economic multilateralism, the underpinning of growth in the world capitalist economy. (Cox, 1992:162; emphasis added)

In order to understand the manner in which trade became partially politicized in the 1970s *despite* the internationalization logic of Pax Americana, we must turn our attention to the crisis of U.S. hegemony that touched the international economic order. Robert Cox has posited that the dominance of economic hegemons (first Britain then the United States) had been assisted because it appeared to take place "according to nonpolitical economic laws . . . [although it] was made possible by the existence of a world economy which was in fact guaranteed by political and military power" (Cox, 1982:38). The economic structure and rules created by the hegemon become part of the "natural" order,[4] and were consequently not the matter of political debate. More specifically, this hegemonic or natural order was constructed around the premise that "the world economy is a positive-sum game in which some businesses and some national economies may benefit more than the others but in which all have the opportunity to gain" (Cox, 1987:217). This central premise of the virtues of liberalization, embedded in the institutional context of Pax Americana, was functional both to the internationalization of capital and the internationalization of the state, for it encouraged the notion that the role of the state should naturally be limited—that "the highest interest of all countries . . . [should be to] facilitate the expansion of the world economy and to avoid restrictive national measures of economic policy that would be in contradiction in the long run with world-level expansion" (Cox, 1987:217).

Despite its ideological component, the outset of the crisis—the partial collapse of Bretton Woods, the oil shocks, the diffusion of manufacturing production to an increasing number of countries, and the rise of multinational and transnational corporations—began to repoliticize what had been accepted as natural under the hegemonic consensus of Pax Americana. In part, the growth of new forms of protectionism can be interpreted within the context of this repoliticization, particularly given the relative successes of the GATT in reducing explicit barriers to trade.

Unsurprisingly, the partial erosion of the consensus around Pax Americana finds its most schizophrenic response within the United States. As the economic crisis began to impose burdens of restructuring upon the U.S. economy, trade quickly became a more parochial concern, finding expression in legislative maneuverings within the Congress. The logic of Pax Americana, however, despite the fact that its benefits were no longer falling as disproportionately to the U.S. *state* as a whole, still dictated that important benefits were to be derived for certain segments of U.S. *capital.* Calls to protectionism from segments of labor and national capital had to be weighed against calls to further liberalization by nationally headquartered international capital.

Paradoxically, as the logic of Pax Americana within the context of the economic crisis encouraged capital nationally based in other countries to internationalize, states other than the United States

equally became subject to increased pressures to liberalize their economic policies—that is, to internationalize—rather than to define
them more restrictively. The irony of the hegemonic order of Pax
Americana is found in the fact that as trade policy is politicized in
the United States as elsewhere—as the benefits of the natural order
of liberalization are questioned—the internationalization pressures
embedded within it have never been manifested more strongly. The
crisis of hegemony, therefore, can thus be seen as one in which the
U.S. state assumes more of the role of a state *comme les autres,* rather
than be construed as a crisis of the order of Pax Americana per se.

It is important to note, however, that multilateralism and the
natural order of trade liberalization has hardly been without its contradictions. Whereas the ethos of multilateralism implied a global
scope and orientation, multilateralism as manifested at its inception
was actually the policy choice of a fairly circumscribed group of
states in the postwar world, and was restricted in important ways.
The Soviet Union and Eastern Europe, for example, devastated eco-
nomically and increasingly isolated politically, limited their participation in the definition of this new multilateral economic order.[5] As
well, given that most of the South had yet to assume an independent
role on the world stage, the voices of developing states were effectively muted in this process. Equally, national and regional regulations and intervention, which contradicted the liberal premises of
the order but had been allowed "temporarily" to facilitate reconstruction and stabilization in specific European countries, remained
in place until the end of the 1950s. In other words, at its inception,
the open, liberal multilateral economic order was neither particularly open nor particularly liberal. Multilateralism as part of an ideology, however, was functional to the *liberalization* implied in Pax
Americana; it sowed seeds instrumental to the expansion of the
world economy and its political component served the internationalization of capital well by encouraging the internationalization of the
state. In the rhetoric of fair and free trade, however, it is important
to remember that liberalization and multilateralism were not then,
nor are they now, synonymous.

U.S. Trade Policy: The Rhetoric of Liberalization

The principles of the postwar multilateral system for trade and
money are well known. These included nondiscrimination and
national treatment; a commitment to progressive liberalization of
international economic relations; a commitment to freely convertible
currencies; and transparency and multilateral surveillance, based on

codified legal principles. Gilbert Winham, in his key work *International Trade and the Tokyo Round Negotiation* (1986), has outlined the extent to which these principles were a reflection of the vision of the systemic hegemon—the United States—at the outset of the postwar era.

Whereas the commitment to progressive liberalization is apparent in the discussion of the internationalization logic of Pax Americana, and stems from the identification of state interests with the interests of capital, the commitment to multilateralism embodied in the principles of nondiscrimination and national treatment is not as easily established. Winham has attributed this commitment to roots founded in a conjunctural definition of a U.S. view of world politics. Historical U.S. opposition to the establishment of regional spheres of influence (particularly by other countries), he has argued, underlay their support for multilateralism and its corollary, nondiscrimination, as the guiding principle of an international trading regime (Winham, 1986:31–32).

Although the interests underlying multilateralism, therefore, could hardly be said to have been as materially based as those supporting the principles of liberalization, their implementation within the multilateral economic order has had implications. Winham has argued, in fact, that the practice of multilateral negotiation based on principles of nondiscrimination remains the most enduring contribution of that postwar agent of trade liberalization—the GATT (Winham, 1992:44). Insofar as the ethos of multilateralism was functional to the ideology of the hegemonic order—that is, inasmuch as multilateral structures convinced "lesser" participants that they promised the potential of shared benefits—multilateralism strengthened the logic of Pax Americana. Given its different material base, however, it might be argued that the ideology of multilateralism thus ironically became more central to other (industrialized) states in the postwar economic order than it did to the United States.

The Unilateral Face of U.S. Trade Policy

Since the advent of the economic crisis in the 1970s, the internationalization logic that dictates the strategies of transnational firms has had repercussions at the level of the domestic economy and thus, necessarily, upon state action and discourse. The first indication of the repoliticization of trade was clearly noted in the rise of the "new protectionism"—the increased recourse to nontariff barriers in order to limit the exports of competitors. In particular, industrialized countries broadened the range of trade remedy actions (especially antidumping and countervailing duty action) in order to "level the playing field." While certainly not limited to the United States—in fact, many would contend that these measures have been enthusiastically adopted by the range of countries in the Organization for Economic Cooperation and Development (OECD)—a partial list of antidumping and countervailing duty actions imposed against competitors since 1987 includes some unlikely targets. Among others, the United States has imposed antidumping duty action against Bangladesh (for the export of shop towels) and Kenya (for carnations), and countervailing duty action against Ecuador (for fresh cut flowers) and Zimbabwe (for carbon steel wire rod) (UNCTAD, 1991:73–74).[6] As the United Nations Conference on Trade and Development (UNCTAD) has argued, "even very small exporters with marginal market shares . . . have become subject to anti-dumping investigations in recent years. The harassment to trade for new and small exporters resulting from the time and costs involved in anti-dumping investigations can be very large" (UNCTAD, 1991:59).

Of course, antidumping and countervailing duties are not the only manifestations of quasi-protectionist actions meant to restrict trade by limiting exports. Voluntary Export Restraints and Orderly Marketing Arrangements have also evolved as specific mechanisms to manage or "administer" the nature and quantity of exports. As sardonically noted in *The Economist*:

> Increasingly, if a powerful government is worried about the harm that imports are doing to its producers, it does not seek a remedy through the GATT. Instead, especially if it happens to be the American government, it requires another government, on pain of retaliation, to restrict its country's exports of the good in question. (*The Economist*, September 22, 1990, p. 8)

The range of targets of these "voluntary" restraints has been quite broad, again including countries that would not normally be considered major export threats.

> The countries selflessly volunteering to restrict their exports include Japan, the newly industrialized East Asian economies, poorer countries such as Brazil, Mexico and Poland, and desperately poor ones such as Bangladesh. Members of the European Community, themselves devotees of the VER as an instrument of trade policy, are reluctant volunteers in one case: the Community has agreed to restrict its exports of steel to the United States. (*The Economist*, September 22, 1990, p. 8)

In addition to steel, most VERs have been imposed to control exports of chemicals, color televisions, footwear, textiles, and automobiles. Patrick Messerlin, an economist at the World Bank, has gone so far as to suggest that "entire industrial sectors—steel and chemicals in the United States; steel, chemicals and electronics in the EC—are increasingly molded by this instrument" (cited in *The Economist,* September 22, 1990, p. 11). These quasi-protectionist measures have also not been used sparingly. Over the period from 1979 to 1988, the United States brought forward 427 antidumping cases and 371 countervailing duty cases (*The Economist,* September 22, 1990, p. 11).[7] An argument might be constructed that these measures at least have some legal status in international trade jurisprudence; however, the same is more difficult to argue in defense of the growth of unilateral action to manage international trade.

The appearance on the international trade scene of unilateral trade strategies, often defined under the rubric of "aggressive unilateralism," has become an important preoccupation of trade scholarship. Where antidumping, countervailing duty, and export restraint actions have been directed to the management of exports (and therefore to the restriction of trade), the advent of aggressive unilateralism has contrarily been pursued in order to broaden or expand trade. The protectionism inherent in the first class of trade-restricting measures is not manifested in the same way in unilateral trade actions, for these ironically appear consistent with the logic of Pax Americana insofar as they move forward a liberalization agenda.

Chapter 1 of Title III of the U.S. Trade Act of 1974 (commonly referred to as Section 301), particularly as revisited in the passage of the 1988 Omnibus Trade and Competitiveness Act, has become the symbol of the trend to unilateral action. Section 301, even in its original inception, was broadly directed at foreign restrictions on U.S. trade and was to be used to enforce U.S. trade rights as conferred by the GATT and by bilateral treaties, if necessary through retaliation against those judged to have violated these rights. Section 301 thus provided the authority and procedures for the president of the United States to enforce U.S. "rights" to respond to the "unfair" trading of specific goods.

Whereas Section 301 was invoked to deal with complaints about goods, its toughened version—known as "Super 301"—is "used to accuse countries of a broad range of unfair trading practices" (*The Economist,* September 22, 1990, p. 11). The 1988 amendments to the original Section 301 imposed timetables on the steps to be followed in the determination of Super and Special 301 cases. These timetables raised the possibility that U.S. trade law could *explicitly* conflict with the more leisurely GATT procedures, greatly increasing the likelihood of Section 301 retaliations by the United States *before* a GATT determination, and thus making U.S. action GATT-inconsistent (Bhagwati, 1990).[8] As well, the 1988 act substantially stiffened the process by supplying a nonexhaustive list of unfair trading practices, including inadequate workers' rights and insufficient anticompetitive policy strictures—matters that have not traditionally been dealt with in trade negotiations but played into the U.S. rhetoric of fair trade and market access.

Most importantly, however, the strengthened Section 301 provision gained its teeth through its automatic imposition.

> Super 301 essentially requires the United States Trade Representative, on schedule, to prepare an inventory of foreign trade barriers, establish a priority list of countries and their unreasonable practices, and then set deadlines for their removal by the foreign countries and, should they fail to comply, for decisions on retaliation by the United States. (Bhagwati, 1990:3)

The 1988 Omnibus Trade and Competitiveness Act also mandated the creation of Special 301, whose provisions are similar to Super 301 but are addressed to intellectual property rights. These measures, although not protectionist in any strict understanding of the term (and in fact consistent with the logic of liberalization), do violence to the basis of the multilateral trading structure. Where the GATT provides at least the illusion of being a neutral arbiter, Section 301 provisions place the United States in the role of judge, jury, and executioner.

More interesting, however, is the list of countries against whom Section 301 provisions have been used or threatened. Originally seen by the U.S. Congress as a mechanism to force Japan to play by the rules set by the multilateral trading structure as it has been interpreted by the United States (within the context of the politicization of trade in the United States), the "priority hit list" published annually by the executive branch is instructive for the countries that have been included *beyond* Japan.[9] On May 26, 1989, the United States cited three countries as unfair traders: Japan, for erecting trade barriers in supercomputers, telecommunication satellites, and wood products; Brazil, for its import licensing policies and high tariffs; and India, for its trade-related foreign investment regulations and for restrictions on U.S. insurance companies (UNCTAD, 1989:69). As of May 1990, four countries remained on the "priority watch list" (Brazil, India, China, and Thailand), and nineteen had been placed on the "watch list" (Argentina, Canada, Chile, Colombia, Egypt, Greece, Indonesia, Italy, Japan, Malaysia, Pakistan, Philippines, Republic of Korea, Saudi Arabia, Spain, Taiwan, Turkey, Venezuela, and the former Yugoslavia).

What is most striking about these lists is the disproportionate number of developing countries cited. Although U.S. trade with developing countries (other than those of Southeast Asia) remains minuscule as a percentage of its total trade, these countries represent the greatest number identified as probable unfair traders by Section 301 mechanisms. What is also interesting is that a disproportionate number of these citations relate to violations of trade disciplines that have not yet fallen under the GATT structures—trade in services, the respect for intellectual property rights, and the imposition of trade-related investment regulations.[10] In cases against Brazil and India, U.S. interest was clearly to promote and advance the multilateral negotiations to codify trade in services under the auspices of the GATT, and more specifically to advance the U.S. interpretation of how this codification should be achieved.

Geza Feketekuty, counselor to the U.S. Trade Representative (USTR), has argued that Section 301 provisions are positive inasmuch as they "encourage" other countries to consider the international codification services trade (Feketekuty, 1990:102). In response to Feketekuty's analysis, however, Claude Barfield, Jr., has argued that Feketekuty

> states flatly what other administration spokesmen have only implied previously—that Brazil and India were chosen because of their resistance to the U.S. administration's multilateral positions on trade issues—and, indeed, exposes once again the 1989 Super 301 process for the procedural and substantially corrupt exercise its critics have maintained it was. (Barfield, 1990:105)

What GATT negotiations have failed to create, the United States through actual and threatened Section 301 actions has been able to impose.

Unilateralism and Internationalization:
The Contradictions of Trade

Under considerable pressure from the United States in the post–Tokyo Round era (specifically from 1982 to 1986), the GATT took up the causes of negotiating the liberalization of trade in services as well as of incorporating agreements on respect for intellectual property rights and international investment as part of the Uruguay Round. The interest of the United States, shared by many other OECD countries, in the negotiation of an agreement incorporating these new issues appeared evident, at least at the outset.[11] Service industries such as banking and finance, telecommunications, transport, shipping, tourism, construction, education, and entertainment, among others, account for well over half the national income of most of the economies of the industrialized world. Nearly 70 percent of the U.S. gross domestic product (GDP) and three-quarters of its employment are found in services (*The Economist*, September 22, 1990, p. 36). Estimates of the significance of exchange in services to current international trade vary from a low of $560 billion per year to a high of $1 trillion, or an estimated one-third of world trade. In the case of intellectual property rights, the interest of the United States is equally apparent, and in many respects its aims are thus clearer than those of other industrialized countries.

> America's interest in intellectual property is by no means altruistic. From movies to microchips, America ran a healthy $12 billion surplus on its trade in ideas in 1990. . . . Most other developed countries, by contrast, pay more for technology licences than they earn from them. Though Japanese companies apply for the most patents at home, American companies apply for many more foreign patents than any of their competitors. (*The Economist*, August 22, 1992, p. 55)

Whereas much of the developed world was at least initially supportive of the prospect of negotiations on services and intellectual property, the United States at the outset faced the challenge of gaining the support of developing countries, particularly—although on different issues—the larger markets of Brazil, India, and Egypt.

> Countries such as Brazil and India feared—not without reason— that rich-country banking and insurance firms would steal business from their own less efficient domestic providers, whereas the rich countries would bar the third world from exporting the services in which it has the greatest comparative advantage. How willing will America be, for example, to let teams of low-paid foreign construction workers compete with its own hard hats? (*The Economist*, September 22, 1990, p. 36)

At the outset, therefore, agreement on services and intellectual property rights was presented as a U.S. condition for substantial reform in textiles, a key demand, along with reform of trade in agriculture, of the developing world. As we have seen, however, such negotiation positions were supplemented with the judicious application of protectionist and unilateral trade actions, which throughout the negotiations were increasingly seen to work.

> As soon as the USTR, Mrs. Carla Hills, named Brazil, India and Japan as unfair traders, talks began. Brazil and Japan made trade concessions and soon escaped from the list. Before the list was ever announced, Taiwan and South Korea made trade concessions in anticipation of being named. . . . Who says realism doesn't pay? (*The Economist*, September 22, p. 25)

In August 1989, the *International Trade Reporter* related that the United States was determined to obtain the broadest possible agreement on services and intellectual property with the strongest possible enforcement language, even at the expense of limiting the number of agreement signatories. Seemingly consistent with the spirit of multilateralism, such an agreement would effectively obviate the need for Section 301, particularly in its Super and Special manifestations, at least for those limited signatories of the agreements. This was particularly clear in the case of intellectual property rights, for which the United States championed the negotiation of strong enforcement measures despite not only the possibility of fewer signatories at the outset but also India's vociferous opposition. The United States promoted the adoption of language that would have the effect of making its own restrictive regulations more GATT-consistent, and urged that countries "agree to measures to enforce protected intellectual property at the border" (*Inside U.S. Trade*, August 25, 1989, p. 3).[12] As "leader" of the charge of developing countries, India argued that enforced protection for intellectual property holders would only widen the development gap between industrialized and developing countries.

In the first formal proposal on trade in services,[13] tabled in Geneva on October 23, 1989, U.S. negotiators appeared to derogate from the potentially inclusive approach they had advocated earlier. The U.S. team now advanced the prospect of appending schedules to a services agreement, in which each country could exclude temporarily certain sectors, or list reservations to some of the provisions dealing with market access and national treatment (Dullforce, 1989:8). In part, this derogation can be traced to the lobbying of the telecommunication industry, which expressed a clear preference for an international agreement that did not limit access to unilateral action. The U.S. Department of Defense, together with major telecommunication firms led by AT&T, argued that basic telecommunication services should be excluded outright from an agreement on services (*Inside U.S. Trade*, September 28, 1990, p. 14). This reluctance to abandon the provisions of Section 301 was to play an ever greater role in the negotiation of the GATT new issues package.

In a new proposal in early April 1990, the United States returned to a more inclusive position, although specifying that any services text would have to contain a clause allowing any government to refuse to apply liberalization provisions to a country it considered was maintaining too many reservations on its schedule (*Financial Times*, April 3, 1990, p. 6). By November, however, even this limited provision was deemed to be unsatisfactory to U.S. negotiators, who announced their insistence that signatories to the agreement should not enjoy automatic rights to nondiscriminatory treatment (otherwise known as most-favored nation [MFN] status). MFN status would be granted only if countries opened up their own services markets on a basis of reciprocal access. In part in response to the concerns of its transnational telecommunication firms, the U.S. administration argued that the possibility of unilateral action had to be maintained within the context of an international agreement. In a letter to U.S. Trade Representative Carla Hills, Commerce Secretary Robert Mosbacher argued that any agreement should "include the continued use of section 301 to open foreign closed markets, the right to retaliate against a country violating an existing bilateral telecommunications agreement and the right to negotiate bilateral agreements that would increase market access bilaterally" (*Inside U.S. Trade,* September 28, 1990, p. 14).

The negotiation of TRIPs was to prove equally problematic, for many of the same reasons. By August 1990, and following the U.S. position, Uruguay Round participants were ready to acknowledge that they were more likely to agree on an intellectual property code with limited membership than an inclusive article within the GATT that applied to all members. Although the telecommunication industry played a key role in the movement to abrogate MFN in services negotiations, unsurprisingly, support for a code with the strongest possible enforcement language came from the Pharmaceutical Manufacturers Association. On this front, the battle on intellectual property rights was drawn as one between developed countries, following the lead of the United States, and developing countries, led by India and Thailand. Developing countries resisted an inclusive code on this issue and argued that intellectual property laws drive up domestic prices, thus depriving the poor of access to patented, trademarked, and copyrighted products. The two positions could not have been farther apart. Asked to outline what a GATT intellectual property code would include, Harvey Bale, spokesperson for the Pharmaceutical Manufacturers Association, argued that

> "it would not be unreasonable" to expect it to provide 20-year patent protection, limitations on compulsory licensing, coverage of all subject matter, including pharmaceuticals, coverage of previously patented products, and coverage of "pipeline" products like pharmaceuticals where there is a lag time between development and commercial availability. (*International Trade Reporter,* August 22, 1990, p. 1306)

Within the context of this gulf between positions, it is unsurprising that Section 301 actions were launched so consistently against developing countries on intellectual property grounds.

Foreshadowing a division between the United States and the European Community on trade in services, the debate over positions on TRIPs was not limited strictly to a developing/developed country split. The EC, on issues such as the audiovisual sector, was less than interested in the negotiation of an inclusive code for intellectual property. Confronted with the giant U.S. film industry, the EC argued for the exemption of audiovisual industries from international obligations such as most-favored-nation status, national treatment, and market access. This position more closely corresponded with that of India and Egypt, two of the world's largest movie producers, who argued that some form of cultural protection would be necessary to promote the survival of their indigenous industries. This similarity of interests was not in specific proposals, however, with the EC advocating national cultural content quotas, which both India and Egypt feared would limit the distribution of their films in their respective regional markets.

For their part, U.S. industry, from films to publishing, returned to unilateral measures as the best fallback position, preferable to many potential negotiated agreements. Industry representatives argued that they would "not sanction a bad international agreement and abandon the success of bilateral negotiations and the so-called special 301 provision in the 1988 trade law that permits the U.S. to take unilateral action against foreign violators of intellectual property" (*Inside U.S. Trade*, November 2, 1990, p. 6). By late November 1990, a draft text of an agreement on intellectual property revealed that developing countries had committed themselves to new rules to curb trade in pirated and counterfeit goods, whereas industrialized countries continued to push for highly detailed and binding rules governing the protection of intellectual property rights and standards, notwithstanding the dispute between the United States and the European Community on how best to achieve this end. The United States continued to maintain the necessity of providing minimum standards of patent protection for all technologies, or else face unilateral trade retaliation.

U.S. retreats from the principle of nondiscrimination were roundly condemned, not only by the developing world but also by the European Community, which began pushing for the elimination of Section 301 provisions in U.S. trade law. In contrast to the U.S. proposals, Brussels put forward its own draft in early December 1990, enshrining MFN status for all signatories and calling for common dispute settlement rules that would supplant unilateral measures such as Section 301 provisions. In an attempt to forge a compromise before the formal December 1990 negotiation deadline, the

United States moved to abandon its insistence that market access commitments would have to be made before extending MFN treatment to trading partners, although it maintained the de facto linkage between the two (*Inside U.S. Trade,* December 14, 1990, p. 10).

Interestingly, although the gulf between the United States and developing countries—and increasingly the European Community —appeared wide on services and intellectual property, trade-related investment measures were less of a source of contention. Not prepared to accept the unequivocal prohibition of measures that inhibit trade, developing countries, particularly from Southeast Asia, proposed that language be developed to discourage the use of investment policies that would adversely affect other GATT contracting parties (*Inside U.S. Trade,* August 25, 1989, p. 4). Known as the "amber light" scenario (as opposed to the "red light" of prohibition), progress in negotiations by the summer months of 1989 suggested that the issue of TRIMs would not be as difficult as had been anticipated. By July 13, 1990, negotiations on TRIMs had produced a relatively harmonious draft agreement, with only modest differences among proposals from the United States, the EC, and developing countries.

In part, and in contrast to other issues, this relative harmony was seen as a consequence of the U.S.'s diminished ardor for a code to deal with the trade impact of specific investment measures. U.S. firms did not identify TRIMs as one of their pressing priorities "because they are generally offered investment sweeteners such as favourable tax treatment in return" (*The Economist,* September 22, 1990, p. 36). Further, the United States had itself begun to toy with local-content rules for inward investment, and the high-profile takeover of a number of U.S. assets by Japanese firms among others had the potential of pushing the United States further in this direction. With TRIMs, at least nominally, the protectionist discourse of U.S. policy challenged its commitment to liberalization.

Once the December 7 deadline had passed and the talks had seemingly collapsed, the links between Section 301 provisions and multilateral trade negotiations became a more significant part of the political discourse in the United States. Senator Max Baucus, chairman of the international trade subcommittee of the Senate Finance Committee and long a supporter of unilateral U.S. trade policy, made the links most explicit. "Our trading partners must realize that the U.S. is firmly committed to opening markets. . . . If we cannot open those markets through the GATT, we will use Section 301" (quoted in *International Trade Reporter,* January 9, 1991, p. 60). Baucus went on to comment:

> In light of the seeming breakdown of the GATT, it is time for
> the Congress to review Section 301. . . . Section 301 has been
> the most successful provision of the trade act. . . . In recent
> years Section 301 has had a much better record of opening markets
> than the GATT. . . . In light of its success in opening foreign mar-
> kets and the apparent failure of the GATT, the Congress should
> now extend Super 301. (quoted in *Inside U.S. Trade,* January 4, 1991,
> p. 2)

Representative Sander Levin, cochairman of a House working group
on the Uruguay Round, emphasized that the Congress would not
"consider changes to domestic remedies such as section 301 and
countervailing duty laws until it sees that a new international system would effectively foster open trade" (quoted in *Inside U.S. Trade,*
December 21, 1990, p. 15).

In response to congressional concerns, Deputy U.S. Trade
Representative Julius Katz signaled the intention of the administra-
tion to support the unilateral provisions of Section 301. U.S. negotiators would not concede Section 301 market access provisions in the
Uruguay Round, for these allow the United States to "achieve rea-
sonable, non-discriminatory trade treatment abroad" (*Inside U.S.
Trade,* January 11, 1991, p. 9). Deputy U.S. Trade Representative K.
Linn Williams commented further that the prospect of Uruguay
Round failure would not signal Armageddon for the United States,
which could quite comfortably pursue bilateral arrangements and
use unilateral trade remedy solutions in various sectors
(*International Trade Reporter,* January 30, 1991, p. 167).

Failure to reach agreement on intellectual property rights saw
calls for further recourse to Section 301 provisions on the part of
industry as well. The Pharmaceutical Manufacturers Association
began to muse aloud about the possibility of launching a petition
before the USTR to begin a Section 301 investigation against
Thailand for its failure to protect foreign-owned patents (*Inside U.S.
Trade,* January 4, 1991, p. 1). Among others, John L. Pickett, president of the U.S. Computer and Business Equipment Manufacturers
Association, expressed concern as to the inadequate intellectual
property protection legislation and enforcement procedures in many
countries. In the absence of an agreement, he warned, "the U.S. may
be forced to turn to Section 301 of the . . . trade law to counter grave
piracy and market access problems abroad" (quoted in *International
Trade Reporter,* December 12, 1990, p. 1,882). What could not be
achieved through negotiation was still open through mechanisms of
unilateral imposition.

Conclusion

This brief review of U.S. trade policy allows us to draw certain conclusions about the potentially competing notions of multilateralism, liberalization, and internationalization, and the role of the United States in defending or undermining these ideals. Whereas liberalization seemed intrinsic to the internationalization logic of Pax Americana, and multilateralism became its functional corollary, the role of the United States in defending these principles has been far from consistent. In fact, the contradictions observed would seem to suggest the extent to which U.S. hegemony may be under siege, although the structure of the international trade system put into place under U.S. leadership at the close of World War II does not appear to be waning as such.

It is clear that the commitment to multilateralism, and in particular to its central tenet of nondiscrimination, has become eroded both in U.S. discourse and trade policy action. Lost in the rhetoric of fair trade is U.S. leadership in the defense of an *internationally* (as opposed to a regionally or bilaterally) defined world trading system. The advent of economic multipolarity is clearly important in this respect—multilateralism would seem a wiser course when economic advantage is clear, for under such circumstances, selfless concessions might more easily be granted. Yet, in this regard, it is interesting to note the extent to which the United States has been pushing for the entrenchment of its advantages, including the right to unilateral retaliation, in negotiations on intellectual property—that issue in which it likely has the clearest comparative advantage. Michael Prowse may well be right in his hypothesis that "whatever happens to the Uruguay Round . . . [it] marks only the beginning of a more assertive—and more *selfish*—U.S. trade policy" (Prowse, 1991; emphasis added).

Equally clear is that the U.S. commitment to liberalization also appears suspect. The increasing adoption of VERs and antidumping and countervailing duty actions has the impact of limiting trade rather than expanding it. In the sectors in which they are most often applied, such trade actions clearly have the effect of protecting U.S. firms, rather than assisting their internationalization. Furthermore, in the negotiation on TRIMs, there is growing evidence of a half-hearted resignation to an amber light scenario, which continues to permit in part a number of investment regulations. This may not be as contradictory to the logic of Pax Americana as would initially be thought, however, largely because U.S. firms continue to benefit from these measures at least as much as they are constrained by them. If the logic of internationalization privileges the transnational firm, then it is perfectly consistent to place limits on liberalization as long as these limits advantage the key "internationalizing" actor.

In contrast, whatever else Section 301 provisions may or may not be, they are in themselves not inconsistent with the logic of internationalization. Whereas the growing permeability of the U.S. Congress has given rise to the rhetoric of fair trade, this parochialism, much decried by U.S. trading partners, is functional to the logic of Pax Americana inasmuch as it has been used to make foreign states accountable to the logic of internationalization. As we have seen, Section 301 actions have been launched less for reasons of an explicitly protectionist nature than to encourage the opening of certain (primarily developing country) markets. Section 301 thus becomes a proxy for the inadequate international institutional structures that might otherwise dictate the "internationalization" of developing country states. The fact that many of the strongest supporters of Super 301 are among the largest of the U.S. service firms suggests the extent to which such policies conform to the demands of the internationalization of production.

The lessons of the discourse of U.S. trade policy, particularly for those who find themselves marginalized by the current configuration of power in the international trading system, are found in these contradictions between multilateralism, liberalization, and internationalization. The logic of Pax Americana appears overwhelming, but its inevitability has been repoliticized through its very success. Derogations from multilateralism and even from liberalization may eventually prove injurious to the underlying logic of internationalization. As Robert Cox reminds us:

> Like the internationalizing of production, the tendency toward the internationalizing of the state is never complete, and the further it advances, the more it provokes countertendencies sustained by domestic social groups that have been disadvantaged or excluded in the new domestic realignments. These countertendencies could prove capable of reversing the internationalizing tendency. . . . There is nothing inevitable about the continuation of either the internationalizing of the state or the internationalizing of production. (Cox, 1987:253–254)

Notes

1. See, for example, Bhagwati and Irwin (1987), or Bhagwati (1990).
2. The incorporation of issues representing up to one-third of total world trade is certainly an ambitious undertaking, particularly given the far greater number of participants in the Uruguay Round negotiations. It is in

many respects unsurprising, given the complexity of these issues and the difficulty of incorporating them into an existing structure, that the Uruguay Round would have extended beyond the deadlines set for it.

3. Robert Cox has described this transition in the following manner:

> The *Pax Americana* created a world hegemonic order in which a *world* economy of international production emerged within the existing *international* economy of classical trade theory. . . . Where the international-economy model focuses on exchange, the world-economy model focuses on production. It consists of transnational production organizations whose component elements are located in different territorial jurisdictions. (Cox, 1987:244)

4. This, in fact, represents Cox's notion of hegemony: "the temporary universalization in thought of a particular power structure, conceived not as domination but as the necessary order of nature" (Cox, 1982:38).

5. Although the Soviet Union was present at the Bretton Woods negotiations, neither it nor the Eastern European nations that came under its influence participated in the institutions that were created.

6. As Jagdish Bhagwati has remarked, there has been a virtual explosion in the number of antidumping and countervailing duty cases investigated by industrialized countries since the conclusion of the Tokyo Round of GATT negotiations. Between 1980 and 1987, 300 cases were investigated in the European Community, and 700 cases were initiated in the United States. Bhagwati contends that this trade remedy machinery, although it remains formally consistent with GATT disciplines, has been used primarily for protectionist ends (Bhagwati, 1988).

7. Comparable figures for the European Community (EC) reveal the extent to which the imposition of countervailing duties is a U.S. trade tactic. From 1979 to 1988, the EC enacted 406 antidumping cases but only 13 countervailing duty investigations.

8. The assessment prepared by *The Economist* is in many respects even blunter. The toughened Section 301 procedures, they argue, violate three of the fundamental principles of the GATT: reciprocity, because the United States is not offering to lower its own trade barriers; nondiscrimination, because the United States is implicitly threatening to block imports from one country; and transparency, because the outcome is likely to involve some nontariff intervention in trade (*The Economist*, September 22, 1990, p. 11).

9. Japan was not a marginal target, however. Wielding the Section 301 stick, the United States was able to negotiate its Structural Impediments Initiative with Japan, covering "Japan's retail distribution system, its public spending on roads and infrastructure, households' savings habits, employment legislation and so on, this list extending to more than 200 issues" (*The Economist*, September 22, 1990, p. 11). To say that the list includes elements not traditionally thought of as trade-related would be an understatement.

10. *The Economist* reports that by far the greatest number of countries listed under priority or other watch lists have been placed there because of their allegedly inadequate protection of intellectual property (*The Economist*, September 22, 1990, p. 11).

11. One of the more comprehensive, and most recent, reviews of the services negotiations of the Uruguay Round is to be found in Drake and

Nicolaïdis (1992). In this review, they point out the difficulty of defining the specific meaning of a service. Citing a phrase usually attributed to *The Economist*, they suggest lightly that "Services are something you can buy and sell but cannot drop on your foot" (Drake and Nicolaïdis, 1992:43).

12. Section 337 of the United States Trade Act of 1930 allows the International Trade Commission to ban imports that violate U.S. patent law.

13. The U.S. position on trade in services, and the progress of negotiations therein, is treated in more detail in Sjolander (1993).

4

The Politics of Violence: Global Relations, Social Structures, and the Middle East

WAYNE S. COX

Q. *Middle East Report:* Within certain university contexts there have been lately two major issues: the Gulf war and multiculturalism. I have not seen any linkage between the two.

A. Edward Said: Even inside the university, the prevalence of norms based upon domination and coercion is so strong because the idea of authority is so strong, whether it's derived from the nation-state, from religion, from the ethnos, from tradition. It is so powerful that it's gone relatively unchallenged even in the very disciplines and studies that we are engaged in. Part of the intellectual work is understanding how authority is formed. Authority is not God-given. It's secular. And if you can understand that, then your work is conducted in such a way as to be able to provide alternatives to the authoritative and coercive norms that dominate so much of our intellectual life, our national and political life, and our international life above all.

—*Edward Said* (1991)

This chapter puts forward a social framework for the understanding of violence in global society. It argues that the basic analytical tool used in the construction of theories of war—the state—is poorly conceptualized within mainstream international relations generally, and within conflict studies particularly. This poor conceptualization has resulted in a research preference toward state-centric explanations of war at the expense of an analysis of the complex social contexts within which these processes develop. Such a preference is largely driven by the fact that states attempt to appropriate "the legitimate use of violence," regardless of the fact that such an attempt is often disputed by subordinate social groups who either reject the authority of the state or reject the international state system altogether. A field of enquiry that defines itself as the study of state actors provides an understanding of conflict from the perspective of a hegemonic system driven largely, but not exclusively, by the United States. For disempowered social groups,[1] however, this picture is incomplete and potentially dangerous.

As E. Fuat Keyman argues in Chapter 8, developing a more nuanced notion of the state is an inadequate way to understand the complex interrelationships between social groups and the state. A theoretical deconstruction of state-centered conflict analysis provides an important contribution to our understanding of violence at the theoretical/political level, as well as the empirical level. In keeping with the tradition of reflexive theory, deconstructed state-centricity reveals the extent to which scholars and practioners of international relations "see" violence. Of course, the way they see the world affects the potential solutions to the problem. Recent history suggests that the solutions (by political and military leaders and state-centric realist and neorealist scholars alike) are almost exclusively thought of in terms of state-controlled military responses to complex international and intersocial relations. In other words, the way you see violence often affects the way you do violence. The Gulf War is a graphic example of this, and its costs in human life should convince even the most committed partisans of state-centric power politics that there "has to be a better way." Moreover, the reflexive mode of theorization might be the only way in which practioners and some scholars of international relations will come to face the fact they are not merely reacting to the world *as it is,* but are involved in the inherently political act of constructing the world *as it will be.*

As an alternative, a sociostructural framework is proposed that assists in analyzing the role of the state and its claim to the legitimate use of violence, and provides more effective theoretical tools to conceptualize both the social and state influences upon the process of violence. In order to begin the construction of this framework, however, we must fully understand the concept of the state as it is now commonly used in the study of war.

The State in the Context of Civil Society

The most basic understanding of the state is that which suggests its rough equivalence to what is usually called a country. In this sense a state possesses population, territory, government, and international recognition. A central aspect of this definition of the state is the notion of political sovereignty. Essentially a legal term, sovereignty refers to the belief that only states can determine and regulate the social rules of conduct and political organization within their respective sovereign boundaries. As such, only states possess political sovereignty.

Beyond the basic definition of state is the concept of the nation-state.[2] The nation-state includes, of course, the legal characteristics of a state, and as such the nation-state possesses population, territory, government, and international recognition. However, the concept of the nation-state also includes the idea that the constituents within states share a relatively homogeneous "national identity." If this is not the case, many contend that states often embark upon a process of national assimilation in an attempt to forge this national identity.

As a state-based theory of global politics, realism tends to gloss over the significance of ethnic, national, and/or civil fragmentation within states. As a result, realism assumes that most states in the international system are nation-states or that the domestic concerns of a multinational state are somehow less significant than its international considerations in the definition of state action on the international stage. Beyond this, however, one must note a more complex assumption of these state-centric classical realist and neorealist theories. State-centric understandings of international relations are unable to theoretically divorce the concepts of state and society. In assuming that states are unitary actors in the international system, these theories do acknowledge that society is composed of all social relations within the geographic boundaries of the country. Despite this acknowledgment, theoretical primacy is given to the state in the international context.[3] This implies that there is no causal link between the complex social relations within and among states and the international state system per se. Morgenthau has confirmed this assumption by defining the study of international relations as *only* the study of states and the international state system. According to Morgenthau, the state unit is the theoretical delineation between domestic civil society and relations at the international or global level. "In other words, what factor making for peace and order exists within national societies which is lacking on the international scene? The answer seems obvious—it is the state itself" (Morgenthau, 1973:479).

Some of the implications of this state-centric approach are clear. To begin, all sub- and/or transstate relations are inevitably reduced to state-level analysis or ignored as having little impact upon conflict outcomes. Within or among states, ideas of nationalism, ethnic self-determination, revolution, economic classes, inter- and intrastate trade, economic development, and regional disputes are treated as elements of a theory in which states are viewed as unitary power-maximizing actors. Political realism and neorealism quite simply assume that states are unitary actors despite theoretical or methodological evidence to the contrary. As Waltz has contended, states "are individualist in origin, spontaneously generated, and unintended" (Waltz, 1979:91).

Diaspora national groups, ethnic minorities within states, and multistate nation-groups are considered by realists only insofar as these groups relate to existing states, and even such considerations are usually relegated to the realm of "low politics."[4] Social divisions within states are equally regarded as subparts of an all-encompassing statewide society. Long-term relationships of exploitation and violence between social groups within any one society cannot seriously be considered by a state-centric theory that rests on unitary state assumptions. The result of such assumptions is that realist conceptions of war pose a theoretical impediment to the full understanding of the social basis of conflict. Such a division between domestic and international levels of analysis must be rejected as wholly inadequate and distorting if we are to capture fully the roots of violence in international society.

The notion of the state as presented in this chapter is necessarily multidimensional. Although states do possess population, territory, government, and political sovereignty, it cannot be assumed that states in the international system are in any way homogeneous. Moreover, there is a clear need to theoretically divorce the concepts of state and society in both the domestic and international context. Social groups are both independent of and conditioned by the state. Although many social groups (particularly those who use collective violence as a means toward political ends) exist within states, many transcend sovereign boundaries. At the same time, states possess the mechanisms that can be used by these social groups to advance some of their interests. As a result, state elites, bureaucracies, militaries, state polices, and so on are involved in a complex dialectical relationship with social groups, the agents of other states, and institutions.

Social Systems, States, and Violence

Having laid out the inadequacies of state-centric analyses, the need for a broader theoretical understanding of the social bases of political violence should be clear. Few (if any) would doubt that states possess the deadliest instruments of mass destruction, but it cannot be assumed therefore that states are the sole actors in organized acts of political violence. The focus upon the state is similar to a focus upon the weapons of destruction themselves, for both sidestep the problem of violence. Both ignore the series of social factors implicated in the process of violent conflict. Whereas violence is often conducted within global society in the name of states, the unitary state-society assumptions implied by political realism tell us nothing about how states deal with social cleavages within and among these "autonomous" actors. Although the theoretical framework for a sociostructural theoretical understanding of collective social violence proposed here relies upon examples of ethnic-national social groups, this is not to imply that ethnic-national social groups are the only ones this model attempts to understand.

Structural Violence: The Actors

Conflict within global society is defined here as the collective use of violence by two or more socially identifiable groups as a means to achieve contending political and/or social objectives. Specific to this notion, the social actors can be identified as groups whose self-identification is sufficient to legitimize the use of violence in the name of the collective. Such a definition can be applied to both state and non-state social groups with a preponderance toward the use of violence as a means to political ends. These social groups may coexist within a single state, may reside in two states, or may be found in a large number of separate sovereign political units. This conceptualization allows us to conceive of a nonstate actor–based definition of conflict.

It is essential that any definition of conflict include those who are involved in the violence itself. The collective social interaction of individuals must also play a role in the definition of a concept of collective, or social, violence. As such, "agency" is an inherent factor in the definition process. Alexander Wendt's arguments with regard to the ontologically primitive nature of the state in realist and neorealist theory examine the limitations of such a "macro" theoretical approach (Wendt, 1987). The need to disaggregate the state is crucial in order to conceptualize those factors considered key in the understanding of conflict below and across the state level. The basic questions to be addressed are: At what level does any theory of conflict assign ontological primacy? Is there a basic (or primitive) agent in the process of conflict? The use of violence in the name of social groups suggests more than individual self-interest. It suggests the perceived need of social groups to maintain a group identity and ensure the collective interests of the social group itself. The ultimate expression of the collective interests of social groups is found in the legitimization of the collective use of violence. Whereas scholars of international relations have been willing to acknowledge this fact since the inception of the discipline, the dominant theoretical analysis has been at the state level. Social identification appears to provide a more inclusive means by which we can conceptualize the crucial actors in the process of violent conflict.

To some extent, the use of collective violence by social groups depends upon their own degree of politicization as well as the degree to which existing political organizations and institutions can accommodate, or are perceived to accommodate, the needs and desires of these groups. Moreover, this definition of social groups is based upon the perceived identity of its constituent members. As such, social groups will often transcend political boundaries, membership in political organizations and institutions, and perceived solutions toward the continued identity and survival of the groups themselves. Social groups can thereby be conditioned and socialized by a variety of different and potentially contradictory forces. Members of a single social group may be subject to differing attitudes about their respective relationships with a variety of state and social structures. They may also coexist with other social groups (and be conditioned by their respective relationships with them) within the context of different state units. Social groups are therefore complex and fluid. However, their desire for a continued identity as a collective provides the basis by which these groups can be conceptualized as distinguishable social groups.

The Process of Structural Violence

The term structural violence is used here to describe a process of existing power struggles between social groups. Whereas mainstream international conflict studies place the focus of their analyses upon the actual physical act of violence (usually the direct result of the use of military force in the name of states), the theoretical framework proposed here seeks to broaden the definition of violence to include structural relations of hegemony between social groups. In effect, the physical act of violence is but the external expression of an ongoing structural relationship between social groups—a relationship built on structural violence. A definition of conflict that focuses upon the physical act of violence can therefore only describe the results of violence rather than understand the overall process itself.

Johan Galtung has provided a basis for the model of sociostructural violence, arguing that "hostile aggression is no inseparable part of the innate structure of the 'minds of men,' but added to it from the outside, e.g. through special socialization processes"

(Galtung, 1964:95). According to Galtung, although the outward observations of aggression (in this case, organized political acts of violence) are worthy of study in themselves, they are merely a reflection, or a result of, existing sociostructural relationships that are arranged by a set of power relations. These relationships result in an "interaction system [which] is a multi-dimensional system of stratification" (Galtung, 1964:96). From here, Galtung set up a series of possible relationships between groups, which are simply characterized as Topdog (T) and Underdog (U). Throughout his discussion, Galtung has focused on the notion of power relationships dictated by the Topdog.

The result of Galtung's early work suggests that structural aggression can be applied to the relationship between social groups, as defined earlier in this chapter. However, Galtung's generalization of groups into the two basic categories of Topdog and Underdog (and the resulting concept of power relations) is not sufficiently developed to be the sole basis of a sociostructural conceptualization of violence. Although it is clear that social groups can be categorized by their respective access to power resources, these resources are only vaguely defined by Galtung, and in any event they depend upon their social context for meaning. Therefore, we must search beyond the theoretical foundation provided by Galtung in order to develop a more sophisticated notion of hegemony and social group power before we can continue.

Robert Cox has provided what is perhaps the best definition of social hegemony for such a purpose. Galtung's basic premise can be extended to suggest that a structured power order exists in the relationship of violence between self-identified distinct social groups. According to Cox, hegemony is the "temporary universalization in thought of a particular power structure, conceived not as domination but as the necessary order of nature" (Cox, 1982:38). This notion of hegemony provides a useful development to our sociostructural theoretical framework of violence.

Social groups exist by virtue of a collective self-identity, which is inherently based upon their relationship with individuals or other social groups. Each social group is different (even if only by virtue of its very self-identification), and each can be located in the context of a distinct relationship to its social environment. Within and among state units, a complex network of social groups interact and interrelate on the basis of collective interests, which may or may not coincide with those of contending groups. The result is a set of structural relations between these groups.

The regularization of the relations between social groups is the "order of nature" similar to that referred to by Cox. In many cases these relations can be interdependent relations of cooperation. However, the relations between social groups can equally be antagonistic, although not necessarily physically violent. In cases such as this, the ongoing pattern of relations is structured to work to the advantage of one group over another. At the same time, each social group has a distinct set of characteristics, or resources, which may permit the attainment of collective interests. These features are so diverse, however, and of such varying political utility as to make the comparative resources of social group power impossible to estimate. In short, social group power is so elusive that its composition is often only apparent in the ability of a social group to achieve a desired political objective. In some cases, the sheer persistence of a group's desire to remain unique (by language, culture, religion, location, and so forth) can be sufficient enough to ensure its survival. In other cases, social groups may control state and nonstate organizations (such as militaries, economic institutions, multinational corporations, access to crucial services, or educational institutions) and utilize these resources to further their own social group interests. In the end, all social groups exist within a complex of relationships with other social groups. Some may act to counter the interests of others, and some may act to further the interests of others. All have varying and inherently unmeasurable resources to further their collective interests.

The pluralism of social group divisions within global society becomes normalized through the structuring of power relations between social groups. The result is found in structured group relations of dominance and subordination. The successful relationship of dominance is one in which both the exploited and the exploiter accept this arrangement as a natural order. In many instances, the naturalness of this order ensures an exploited group is unaware of the hegemony of the dominant. Through state mechanisms, assimilation tactics, economic relationships, and other structural means, the hegemon can regularize a relationship of structural violence. However, as long as the dominated social group maintains its perceived notion of a distinct identity, such tactics cannot effectively dismantle or assimilate contending social groups. Should the legitimacy of the natural order become challenged by a subordinate social group, the potential exists for a relationship of structural violence to move into the use of collective *physical* violence as a means toward political objectives. Although the level and magnitude of the violence have changed dramatically in such a situation, the violence remains consistent in terms of the groups involved and the objectives sought.

Our understanding of violence within global society is further complicated by the dynamics of social group relations and their relationship to state structures. Dominant groups may use mechanisms within their control, including state mechanisms, to forge support for their objectives, contrary to the interests of subordinate social groups. The outbreak of physical violence can thus be viewed as the consequence of a breakdown of the natural order, which results from power relations between social groups. Using the above conceptualization of structural violence, we can see that a theoretical focus upon the outbreak of physical violence is wholly inadequate to an understanding of the social basis of conflict. In effect, the dominant theoretical understanding of conflict within the study of international relations (state-centric) can only partially "describe" conflict, as opposed to making any serious theoretical attempt to "understand" it.

A social group definition of collective violence also allows us to pursue another avenue of research ignored by state-centric perspectives. As has been stated, the domestic/international division of conflict tends to focus analysis upon violence conducted in the name of state actors. The horrors of destruction inflicted by states in interstate conflict have been obscene, and collective acts of violence by social groups within states have also cost humanity dearly. Are we to assume that violent conflict within states is somehow less significant or important? Military interests, bureaucratic interests, the interests of elite state managers, and the structures these entities control can be contrary to the interests of all social groups within states. These so-called mechanisms of sovereign defense can be and are utilized against what are perceived to be threats from within. Furthermore, the perceived interests of those who claim to be in control of the mechanisms of states can also diverge. In some cases, this can lead to bloody conflict of enormous proportions within states. Are we to accept that these acts of organized violence are less relevant because they take place within rather than across sovereign borders?

Structural Violence and State Systems

Although structural violence may be the outcome of a relationship of hegemony, such relations do not exist independently of the international state system. We cannot ignore the fact that the mechanisms available to states include the deadliest instruments of violence deployed in the name of national self-defense, as well as the institutional structures that often reinforce relations of structural violence. Earlier sections of this chapter were critical of state-centric theories of conflict, but we cannot set them completely aside in the development of a holistic notion of structural violence when looking at conflict within global society.

The Iran-Iraq War

In terms of the number of military and civilian casualties incurred in a violent military conflict, the Iran-Iraq War ranks as one of the most serious wars since World War II. Although there have been conflicting, and often contradictory, claims as to the total number of deaths resulting from the conflict, this war was clearly of immense magnitude. Ruth Leger Sivard has estimated the number of deaths to be 377,000 as of the end of 1988 (Sivard, 1988:30). These numbers do not include ongoing internal religious and ethnic disputes in both Iran and Iraq, which had become crucial aspects of the overall war by the end of the conflict in 1988. As well, numerous factions within Iran (who were variously associated with the former Shah) continued fighting until at least the middle of 1985 (Sivard, 1988:30).

A full understanding of all events during the Iran-Iraq conflict is not necessary to gain an understanding of the relationship of violence that existed before, throughout, and after the war. A structural conceptualization of social violence allows for an expansion of the parameters of scholarly examination to include factors that otherwise would have been ignored by a perspective focused solely upon the physical act of violent conflict. First, the Iran-Iraq War *must* be understood within the context of the domestic social structures and relations within both Iran and Iraq. Within Iran, the war with Iraq can easily be viewed as a continuation of the process that led to the revolution in 1978.[5]

Although the overall history of the Shah's tenure in Iran is both interesting and significant, the political environment for the Shah within Iran had become extremely tenuous by 1976. Political corruption and a rash of high-profile scandals rocked the government from 1973 through 1976, and the domestic economic situation was deteriorating rapidly. Urban incomes had increased to five times the level of rural incomes, massive unemployment was complicated by an influx of rural job-seekers, inflation was running at 35 percent, $2 billion worth of food was imported in 1978 to avoid famine, and the gap between rich and poor was widening at a rapid pace (*Strategic Survey*, 1978:50). At the same time, the material excesses of the corrupt leadership seemed to exacerbate the frustrations of many Iranians.

Although essentially a less institutionalized form of religious organization than Western Christian churches, the mosque became a significant political force in the rejection of the Shah's leadership and his support of Western-style modernization. Traditionally antagonistic factions of Islam became increasingly united under the mullahs in their opposition toward the Shah's regime. Moreover, middle-class civil servants and industrial workers became offended by the excesses of the political leadership in Iran, and they joined the movement of a fundamentalist Islamic rejection of Westernization. An overthrow of the Shah became the objective that united traditionally antagonistic factions of Islam. In structural terms, the relations of hegemony between the Shah's regime and the various Islamic factions within Iran was so complete as to unite traditionally fractionalized groups under a common cause. The social group identification had become one of community, as all agreed that they shared a common exploitation by the Shah's regime. Fundamentalist Islamic values provided both the doctrine and the leadership for an emerging alliance of social groups that sought to address their exploitation by a hegemonic and corrupt regime.

Ayatollah Khomeini (exiled to Iraq in 1963 as a potential threat to the Shah) gained credibility as a legitimate Islamic leader who wholly rejected the Shah and all that his leadership came to symbolize in the eyes of most Iranian citizens. Attempts to resolve the growing crisis by moderate Islamic leaders in Qom (i.e., Ayatollah Shariatmadari) were rejected as unreasonable solutions to the situation. From his new base in Paris in 1977, Khomeini's calls for the establishment of an Islamic republic brought on cries for a return to the 1906 constitution, which gave the full right of veto to a committee of five religious leaders. The uniting influence of Khomeini was sufficient to successfully organize a protest strike throughout the oil fields by December 1978. Oil production was reduced from more than six million barrels per day to less than half a million. As a result, the Shah's regime lost more than U.S. $3 billion in revenue, financially destroying an already beleaguered regime.

Throughout 1978, the political situation in Iran became increasingly violent. At least 2,000 were killed in an escalating number of clashes with government troops and police forces. In June 1978 the head of SAVAK, the secret police, was replaced in response to violent rioting in the city of Tabriz. The new head of SAVAK, a moderate, pushed for the adoption of martial law after further violent clashes in Isfahan in August 1978. After an attack on a cinema in Abadan, in which 430 were killed, the Shah was forced to replace Prime Minister Jamshid Amuzegar with Jafaar Sharif-Emami, whose religious connections it was hoped would help resolve the crisis. However, the responses of the Shah's regime reflected its total inability to fully understand the changing social environment in Iran. As a hegemonic social regime, it responded with the use of political and military force, which had successfully maintained the Shah's reign for years.

By 1978, however, social group factions within Iran had successfully forged a common objective to address the unequal power relations within the state. Factions within the new alliance (such as moderate Islamic oil workers or civil servants) were now willing to pay the perceived economic, social, or political costs that would result in the attainment of their goals. In short, their self-identification as members of a political and religious movement toward an objective of Islamic leadership had surpassed their self-identification as industrial or civil workers whose principal interest was the maintenance of the status quo. The solidarity of social group identification within the Islamic revolution was sufficient to render any structural adjustments by the hegemonic regime useless. The forging of a coherent social group identification by various opponents to the Shah's regime was a direct result of the persistent power relations that existed between a complex network of social cleavages. In short, subordinate social groups no longer accepted domination by the Shah as part of a natural order. As such, the Shah's reign was destined to collapse.

Successive attempts by the Shah to appease the calls for political change (from a now seemingly united opposition) brought on a rapid series of concessions by the Shah, none of which were sufficient to satisfy an opposition that would settle for nothing less than his complete fall. By late December 1978, the Shah appointed one of the leaders of the National Front (his primary opposition for more than twenty-five years) as the new prime minister. However, the newly appointed Prime Minister Bakhtiar was considered too moderate by followers of Khomeini and was unsuccessful in calling off a strike by civil servants and oil workers. Bakhtiar was also unsuccessful in persuading fundamentalists to favor a more secularized form of political leadership. On January 16, 1979, the Shah left on an "extended vacation" and never returned to Iran. Within days, the Regency Council, designed to preserve the monarchy, was dissolved. With the Shah officially the commander in chief of the armed forces, the loyalty of the powerful Iranian military was uncertain. Leaderless and unable to follow a political situation that changed from day to day, the military proclaimed itself neutral in the domestic power struggle on February 9, 1979 (*Strategic Survey*, 1979:53). Within forty-eight hours, Ayatollah Khomeini was back in Iran and his new prime minister, Mehdi Bazargan, was forming a new government.

Although the Iranian military proclaimed its neutrality in the conflict, the revolution in Iran was not without violence. An estimated 2,000 supporters of the Shah were killed in uprisings throughout 1978 (*Strategic Survey*, 1980:55). Moreover, roughly 1,000 civil servants and military police were killed in the week following the arrival of Khomeini in February 1979. Sivard has estimated that about 20,000 Shah loyalists were killed throughout the conflict with Iraq from bases far outside of Teheran (Sivard, 1988:30). Perhaps more importantly for this analysis, the revolution in Iran was instrumental in the outbreak of hostilities between Iran and Iraq that same year.

The domestic situation in Iran was met with great concern by the Ba'th regime in Iraq. First, Iran was clearly a regional power, and the pro-Western policies of the Shah were part of a complex set of regional state relations that saw Iran and Saudi Arabia as Arab counterweights to Soviet and anti-Israeli states in the region. Although superpower attempts to play states off against one another in the volatile Middle Eastern political environment were anything but successful, no one could ignore the massive military the Shah had built in Iran with the aid of the United States. Relations between the Shah and Iraq had been uneasy, but by comparison to other relations in the region, the Shah and Iraq could have been considered allies. In fact, in 1975 Iran and Iraq signed a treaty that redefined their common border. The widespread hatred of the Shah within Iran could only spell trouble for his friends in Iraq.

Second, and more importantly, the Ba'th regime in Iraq was supported by the Sunni minority. This minority had successfully established itself as the dominant social hegemon throughout the political, military, and social structures of Iraq. The Shi'ite majority had begrudgingly accepted Sunni political domination for decades. However, the new Khomeini regime in Iran was supported largely by Shi'ite fundamentalists in Iran and elsewhere. The Ba'th regime in Iraq now saw great potential for this fundamentalist revolution to spread into Iraq and threaten the Ba'th hold on power. Iraqi president Saddam Hussein felt threatened by the Iranian revolution and seemed compelled to act.

A delineation between the Iranian revolution and the Iran-Iraq War thus seems merely academic. While supporters of Khomeini were busy seeking out supporters of the Shah in Teheran in May 1979, Iraqi troops were attempting to take advantage of the turmoil caused by the revolution. The Iraqi government and military had assumed that the leadership of the powerful Iranian military (formerly loyal to the Shah) would be purged. Sporadic Iraqi raids on Iranian borders began as early as May 1979. Hussein began to expel 30,000 Iranian workers, fearing that they would instill Islamic revolutionary doctrine in the Iraqi Shi'ite majority. On September 17,

1980, Hussein cancelled the 1975 border treaty with Iran and reclaimed sections of the Shatt-al-Arab waterway, which had been taken from Iraq during an Iranian intervention into a "domestic" dispute in November 1971. On September 20, 1980, Iranian president Bani-Sadr called up Iran's reserve forces in order to stop the advancing Iraqi incursions into Iranian territory. Initially, Iraq made great advances and took the waterway as well as important oil refineries and several border cities (*Strategic Survey*, 1981:50).

In strategic terms, the war opened quickly and Iraqi military advances were extremely fluid, due to the total disorganization of the Iranian military—a direct result of the Iranian revolution. By early 1981 the oil production of both Iran and Iraq had been cut to less than 600,000 barrels per day, as opposed to the prewar daily totals of 3.5 million barrels for Iran and 1.4 million barrels for Iraq. Although initially a rapidly moving military conflict, the Iranian Revolutionary Guards had begun to successfully hold off Iraqi advances by October 1980. From that point on, the conflict became a bloody, stagnant, labor-intensive war of attrition in which months of intensive fighting would result in the movement of the front by only several hundred yards.

Although the war continued to remain stagnant throughout its duration, it did bring about serious internal social divisions in both Iran and Iraq. Challenges to the legitimacy of the Khomeini regime in Iran came almost immediately after the revolution. Whereas most religious and ethnic factions in Iran agreed that the Shah must be deposed, there was no such agreement with regard to an Islamic republic. Ethnic minorities compose nearly half of Iran's 36 million citizens. In January 1980, Turkish minorities and moderate Islamic clergymen engaged in bloody clashes with Khomeini supporters around the city of Tabriz. Throughout the duration of the war with Iraq, ethnic unrest was widespread in Iran, although Khomeini's Revolutionary Guards did gain legitimacy as the defenders of Iran against their primary adversary—Iraq. In any case, Iraq used every opportunity to exploit ethnic unrest in Iran by the supply of food, men, and arms to groups in Iran.

The stability of Iraq's Saddam Hussein was also seriously challenged by the events of the war with Iran. Hussein, a Sunni Muslim, had to contend with an ethnically and religiously fractionalized state. In terms of ethnic identification, Iraq's population is 75 percent Arab, 15 percent Kurd (most of whom are separatists),[6] and 5 percent Turk. Although 95 percent of the population is Muslim, 60 percent is Shi'ite and the remaining 35 percent is Sunni (*UN Statistical Yearbook*, 1988). President Hussein had assumed power only in July 1979 and his hold on power was not secure by the time he cancelled the boundary treaty with Iran later the following year. In fact, Hussein used the conflict with Iran as an opportunity to eliminate the Kurdish Democratic Party (KDP) and communist cells of his military. For Hussein, the war with Iran was a serious risk, and his political survival hung in the balance. By 1982, Khomeini had stated that Iran would not settle for anything less than the downfall of Iraq's Hussein as acceptable terms for a negotiated peace. Hussein responded in kind, and claimed that Iraq would never end the war as long as Khomeini was alive and in control of Iran. The duration of the war saw a series of moves by either side in attempts to play off the domestic instability of each regime as a means of political advantage in the conflict. Both Iran and Iraq spent huge resources fighting political and military threats from within their respective states.

The Iran-Iraq War in a Structural Perspective

Although the Iran-Iraq War has been considered by many realist international relations scholars to be another example of state-state war, we have seen that the complexities of this war suggest that such an assumption is a serious oversimplification. To draw a theoretical line between the Iranian revolution and the Iran-Iraq War presents a serious theoretical impediment to an understanding of the full *process* of structural violence. Relations of domination had become the normal means of political organization in Iran, as seen in an alliance of political elites controlling virtually all aspects of, and social structures within, the state. Moreover, this political regime displayed excesses that reflected the Western values of the external powers that supported the regime. Subordinate social and religious groups in Iran were expected to accept this relationship of domination as the natural order.

In the end, these groups rejected the natural order and put aside their traditional differences in an alliance to overthrow a repressive elite. Islam became the link uniting these groups into a common front of the oppressed. So successful was the legitimization of their common goals that members of the Shah's elite abandoned their traditional support of the status quo in favor of the objectives of the new social alliance. The response of the ruling elite was the use of military force, moving a relationship of structural violence into the realm of physical violence. However, without effective control over the mechanisms of physical force (the police and the military), the hegemon's control over subordinate social groups collapsed quickly.

The rapid collapse of the status quo in Iran became an immediate threat to the stability of the emerging, albeit tentative, hegemonic consensus in Iraq, which was still in the process of consolidating its hold over the social structures within that state. The response of the regime in Iraq was to exploit the political instability in Iran and divert internal social concerns to an external threat. The Hussein regime in Iraq had an instinctive distrust for the new leadership in Iran, given that the interests of the former Shah had included stable and friendly relations with Iraq. The alliance of hegemonic elites in Iran and Iraq dissolved with the Iranian revolution, and the out- break of hostilities between the two should be considered an impor- tant aspect in the process of violence. The existing relationships of structural violence in both Iran and Iraq permit us a richer under- standing of the social environment from which the Iran-Iraq War emerged.

Pre–Gulf War Developments

Since the Iraqi invasion of Kuwait in August 1990, and the subse- quent United Nations action, most political analysis has focused pri- marily upon the leadership of Iraq and the perceived Iraqi quest for military supremacy in the region.[7] A focus solely upon the Iraqi leadership, however, glosses over the complex civil relations upon which Saddam Hussein has established his power base, as well as the existing and recently transformed regional tensions that are an integral part of his strategy to remain in power. A brief description of some of the most important of these considerations will highlight the extent to which this conflict is consistent with the existing sociostructural relationships in the region and their implications for international politics.

In purely economic terms, the greatest impact of the Iran-Iraq War upon Iraq was the rapid decline of its foreign reserves[8] and a growing economic dependence upon Saudi Arabia, Kuwait, Turkey, the former Soviet Union, and the United States (Farouk-Sluglett and Sluglett, 1990:21). Saudi Arabia and Kuwait began to sell "war relief crude" from the damaged Iraqi oil fields in an attempt to raise funds for the war effort. These states also guaranteed export credits to OECD countries on Iraq's behalf. Food import bills were paid by the United States and Turkey. At the same time, the Soviet Union wrote off massive debts accumulated by Iraq in the acquisition of military hardware. At the end of the war, Iraq had amassed foreign debts of between $60 and $80 billion, exhausted its foreign reserves of $35 billion, watched its annual oil revenues fall from $29 billion to $7 bil- lion, lost a good part of its industrial and oil-producing infrastruc- ture, spent countless billions of dollars on the war effort, and received billions of dollars worth of both economic and military aid from several states (Farouk-Sluglett and Sluglett, 1990:20–21).

At the same time, Iraq ended the war with a massive million-man army, large numbers of relatively sophisticated weapons, and a developing armaments industry. Ending in a cease-fire, the war left the larger political disputes between the Iraqi and Iranian governments unresolved. Neither side was successful in dealing a definitive military blow to their respective Kurdish nationalist groups (Khan, 1988:25). Although Hussein wound up with easy access to massive amounts of military hardware, so too did many of his potential adversaries. Most notable among these were the Shi'ites pressed into military service (at both the enlisted and officer level) and Kurdish nationalist groups.

The prolonged Iran-Iraq War also succeeded in transforming relations among Arab states and nation-groups. While Iraq became increasingly dependent upon foreign sources to finance the war effort, Hussein made explicit claims to the leadership of Arab nationalism as a consequence of Iraq's "victory" over Iran. Although many of his Arab allies in the war with Iran were skeptical of his claim to leadership (and increasingly nervous given the buildup of Iraq's military capabilities), Hussein did establish a solid basis of support from Iraqi citizens as well as from many Arab nationalists. Iraq's portrayal of Kuwait (and, to a lesser extent, of Saudi Arabia) as a war profiteer struck a chord among many Palestinians and Jordanians. This became apparent when the Palestine Liberation Organization opted to support Iraq during the Gulf War and throughout Jordan's difficult attempts to remain neutral.

The end of the Iran-Iraq War solidified Hussein's leadership position at least within Iraq, and to a lesser extent among some Arab nationalists. Although many have speculated on the initial Iraqi decision to move into Kuwait, the fact that Iraq claimed to be acting on behalf of an anti-Western pan-Arabism cannot be discounted altogether.

> Iraq's claim of all of Kuwait was not the reason Baghdad invaded in August 1990. Rather, it served as a justification after the fact. What gives the Iraqi argument currency in the Arab world is less the merits of this territorial claim than the powerful sense that the political and economic order prevailing in the region as a whole has been constructed and maintained primarily for the benefit of Western powers. (Stork and Lesch, 1990:13)

From 1988 onward the Iraqi leadership attempted to exploit its position in an effort both to secure political support in Iraq and to play the role of regional power in the Middle East. By the spring of 1990 Hussein began once again to play upon Iraqi nationalist sentiment[9] and restate the 1930s Iraqi intention to "restore" Kuwait to Iraqi control. In the late 1930s the Iraqi monarchy proclaimed its desire to have Kuwait restored to Iraqi control. Again, after the formal independence of Kuwait in 1961, Iraq's nationalist leader (Abd al-Karim Qassim) attempted to gain political control of Kuwait (Stork and Lesch, 1990:12). The British responded by sending troops to the newly independent state. By 1963, Iraq formally recognized the independence of Kuwait.

The renewal of Iraq's territorial claims on Kuwait are clearly tied to Iraq's economic situation since the end of the Iran-Iraq War. Given the debt burden carried by Iraq at the end of the war (and its continued arms procurement afterward), Iraq sought to rebuild its oil-producing infrastructure as rapidly as possible. At the same time, Kuwait, the United Arab Emirates, and Saudi Arabia had developed oil production outputs that surpassed the export quotas of the Organization of Petroleum Exporting Countries (OPEC) (Farouk-Sluglett and Sluglett, 1990:24). Iraq was desperately interested in having all Gulf states lower their oil production in order to push the price up to between $18 and $20 per barrel. Throughout the spring and early summer of 1990, OPEC negotiations failed to produce agreements to limit oil production among OPEC members. As far as Iraq was concerned, Kuwait was the largest stumbling block in the way of securing reduced oil production quotas. While these negotiations were under way, Hussein began to publicly state Iraq's position that it had a long-standing claim over Kuwait's territorial sovereignty. Although many dismissed these claims as overt political pressure to force Kuwait to accommodate Iraq's request for lower oil production quotas, Iraqi military forces began to position themselves along the Kuwaiti border throughout the spring and early summer of 1990.

The United States was paying close attention to the Iraqi-Kuwaiti standoff at the negotiating table for two basic reasons. First, the United States was concerned that an agreement would bring about a sharp increase in world oil prices, and second, the U.S. intelligence service was watching with concern the buildup of Iraqi troops. The now public Baker memo reveals the extent to which Washington felt helpless, particularly in terms of the degree to which U.S. military pressure could deter an Iraqi invasion.[10] The memo instructed the U.S. embassy in Baghdad to make it clear to the Iraqis that although an invasion of Kuwait would not be without political consequence, the United States was in no position to respond in military terms. It seems likely that this information weighed heavily upon Iraq's decision to move into Kuwait in August 1990.

Conclusion

The Iraqi decision to move into Kuwait in 1990 was obviously based upon a number of considerations, many of which are beyond the scope of this analysis. For the purposes of this chapter, however, several crucial links can be made to the Iran-Iraq War. First, the 1988 cease-fire did not resolve any of the outstanding political and social differences within and between the two states. Iran remains the leader of a fundamentalist Islamic political vision. At the same time, Saddam Hussein attempted to lay claim to the leadership of a non-fundamentalist pan-Arabism (regardless of his recent incarnations). Perhaps most significantly, the immediate postwar era saw the Iraqi leadership continue the externalization of aggression in an attempt to remain in power. This is consistent with the decisions to take the Shatt-al-Arab waterway in 1980 and the annexation of Kuwait in 1990. In both cases, Iraq assumed that the military prospects for victory were good and that the political consequences would ultimately be positive for the Iraqi leadership. At the same time, economic considerations within Iraq clearly had an impact upon the decision to take military action. It is also reasonable to assume that Hussein felt compelled to act in order to maintain his hegemonic status as the leader of Iraq as well as a regional power.

This analysis effectively displays the merits of theoretical constructions, which are sensitive to the social environment from which social relations emerge. Relations of violence between social groups cannot be aggregated solely to state-level analysis. At the same time, they cannot be effectively understood merely by looking at social relations within states. As the Iran-Iraq case displays, the physical outbreak of violence by state and nonstate groups is merely an expression of existing relationships within and among state units. The need to move beyond the simplistic state-centric assumptions of many approaches in the study of international relations should be clear. The subject matter of international relations is vast, and we cannot base our understanding of global relations solely upon the state and the international state system. If Morgenthau, Carr, and others claim that the state is the basis of the subject matter of international relations, then attempts to fully theorize the state must be the key to understanding the social basis of global relations. In and of themselves, however, attempts to further theorize the state, while deepening our understanding of these key actors, may not advance our understanding of the underlying structure of social relations of violence in any substantial way.

As Mark Neufeld has contended, reflexive theory is theory that can reflect upon its own assumptions and come to grips with the political nature of its implications. Clearly, state-centric realist and neorealist theory privileges the state in its understanding of violence and war in the international system. Moreover, the political nature of theories that privilege the existing empowered elites and structures in the international system should be called into question. A sociostructural understanding of violence helps to reveal those crucial social interrelationships that perpetuate (and often legitimize) acts of violence by state and nonstate social groups. An alternative approach to the orthodoxy in conflict analysis is not without problems; it must be integrated into empirical analysis in order to reveal the limitations of the state-centric approach, as well as to direct scholarship toward those social issues that the orthodoxy tends to ignore.

Technological progress in the name of modernity has given "modern" society the ability to perfect the means of violence and destruction. If the results of our progress reflect both our social values and the dominance of Western-style modernity, then so-called social progress has not kept pace with technological progress. The modern state system (and the complex social relations within it) seems to perpetuate structural relations of domination and violence. Perhaps it is time to begin the search for appropriate means of social organization to deal with our continued acceptance and legitimization of organized acts of political violence.

If we continue to see violence in the international system only at the level of states, we will continue to ignore (or gloss over) a number of social conflicts that individual states and the international system will eventually have to face. In the post–Cold War era, it has become clear that this is not merely an empirical or a theoretical question—it has became the social responsibility of all people who are committed to the elimination of the intolerable pain we are inflicting upon ourselves in the name of social, national, religious, ethnic, economic, or political causes.

Notes

1. The term "social" in this context must be fully understood. For the purposes of this chapter, social groups are those who share a common lan-

guage, culture, religion, sense of history, economic class, gender, or ethnic identity. Not all of these distinguishing characteristics need be present at the same time for a group of people to be considered a social group. However, the people must be able to identify themselves as a distinguishable group and this affiliation must be the basis upon which their collective political action is derived. At the same time, their social consciousness *does not* necessarily lead to political action or ideology.

2. See Chapter 8 by Keyman for the full implications of the inadequacies of an undertheorized concept of the nation-state.

3. See Wendt (1987) and Ashley (1984) for a full discussion of the ontological primacy of the state unit in both classical realist and neorealist theory.

4. Of 161 sovereign states identified in 1985, only 45 could be considered nation-states (those with 95 percent or greater of their population belonging to a single ethnic-national group). Another 62 had majorities of a single ethnic-national group. The remaining were multinational states with no clear ethnic-national majority. In addition, Gunnar Nielsson identified 589 distinct ethnic groups within global society. In only 13 cases did most of an ethnic group reside in a single state. Of these groups, 399 were minorities of less than 10 percent in the state of their residence (Nielsson, 1985:27–56).

5. The following description of events within Iran through the 1980s is based upon an overview of factors considered crucial to the Iran-Iraq War in the *Strategic Survey*, compiled by the International Institute of Strategic Studies. To gain a comprehensive overview, these observations were drawn from editions of *Strategic Survey* from 1978 through 1989; however, for reasons unknown, no analysis of the Iran-Iraq conflict was provided in the 1979–1980 edition.

6. The Kurdish separatist movements in both Iran and Iraq have been active for decades. In fact, the 1975 boundary treaty between Iran and Iraq was a direct result of Iraqi Kurdish groups moving in to support fighting between the Iranian government and the Kurds in Iran. During the Iran-Iraq War, Kurds were fighting both Iran and Iraq simultaneously from both sides of the border. At the same time, Kurds were fighting Kurds (both across borders and within each state) as both Iran and Iraq had made desperate pleas to each in an attempt to secure their support in the broader war. As well, Kurdish groups were fighting other ethnic minorities in both Iran and Iraq, as other separatist and nonseparatist groups saw the war as an attempt to settle long-term disputes with Kurdish nationals.

7. The cost in human life of the Gulf War has been staggering. Considering the intensity of the killing in a period of forty-one days, this war might well go down in history as less of a military conflict and more of a slaughter. Hooglund (1991) has given estimates of both U.S. and UN casualties. U.S. forces' casualties included 144 dead and 479 wounded, whereas estimates for the Iraqis are as high as more than 200,000 killed and 300,000 wounded. Refugees and refugee-related deaths are extremely high. As many as 1.7 million refugees were estimated to be in the region before the war, and as many as 3–4 million since the end of the war.

8. At the outset of the conflict, the Iraqi state had a foreign reserve surplus of U.S. $35 billion. Within the first two years of the conflict, that surplus was reduced to zero, and the Iraqi state was forced to borrow.

9. Iraqi nationalism may not be the best term to use in this context. Iraq has often laid claims to be the heir of the great Arab empire, as well as

the political heir of Islam. With regard to Kuwait, Iraqi leaders since 1932 have on several occasions claimed that European colonialists (British and Ottoman) wrongfully took Kuwait from Iraq, as Kuwait was once part of the province of Basra.

10. Manfred Bienefeld, in an April 1991 roundtable at Queen's University, Kingston, Ontario, Canada, discussed the Baker memo at some length. Bienefeld contended that although the U.S. State Department was unwilling to put political pressure on the Iraqi government throughout the early political development of the crisis, the Defense Department was ready (in fact anxious) to respond to a potential Iraqi invasion of Kuwait. Bienefeld further speculated that such a display of U.S. military capability in the region had been desired by the Pentagon as early as 1985.

5

Neorealism or Hegemony?
The Seven Sisters' Energy Regime

GREGG J. LEGARE

Judging from the back issues of *International Organization* from the past few years, regime theory and neorealism have taken the field of international relations by storm.[1] Neorealism has reasserted the theoretical primacy and centrality of states as the key ontological category in international politics and continues to characterize the international political system as essentially a state of anarchy, due to its lack of a global central government to regulate and restrain the competition among states for power, wealth, and prestige. Neorealism has thus recycled two of the core axioms of classical realism: the system as anarchy and its components as states. Regime theory is an attempt to account for international cooperation between states within this anarchic, self-help framework.

Recent scholarship has detailed important critiques of regime theories that level the terrain for postpositivist and postrealist research (Ashley, 1988, 1987, 1984; Klein, 1988; Lapid, 1989; Walker, 1987). In its analysis of international energy relations in the past sixty years, this chapter also seeks to evaluate the contributions of regime theorists and neorealists. In so doing, however, it adopts a different strategy from these previous philosophical critiques of neorealism. In particular, through the case study presented, this chapter evaluates the contention that state power and hegemonic stability are the key features that explain the development of the international system and the level of order-cooperation/disorder-discord within it. Because Robert Keohane is among the most subtle of the neorealists and because he has written extensively on international energy matters, we take our exemplar of regime theory from his writings, chiefly from his book *After Hegemony* (1984).

There are several considerations that make regime theory highly misleading as an analytic tool for examining the international energy economy. Foremost among these is the proposition that state power sets the conditions for societal power and brings order to international relations. On the realist model, political hegemony over oil resources was a key to U.S. hegemony in the postwar period. We do agree that order, prosperity, and growth in the industrial world since 1945 (and also before) were crucially dependent on cheap and secure oil supplies. The global hegemony of the West was largely grounded in access to the energy resources of the South. However, these were provided by a regime composed *not* of state actors but of private multinational oil corporations (the "Seven Sisters"), linked by a series of formal cartel arrangements. Periodic attempts by states to move in and secure control were, until 1970, defeated by this constellation of private power.

In contrast, the realist formulation of the international political economy and its emphasis on state power glosses over the central fact that in a capitalist economy, preponderant economic resources are in private hands and are not the property of states. Thus, although hegemony is ascribed to states, the economic power resources for hegemony are largely private property, in this case the property of transnational oil companies. What is missing here is a theorization of the linkages between the two (the public and the private) and how a hegemonic state might either control those resources or be controlled by their owners. Thus a crucial gap in realist international relations is the lack of a thorough analysis of state-society relations *at an international level*.

Hegemony and Counterhegemony

A better explanation of the development of the international oil regime is through the use of a framework employing a hegemony-counterhegemony dialectic. We will demonstrate this by taking the salient issues treated by Keohane in statist terms and reinterpreting them in this alternative framework. This, we argue, provides a more compelling explanation than regime theory. Furthermore, the alternative explanation can also incorporate the key features of the private regime in oil, which Keohane's framework glosses over or treats as an anomaly. Anomalies, of course, may exist, but it is deeply suspicious when the anomaly happens to be the structure of the world's largest and most international of industries!

Hegemony, in our framework, combines the notion of preponderant private power with the Gramscian notion of intellectual, moral, and political leadership clustered around an ideologically instilled consensus on the pursuit of particular political projects. The dialectical combination of material power and ideological-political leadership gives the concept great nuance; but because of this combination, its analytical precision is diluted. Among the reasons for this are hegemony's dual usage. Hegemony, of course, refers to a preponderantly powerful state and its power over other states. In short, it resides in the public interstate sphere. Its other use, pioneered by Gramsci, refers to the domination of the worldview and political projects of a ruling class that pervades civil society, the private sphere. The latter sense of hegemony implies that this ideological dominance acts to define the common-sense view of reality in a way biased toward the interests of this ruling class, but the nature and extent of this bias is masked.[2]

By stressing the latter usage we can explain the process whereby a system of international order was set up by Britain and the United States over the oil-producing areas of the South. In the first usage, they are the hegemonic powers providing a political-military framework for domination. However, it was the multinational oil companies (MNOCs) that set up the hegemonic oil regime within the context of the British-U.S. capitalist hegemony and they themselves were the dominant actors in it. When the hegemonic states intervened it was almost always to assist the MNOCs in battling resistance and counterhegemonic demands from the subordinated.

In a hegemonic system, the dominant groups define international reality in their own interests. They do so, however, in a universalist manner such that those whose interests are subordinated accept the same definition of the way things are; in short, the subordinate share the hegemon's worldview and, in general, its policy direction and analysis of what needs to be done. The acceptance of these definitions by the subordinates is crucial in persuading them to cooperate in a consensual manner with the political projects of the dominant actors. They must be persuaded that the goals of the dominant actors are, to a large degree, also of benefit to them. It is in this process that hegemonic international leadership is manifest. Otherwise, the legitimacy of the leadership claims of the hegemon will be rejected and alternative, counterhegemonic definitions of reality may emerge, themselves competing for consent and hegemony.

A hegemonic framework thus stresses the need for the dominant actors to make compromises in their interests and policies in order to confer benefits on the subordinates to maintain their active consent. We can view this as the need for the dominant actors to provide a material basis of consent via a political and ideological bargaining process. Robert Cox's summary of hegemony is most apt. Hegemony is:

> in Marxian terms, a unity of structure and superstructure—in which power based on dominance over production is rationalized through an ideology incorporating compromise or consensus between dominant and subordinate groups. . . . A hegemonical structure of world order is one in which power takes a primarily consensual form, as distinguished from a non-hegemonic order in which there are manifestly rival powers and no power has been able to establish the legitimacy of its dominance. (Cited in Keohane, 1984:44–45)[3]

There can be no doubt that the MNOCs had dominance over energy production. But it is this element of political-ideological leadership with the consent of the led coupled with the potential power to coerce and reward that makes the idea of hegemony a helpful analytic tool for the analysis of the international oil system before OPEC's counterhegemonic actions.

A hegemonic system in which the dominant actors are multinational corporations is much more than a set of economic arrangements. Of major, indeed crucial, importance for a private-sector cartel is the securing of political toleration and protection for its arrangements from both the producing country governments and the consuming country governments. Indeed, the maintenance of dominance by the cartel rests, in large measure, on the continuing ability to keep the various state actors reasonably happy and to secure their cooperation and assistance when necessary. For instance, it was periodically necessary to secure the friendly intervention of state political or military power on the side of the cartel to counter the use of state power that was hostile to the cartel (e.g., U.S. and British intervention against the Mossadeq regime in Iran).

A key element in a hegemonic regime of control in which the dominant actors are firms rather than governments is the ability and willingness to keep governments satisfied enough to leave control in private hands. For the British and U.S. governments, the ideology of private enterprise provided considerable legitimation for this. Thus, in 1951, on the heels of the nationalization of the Anglo-Iranian Oil Company by Iran, John Loftus, the head of the U.S. State Department's Petroleum Division, laid out the support of the United States for private ownership of foreign oil:

> While recognizing the sovereign right of any country to assume ownership . . . of the petroleum industry or any of its branches, this Government must nevertheless recognize and proclaim that inter-

national commerce predicated upon free trade and private enterprise (which is the conceptual core of U.S. economic foreign policy)
is, in the long run, incompatible with an extensive spread of state
ownership and operation of commercial properties. (Cited in
Shaffer, 1983:108–109)

Thus U.S. political support, at least in the executive branch,
could be expected for the private nature of the hegemonic oil regime
and the MNOCs' dominant role in it. Because they shared the hegemonic definition that the oil regime was private, state managers
could be counted on to work to keep it so. Moreover, once they had
grown to be very large corporations, the political influence of the
MNOCs with their home governments also afforded a measure of
protection against hostile state intervention. However, because oil
became a highly strategic commodity both militarily and economi-
cally, the MNOC cartel also had to be able to provide consumer
countries with large amounts of oil at reasonably economical cost.
Otherwise, imperatives of economic security might prompt these
powerful states to intervene to secure direct control over oil supplies, as was almost done by the United States in World War II. The
United States, in particular, saw the unfettered overseas operations
of the MNOCs as an important contribution to national security,
even to the point that it would waive antitrust prosecution from
other executive departments, such as Justice and Commerce, aimed
at breaking up the cartel. In many countries the local cartel arrangements and collusive practices were clearly in violation of antitrust
legislation. Prosecution and the resultant breakdown of the cartel
had to be avoided both by secrecy and by securing the political protection of the executive branches of these governments to block liti-
gation or, better, to gain exemption. In the United States, in particular, this was very successfully done. The clinching arguments were
the importance of the oil companies to the U.S. economy and national security.[4]

For many years, the separation of public and private spheres
functioned in the interests of the MNOCs, who claimed they owned
or had leased the rights over production to the oil resources of the
producer countries and that energy was no more than a competitive,
free-market business. In advanced capitalist countries this claim met
with little resistance. Initially, producer governments accepted this
claim as well, but in the late 1960s they began to challenge it. They
began to make counterhegemonic claims to challenge the organizational structure and power relations within the hegemonic oil
regime.

This underscores the fact that once established, hegemonic structures are not static nor do they necessarily endure of their own accord. Rather, they have to be constantly remade and reproduced. It is here that international events can undermine the conditions conducive to the hegemony's continued operation and reproduction and create the conditions for counterhegemony. The legitimacy of the hegemonic structure may be broken by ideological change and the emergence of counterhegemonic challenges to the structure. Moreover, it can also be undermined by an inability and/or unwillingness of the dominant actors to any longer make the compromises and concessions necessary to purchase the consent of the subordinates. In the first case, the dominant actors lose their moral-ideological claim to leadership among the subordinate ones, whereas in the second case the subordinates perceive that their interests are no longer being met within the hegemonic structure.

It is in these conditions that counterhegemonic projects can easily emerge from the subordinates. As opposed to a reformist project in which claims to improve the material benefits for the subordinate actors within a hegemonic structure are made, a counterhegemonic project implies a challenge to the hegemonic structure itself—a restructuring of its essential power relationships. The latter project can emerge out of the former if the former is denied. Thus, OPEC nations long sought an improvement in their material returns from oil exports without demanding control over pricing and production decisions. This was accomplished via taxation agreements and the royalty regime. As long as increased revenue demands could be met within the hegemonic oil regime, producers were not discontented enough or unified enough to reject it. Nationalist claims amounted largely to participation in and consultation on major upstream decisions, not control of them.

The counterhegemonic project of OPEC emerged out of the denial, indeed the rollback, by the MNOCs of previous revenue arrangements. The resistance to the claims of the subordinate producing countries to improve their role in the hegemonic oil regime ultimately resulted in producer governments taking direct control of their own oil industries and making production and pricing decisions among themselves, without serious regard for the MNOCs. The companies essentially became middlemen, or "OPEC tax collectors," as some angry Western commentators referred to them.

This represented a fundamental alteration of the power relations in the oil business, a transfer of control of supply to the suppliers. The other aspect of the OPEC project that made it counterhegemonic was the basic reevaluation of what oil represented and of the ends to which petroleum exports would be put. OPEC rejected the MNOC claim that oil was merely another energy commodity whose price and supply was governed by market relations. They substituted a notion that oil was national capital, which was undervalued in a system of unequal exchange through the MNOC-administered price system. As capital, oil's role was not only to provide consumers with energy, but also to act as the means of promoting economic development in underdeveloped OPEC economies. Therefore, the priority in oil production decisions became not the interest of the industrial North in cheap energy, but the developmental interests of the South and requirements for state revenues for OPEC nations' development projects.

It was not until market conditions changed markedly in the 1970s, however, that the counterhegemonic project became *practical*. Specifically, the reversal of market conditions and other changes in the international system opened up the opportunity to implement the detailed changes the counterhegemonic project required. Nevertheless, the counterhegemonic project was successful for only a few short years, for the problems of the control of oil returned to plague OPEC's attempts at international energy management.

Thus the hegemonic oil regime and the dominance of the "Seven Sisters" was broken in the 1970s because of economic nationalism in the producer countries (the ideological-political challenge to hegemony) and the increasing competition between the MNOCs and the independents in retail markets (the erosion of the material basis for consent). The MNOCs were no longer able or willing to meet the demands of producer governments for more benefits from the extraction of their oil. It took the OPEC producers some time to arrive at the realization that they could set up their own counterhegemonic oil regime, and even longer for international conditions to provide the opportunity to do so.

The Foundations of the Hegemonic Oil Regime

The hegemonic oil regime, with the blessing of the British government, began as a private sector affair. Prior to World War I, two Western entrepreneurs, Calouste Gulbenkian and William D'Arcy, secured large tracts of land from Iraq and Iran, respectively. D'Arcy established the Anglo-Persian Oil Company, which later became British Petroleum. Royal-Dutch Shell, with links to Gulbenkian, soon became Anglo-Iranian's partner in setting up the Turkish Petroleum Company (later the Iraq Petroleum Company [IPC]). In early 1914 at the British Foreign Office the British-Dutch group signed an agreement that included a key clause stipulating that the two partners "would not be interested, directly or indirectly, in the production or manufacture of crude oil in the Ottoman Empire . . . otherwise than through the Turkish Petroleum Company" (Blair, 1977:31).

This agreement established Turkish Petroleum as the monopolistic developer of Iraqi crude oil.[5] From 1922 to 1928 U.S. and British-Dutch oil interests negotiated for the entry of U.S. companies into the consortium in Iraq. Despite the attempts of IPC to exclude them, in 1928 two of the U.S. "Sisters" finally succeeded in breaking into the BP-Shell monopoly in IPC.[6] The possibility of new companies securing Iraqi exploration leases was circumvented by allowing IPC itself to become a bidder on any lease, thereby permitting it to outbid any potential interlopers at no cost because the proceeds of any sale were to be paid to IPC (Blair, 1977:33)! This feature was incorporated into the infamous Red Line Agreement, named after borders drawn with a red pen on a map of the Turkish Empire. As a result, within Turkey, Iraq, Saudi Arabia, and neighboring shaikhdoms, the IPC partners agreed to pursue all oil matters through IPC. Once in the consortium, the formerly competitive relation between the European and U.S. oil companies turned to one of collusion to maintain their joint control over Iraq's low-cost oil and to prevent the development of other Middle Eastern reserves that would compete with Iraq and Iran.

The Red Line Agreement, limiting exploration and production activities within the old Turkish Empire, marked IPC's formal emergence as a supply control cartel. It functioned to insure that consortium members did not take independent action, but could not, by itself, prevent outsiders from seeking exploration concessions within the line or outside of it. Despite IPC's best attempts to secure all concessions within the Red Line to preempt outsiders, an outsider, Standard Oil of California (Chevron), discovered petroleum in Bahrain and subsequently found huge reserves in Saudi Arabia. The IPC partners now faced the prospect of this low-cost and uncontrolled supply entering into competition with Iraqi oil. Fears of an oil glut and a price war were set in motion once again.

It is important to underline that during this period there was a good deal of international rivalry among British, Dutch, French, and U.S. oil interests, and although the industry was largely in private hands, these governments were concerned with the security of their oil supplies. Despite its early sanctioning of the petroleum industry as a private sector affair, the British government appeared to seek a greater degree of control over oil when it secured 56 percent direct ownership of the Anglo-Persian Oil Company. This decision was legitimized on the grounds of assuring supplies of oil for the Royal Navy, and ensuring a place for primarily British interests in oil, then dominated by Shell (Dutch) and Standard Oil (U.S.). The agreement prevented Anglo-Persian from selling out to foreign interests, insisted that all directors be British, and gave the government the right to appoint two of these directors who would in turn have veto powers, applicable only in matters relating to British foreign and military policy (Sampson, 1979:66). On the face of it, this appeared to give the British state control of the company, and thus support realist tenets. In practice, however, the directors named by the state were generally treasury people or political appointments with little background to independently assess company policies (Sampson, 1979:68). As a result, BP never became an effective arm of public policy and remained largely autonomous from the British state, with its main interests in dividends and the political security of BP concessions.[7]

In contrast, while the U.S. government was instrumental in breaking down French and British attempts to exclude U.S. private oil firms from the Middle East, it left the task of going abroad and developing oil resources to the MNOCs. Whereas Washington would go to the aid of the companies with diplomatic and political pressure when they were in conflict with other governments, it took little direct interest in oil matters itself. At the same time, the companies had close personal and political links with various governments and their officials when these were important to them.[8] Through lobbying, campaign contributions, exchange of staff, personal friendships, and other devices, the MNOCs had close and influential ties with the U.S. state, which at least ensured an influential audience for their point of view.

The Arabian-American Oil Company

Chevron was a member neither of IPC nor the Anglo-Iranian Oil Company consortium and thus not bound by their collusive arrangements. As a partner in Saudi Arabia, it brought in Texaco, forming Caltex. The ARAMCO (renamed from Caltex) concession is an exemplar of both the strategy of collusive control of oil and the problems of hegemony.

During World War II, Texaco and Chevron found themselves in an intermediary position between the home and host governments, a situation that came close to costing them the Saudi concession. Disruptions caused by the war meant that Saudi Arabia's chief source of income, the *hajj* to Mecca, dried up. The king, anxious for money, was pressing the companies for increased revenue, and Caltex began to fear for its concession if he were not accommodated. Caltex faced the interesting problem of persuading the Allied governments to subsidize Ibn Saud until the situation improved, in effect interceding with these governments on his behalf. Initially, however, it was the British who loaned the king money, which caused fears at Caltex that the British would become too influential with him and he dependent on them. If so, they feared, he might take the companies' concession rights away and award them to British oil interests, a prospect not unwelcome to BP or Shell. Caltex was thus forced to enlist U.S. support for the king or risk losing control of the Saudi oil fields.

In 1943 top executives from the U.S. companies met with Secretary of the Interior Harold Ickes and managed to persuade him to secure Lend Lease funds for Saudi Arabia to counter British influence and sustain the king. In return, Caltex undertook to create a Saudi Arabian oil reserve that would be available for U.S. government purchase at prices below world levels (but still well above cost). However, the administration in Washington went too far for the oil men, declaring Saudi Arabia's defense vital to the United States. Washington feared a postwar oil shortage, and the fears conjured up by Chevron and Texaco of the British gaining control of the Saudi Arabian concession caused the U.S. government to contemplate direct state participation in the concession, like the British in Iran. Under prodding from Ickes and the Navy, the U.S. government planned to buy a controlling interest in ARAMCO, arguing that U.S. oil security was too important to be left to the private companies. President Roosevelt authorized a plan to gain 100 percent of the Saudi Arabian concession through a federal government corporation, the Petroleum Reserves Corporation.

Chevron and Texaco had succeeded in keeping out the British government only to be now threatened by their own (Sampson, 1979:112–116). Although the plan was foiled when Texaco refused to sell its share of ARAMCO to the U.S. government and pulled out of the negotiations, it generated considerable opposition from a variety of sources. Exxon and Mobil, not yet partners in ARAMCO, pressured the administration to jettison the idea, arguing, in accord with the ideological cornerstone of the hegemonic oil regime, against government involvement (Keohane, 1984:153). For their part, the British perceived the Petroleum Reserves Corporation as a challenge to their interests in the Middle East, although they did not push the matter and left the international management of oil in the hands of the Seven Sisters.

After the United States had relented on the Petroleum Reserves Corporation, plans were made in Washington for an Anglo-American Petroleum Agreement. This agreement proposed setting up an international petroleum commission to "recommend production and export rates for various Middle Eastern concessions [in order] to prevent disorganization of markets which might result from uncontrolled competitive expansion" (memo from John Loftus, cited in Keohane, 1984:153). Such a scheme would replace the private cartel arrangements with a formal, interstate cartel. In the Senate Foreign Relations Committee, however, it ran into powerful opposition from a coalition of independent oil interests, anti–big business liberals, and the Justice Department, and was finally unsuccessful.

Keohane has suggested that the defeat of the proposed Anglo-American Petroleum Agreement represented a defeat for both the U.S. state and the MNOCs,[9] but a different interpretation of hegemony suggests that the MNOCs won clear victories, and these against the projects of dominant, not subordinate, states. Why would the MNOCs favor the governmental sanction and management of energy cartel arrangements implied by the proposed Anglo-American Petroleum Agreement when they had already constructed an oil regime favoring their interests?

The defeat of both the Petroleum Reserves Corporation and the Anglo-American Petroleum Agreement did not resolve Saudi Arabia's longer term demands for increased revenue, however— demands that increasingly threatened to pressure corporate revenues. A solution to these pressures was found in the U.S. government's offer to alter its taxation of the ARAMCO companies, an offer eagerly accepted by both the U.S. MNOCs and the producer governments. From 1951 the tax status of payments to Saudi Arabia and other producer governments was considered a foreign income tax, deductible from U.S. taxes, effectively becoming a foreign aid subsidy paid by the U.S. Treasury and administered by ARAMCO. The details of this foreign tax credit were, to say the least, extremely beneficial to the MNOCs and once again displayed their ability to gain highly favorable treatment from the U.S. government.[10] The MNOCs were able to prevail on the U.S. state to significantly alter the fiscal regime under which they operated. The material compromise made in Saudi Arabia's favor was thereby funded by the U.S. state (and the U.S. taxpayer) rather than the MNOCs. It had cost these corporations very little to accommodate the producers, and through the accommodation their relations with the Saudi Arabian government remained favorable.

The Anglo-Iranian Consortium

The Anglo-Iranian Oil Company, the Iranian consortium, exhibited behavior similar to that of ARAMCO in incorporating outsiders, but with more conflict. Anglo-Iranian was a major crude supplier to those "Sisters" who had far larger marketing networks than sources of production. However, this tidy arrangement was disrupted when the Mossadeq government in Iran nationalized Anglo-Iranian's

assets in 1951. Mossadeq represented a nationalistic and statist counterhegemonic challenge to Anglo-Iranian, which would not be toler-
ated by the MNOCs. If Iran were to succeed, it would show other
producers they need not depend on the consortia to market their oil,
but rather that they could do it directly through state-owned corporations. This would represent a threat to private ownership of Third
World oil supplies, which would undermine the hegemonic oil
regime and the dominant position of the MNOCs.

The Mossadeq government tried to sell its oil directly on the
international market, a move successfully blocked by Anglo-Iranian
legal action against prospective buyers and the support shown by
the other MNOCs in boycotting Iranian exports of oil. Mossadeq
himself was overthrown by a CIA-inspired coup d'état, and the
rights of the consortium were restored by the new Iranian government. This use of coercive power by the United States on behalf of
the oil companies, taken together with the actions of the MNOCs in
the defense of their own interests, demonstrates the domination of
the MNOCs and their ability to enlist state power to ensure the subordinate status of producer states.

The actions against the Mossadeq government in Iran were not
without their consequences. To make up for the loss of Iranian oil
exports during the MNOC boycott, production in other producing
countries was boosted by the oil companies. Once Anglo-Iranian
was restored in Iran, room had to be made for the resumption of
Iranian production. This required that other Middle Eastern producers suffer reductions, an unpopular move with their revenue-hungry
governments. In addition, because of the U.S. role in removing the
threat Mossadeq represented to Western oil interests, both the U.S.
government and the U.S. oil companies wanted an end to the British
monopoly over Iranian oil fields.

The U.S. government first argued for the inclusion of the crude
short independents, which were excluded from the ARAMCO
expansion, in a reformed consortium. Once again, however, the integrated majors managed to prevail so that eventually the share of the
independents in the reconstituted concession was a mere 5 percent.[11]
MNOCs argued that only they could market oil in the quantities
needed to restore the Iranian economy (after the serious effects of
the BP-led boycott), an argument that neutralized the stated desire
of the U.S. government to encourage competition in the industry. Of
course, one should not forget that the MNOCs in the Anglo-Iranian
Oil Company were not only responsible for the damage, but also
that they were the only ones big enough to absorb Iranian production without undermining the cartelized price structure, again a
clear victory for MNOC interests.

Through joint-venture supply consortia and long-term supply contracts, which placed restrictions on the end destination of crude oil supplies, the MNOCs were able to establish their domination over oil-producer governments, and through royalties and taxes bring them into a partnership as junior players. Day-to-day control over the industry remained in the hands of the MNOCs, leaving producers heavily dependent on the companies for their economic health. Without the MNOCs, producer governments would have neither the capacity to produce their own oil nor the access to MNOC-dominated markets in which to sell their oil. Thus, there was no *practical* alternative for the producers but to play the oil game by MNOC rules. The system also allowed the MNOCs to closely tune oil production to demand, allowing a price structure considerably in excess of production costs. The high profits implied in the manipulation of the oil price structure enabled MNOCs to offer lucrative rewards to producer governments, and cemented their consent to the hegemonic oil regime and the leadership of the oil companies in the system.

Multinationals and the Control of Markets

To manage the demand side of the oil industry the Seven Sisters set up an equally elaborate system of orderly marketing arrangements to complement their joint efforts at supply management. These, combined with their vertical integration, closed the circle and gave them effective control over all major facets of the industry.

The first of these arrangements dates from the 1920s, the "as is" agreement reached at Achnacarry Castle in Scotland by the chief executives of Anglo-Iranian, Exxon, and Shell. The agreement protected existing market positions and the production cost advantages of existing oil fields, prevented the addition of surplus refining capacity, and defined price structure guidelines. In effect, the Achnacarry agreements formed the basis of an elaborate system of regulation designed to limit competition in consumer markets and to protect the price structure from underselling by freezing existing market shares. These principles formed the guidelines for a series of subsequent agreements setting up cartelized local and national markets, covering the difficulties and problems of detailed control of oil.

Given the nature of these private supply-and-demand control arrangements among the major integrated MNOCs, there was neither the need nor the room for an intergovernmental regime to govern the international oil trade. The MNOCs integrated the producer governments as junior partners in the regime and provided consumers with relatively low-cost oil. The system brought relative stability to the international petroleum economy and removed the threat of cutthroat competition and supply gluts. At the same time, it paved the way for the major expansion of petroleum consumption, which characterized the post–World War II era. The self-administered arrangements governing market shares, pricing, production levels, and so forth were the key mechanisms of control in the hegemonic oil regime and were the secret of its long endurance. As long as producer governments could be kept in the game and new entrants prevented from securing independent access to low-cost oil supplies, which would compete with the MNOC cartel, the system would function very effectively. The fact that there were, at most, eight major players in the regime (the Seven Sisters and Compagnie Française Pétrole [CFP]) and that they were interlinked via the production consortia was a great aid to their cohesion as a bloc. Such cohesion was necessary to limit their own competition, to keep the producer governments from playing them off against each other, and to put up a solid front against the attempts by the independents to secure their own sources of foreign oil.

The Foundation of OPEC

The changes made to the U.S. tax structure in response to Saudi Arabia's pressure for increased revenue had important international consequences, which are revealing of the hegemonic oil regime. Due to the international nature of the industry, other consuming countries were compelled to adopt tax loopholes similar to those of the U.S. government so that their companies could remain competitive with the ARAMCO MNOCs. This effectively changed the incentive structure within the industry. It provided a major incentive for U.S. companies to invest outside the United States so as to capitalize on the foreign tax credit and minimize their tax burdens. It also led to a transfer by these companies of their profit centers, and encouraged them to declare profits in the overseas, upstream end of the industry, again minimizing their taxes to consuming governments where most of the downstream operations were located. The shifting of profit centers also raised the revenues flowing to producer governments, albeit lower than the savings on the U.S. tax rate.

Producer governments insisted that the companies post the prices they paid for crude oil, which made prices public rather than proprietary information. The posted price thus became the price on which taxes and royalties to all governments were calculated (Sampson, 1979:131–134). The posted price was not a real market price but rather a declaratory price arrived at through a complex structure of administrative pricing and tax laws, which was marginally favorable to producer governments and extremely favorable to the oil companies with international operations. The drawback of this system was a more general problem for the MNOCs and the hegemonic oil regime. The posted price accustomed the producer governments to a relatively stable and upwardly trending posted price for oil. This was not a problem as long as markets remained under the control of the MNOC cartel. However, it was to cause great friction between the producers and the companies when the MNOCs began to encounter price competition from the independents and felt compelled to lower the posted price in order to compete. This, in fact, led directly to the creation of OPEC in 1960.

When the multinationals began to lose control of the international supply and price structure, the hegemonic oil regime began to crumble and producer governments, which had become accustomed to relatively stable and steadily increasing revenues with the global growth of the industry, became highly disenchanted with the system as the MNOCs tried to cut back the posted oil price. Iraq and Iran, among the producers, were the most dissatisfied with the MNOCs because their oil exports were held down to make room for those of Saudi Arabia, which was the jewel of low-cost Middle East oil concessions and the major crude source for the four big U.S. MNOCs. As long as their resources were under the control of a single concession of MNOCs, it was difficult for producers to boost oil production. What was wanted were concessionaires who were heavily dependent on a single source because they would tend to maximize production. In the 1960s, oil producers began to offer concessions to interlopers, who then began to undercut the MNOC price structure.

In 1960 the price competition from the independents prompted the MNOCs to reduce the posted price they would pay the producer countries. This eroded the material basis of consent among the producers, and the result was the founding of the Organization of Petroleum Exporting Countries. OPEC was founded to resist oil price cuts and to be a forum for negotiation with the MNOCs, a forum the companies initially shunned. The founding members of OPEC had more than four-fifths of the world's oil reserves at the time and potentially were in a commanding position, but it took them several years to realize their power.

As long as OPEC members continued to rely on their concessionaires for markets and to actually operate their oil fields (as most of them did), effective control remained largely in MNOC hands, even if their decisions now required more consultation with the producers than before. However, OPEC was successful in preventing any further price reductions. The companies tried to lure the members separately into giving them tax rebates in exchange for extra production, but member governments held firm. OPEC did limit the ability of the companies to play one producer off against another, largely nullifying their divide-and-conquer tactics.

The Libyan Concession

Increasing Western oil demand in the late 1960s led to a tightening of the supply-demand relationship in the international oil industry. To meet this demand, a series of new Third World oil producers came on line in the latter half of the 1960s and the early part of the 1970s. Chief among these were the United Arab Emirates, Nigeria, and Libya.

In Libya the most important breaks with the regime of the Seven Sisters occurred, both in the consortia arrangements themselves and in the vigor with which the Qaddafi government extracted concessions from the oil companies. Libya clearly demonstrated the bargaining leverage that producer governments had acquired against the companies in a tightening market. It also showed that the MNOCs were unwilling to step in and aid the Libyan independents when they got into trouble with Qaddafi's government, a failure of hegemonic leadership.

Libyan oil was highly coveted because of its proximity to Western European markets as well as its very low sulphur content, which was important in minimizing pollution. Equally significant, by deliberate policy, the monarchy leased a much higher proportion of concessions to independent and nonintegrated companies than was the case elsewhere. This policy facilitated the entry of newcomers into the upstream end of the industry. It was designed to avoid the situation of other producers who were dependent on the MNOCs and therefore subject to their supply restriction systems. Instead of turning Libyan oil over to the MNOCs, independents were chosen, due to the fact that their overall success would depend heavily on exploration and production in Libya because they lacked the multiple sources of crude oil available to the MNOCs. By 1970, 55 percent of Libyan oil was produced by independents compared to a 15 percent overall OPEC average (Sampson, 1979:212).

However, the independents—Oasis along with Occidental and Bunker Hunt—had insufficient established marketing networks for the quantities of oil they could produce, leading them to engage in a price war with the MNOCs in order to market the new Libyan crude. In their contracts to third parties the majors had little choice but to match the independents' prices. This price competition initiated the decline in wholesale oil prices that characterized the 1960s.

The MNOCs had an ambivalent attitude toward Libya and the independents. The closure of the Suez Canal after the 1967 Middle East war further enhanced the transportation advantages of Libyan oil. The MNOCs benefited from the concessions they had secured in close proximity to Europe, but the flood of oil beyond their control into Europe meant they had to match the price competition of the independents or shut down production in other Middle East concessions. The latter course might preserve the price structure but would reduce the volumes in MNOC networks and thereby reduce their profits. It might also cause major political difficulties with the increasingly disenchanted governments of the other Middle East oil-producing countries, thereby threatening those concessions. On the other hand, if the MNOCs abandoned Libya, they would no doubt lose the Libyan supplies.

In 1969 the Libyan monarchy was overthrown by a coup d'état of radical army officers, and the Qaddafi regime wasted little time in confronting the oil concessionaires. What began as an attempt to get a bigger share of oil rents ultimately resulted in Libya's assuming control over its oil industry, and thus the state, rather than the Western oil companies, would henceforth determine production levels. Thus, an initial attempt to elevate its subordinated status within the hegemonic oil regime was transformed into a counterhegemonic project[12] to wrest control of the upstream end of the industry from the MNOCs and the independents.

The Libyan government decided to attempt to drive a wedge between the MNOCs and the independents by singling out Occidental Petroleum and demanding a tax rate of 55 percent on Occidental's Libyan production. Further, Libya curtailed Occidental's operations pending its agreement. Occidental was completely dependent on Libyan crude for its European operations and was also one of the worst price-cutting offenders in the eyes of the MNOCs. Faced with these cutbacks, Occidental's president, the redoubtable Armand Hammer, went to see Ken Jamieson, his counterpart at Exxon. Hammer warned that Libya's action placed his company in an untenable position and that he could not resist the tax demands unless he was assured an alternative supply of crude at cost. Here the Libyan strategy of playing off the competitors bore fruit. Jamieson, faced with Occidental's price competition both in Europe and the United States, turned Hammer down. Within a month of this meeting Occidental capitulated and signed an agreement accepting Libya's terms, which then became the minimum condition for operating in Libya. The MNOCs and the British and the U.S. governments responded with high-level meetings in New York and Washington in order to build a common front in opposition to the Libyan action. Despite this, Chevron and Texaco broke ranks and signed an agreement with Libya similar to that signed by Occidental. Subsequent to this clear Libyan victory, Iraq, Iran, Algeria, and Kuwait followed suit and raised their tax rates to the same level. Soon after, an OPEC resolution stipulated that the 55 percent figure would henceforth constitute a minimum tax floor in all member countries, and generalized it across the main producers.

The Teheran and Tripoli Agreements

The negotiations surrounding the Teheran and Tripoli agreements constituted the last attempt by the MNOCs and the producers to reach an accord within the framework of the old hegemonic oil regime. The companies now found themselves in a relatively weak position in their negotiations with OPEC. In addition, in the early 1970s, oil market conditions changed from a buyer's to a seller's market, further enhancing the leverage of the producing governments and encouraging OPEC to push for higher oil prices.

In response particularly to Iran's threat to nationalize the oil industry within its borders, the United States convened a special OECD meeting in order to consult with other importing governments. Faced with threats of nationalizations, however, it became clear that the other consumer governments were not prepared to resist higher OPEC prices. In the absence of a unified consumer government front, therefore, oil companies were largely left on their own in the negotiations.

In early February 1971, talks between OPEC and the MNOCs broke down, and OPEC convened a ministerial conference. At this conference, OPEC issued an ultimatum stating that each OPEC member would legislate new terms independent of any negotiations with the companies, and any of the companies failing to comply with the new terms would face an embargo. Confronted by the threat of nationalization and the loss of their oil supplies, and with little support from their home governments, the companies saw no choice but to give in to OPEC.

The Teheran agreement secured producer governments an increase of thirty cents per barrel in the posted price, which would rise to fifty cents by 1975. Despite the Shah's claim that there would be no "leapfrogging" to the Mediterranean, a few months later the Libyans got a better deal. While the MNOCs attempted to put forward a joint negotiating team, the Tripoli negotiations were conducted on a one-on-one basis between the government and individual companies, capitalizing on the weakness of those heavily dependent on Libyan oil. In support of the Libyan initiative, Algeria, Saudi Arabia, and Iraq threatened a Mediterranean embargo if the companies did not agree to Libya's terms. A further show of OPEC solidarity was reflected in the arrival in Tripoli of Saudi Arabia's minister of oil and minerals, Shaikh Yamani, to lend his support. In April 1971, nineteen companies settled with the Libyan government on a $3.30 posted price for Libyan oil, an increase of $0.76. Premiums brought the posted price up to $3.45. Similar agreements soon followed with OPEC's newest member, Nigeria (Sampson, 1979:272).

The Participation Agreements

The participation agreements were designed to meet two problems experienced by the producing governments in their efforts to gain control over the production and pricing of their oil: how to gain control over output levels and at the same time how to retain markets to which they had access only through the oil multinationals. The example of Iran in the 1950s showed the futility of nationalizing oil concessions if access to markets was blocked. Participation was conceived as a process of gradual and negotiated nationalization, based on joint-venture partnerships between consortium companies and OPEC national oil companies, giving OPEC governments greater sovereignty over their oil resources. It aimed to ease the producers into the international oil system without disrupting the managed markets for petroleum. OPEC argued that participation would also be in the interests of the oil companies, as it would save them from ultimate nationalization.

At a June 1971 meeting Yamani persuaded governments to demand an immediate 20 percent interest in their oil concessions and to agree to raise this to 51 percent subsequently (Sampson, 1979:277). Once again the Gulf producers banded together and appointed Yamani to negotiate the terms with the companies' common front. At the same time, nationalizations were proceeding in several countries, most notably in Algeria, which nationalized 51 percent of French oil interests, and in Libya, which seized BP's assets at the end of 1971. The success of these moves only encouraged the other OPEC governments to push further against the weak bargaining position of the companies. In early 1972, OPEC governments sat down with the companies in Geneva. This meeting also set out the details of participation—details the companies disliked intensely and that led to a new confrontation. These details promised to reduce the once-mighty MNOCs to the position of OPEC tax collectors (Sampson, 1979:279).

By 1973, the Libyan government had nationalized 33 percent of its proven reserves and had assumed controlling interest (51 percent equity) in the oil consortia in Libya (Blair, 1977:328). Production restrictions were also imposed on several of the concessions in the expectation that controlled production would increase the barrel price. From the MNOCs' point of view, however, this had the beneficial effect of removing the feared glut of Libyan oil in nonadministered markets. Had the cutbacks not occurred—that is, had the Libyan government not seized control over production levels—an extra 1.5 million barrels per day (MBD) would likely have entered world markets, making the price increases of 1973–1974 extremely difficult to sustain.

The ARAMCO consortium in Saudi Arabia became the critical battleground for the participation question. As shortages of crude increased, the Saudi Arabian oil fields assumed an ever-greater importance in the supply requirements of the ARAMCO partners. Serious negotiations began between Yamani and ARAMCO in 1972. Despite the predilection of the ARAMCO president to accommodate Yamani, the four consortium partners took a no-compromise stance. They refused to sell equity in the company and instead offered to give the government a 50 percent share of any future projects, an offer rejected out of hand. Exxon had persuaded U.S. president Richard Nixon to pressure the Saudi Arabian government, a move that backfired when Yamani secured the personal intervention of King Faisal, who threatened to implement participation unilaterally if "obliged to by the failure of the companies to cooperate" (Sampson, 1979:281).

Yamani also turned to OPEC and convened a special ministerial conference at which he warned that the producers must prepare themselves for battle with the oil companies. On the eve of this conference, ARAMCO had conceded the principle of immediate government participation at a 20 percent equity level. Chevron, for its part, refused to sell any portion of its share in the company. Other OPEC producers set the precedent when the United Arab Emirates, Kuwait, and Qatar secured 20 percent participation agreements with their concessionaires. Further pressure was added when Iraq nationalized IPC outright. At the end of 1972 an agreement was finally reached between OPEC and ARAMCO, which called for an immediate 25 percent share, rising to 51 percent by 1983 (Sampson, 1979:283).

The participation agreements signaled the entry of OPEC governments into an equal but uneasy partnership with the MNOCs and established strong pressure for upward price hikes at the retail level. Price competition with the independents had resulted in a posted price unreflective of the true selling price of crude oil. The erosion of the hegemonic oil regime and the vanished dominance of the MNOCs over the international oil industry were made abundantly clear during the oil crisis of 1973, which signaled that effective control over production levels and prices had truly passed to the OPEC governments.

Conclusion

What, then, are the implications of the rise and decline of the hegemonic oil regime for international relations theory? To begin, this case demonstrates the extent to which the realist preoccupation with the state as a central actor is misplaced, for such a perspective ignores—at least in theoretical terms—the links between states and private capital. It is all but impossible, after all, to describe the outlines of the hegemonic oil regime without describing the role of the Seven Sisters. Perhaps even more significantly, a notion of hegemony based upon neorealism's state-centric assumptions limits our understanding of power in such a way as to gloss over the private constellation of forces that so significantly affected the international energy regime for the past fifty years. Reflexive theorizing allows for the questioning of neorealism's state-centric assumptions, and opens space for a Gramscian understanding of hegemony, which better conceptualizes the complex interrelationships between private and state power. In fact, this case displays that only through an approach founded on reflexivity is it possible to begin to understand the truly illusive nature of "power" in the international political economy. The inherently critical nature of such a reflexive approach suggests that the insights of realism must be challenged, that the role of the state must be questioned, but that any consequent new understandings must themselves be subject to similar critical introspection.

This case reveals flaws in the claim that the lobbying successes of the MNOCs were a result of the national interest of the dominant states in the system. If this is at all true, it would seem to be of only secondary importance. Under the hegemonic oil regime, key interests were defined by the major integrated companies and, to a lesser degree, by the subordinate producing states. The development of the oil import dependency of the OECD countries in the postwar period, after all, can hardly be argued to have been in the rational interest of those dominant states, but it was quite consistent with the interests of the international oil companies. Only through the abandonment of the straitjacket of neorealism's basic assumptions can such an observation become obvious.

The oil case points to the need to move beyond international relations as the study of *interstate* relations and interactions. International relations theory needs to broaden its focus to encompass the study of international *social* relations, of which interstate relations are only one variant. The oil case demonstrates the capacity of international resource capital (organized as MNOCs) to structure a major sector of the world economy in its own interests. A wide variety of other sectors of capital rested on, and were highly beholden to, this structure. Once set up, this economic structure was even beyond the strict or narrow control of the systemic hegemon, the United States, as it attempted to pursue its energy objectives. State power, while providing assistance to the establishment and maintenance of the hegemonic oil regime, was of secondary importance. Thus, the interrelationship between private and state power is such that any adequate understanding of the international energy regime cannot be reduced to either level of analysis. The hegemonic oil regime can hardly be said to have been a *state* project. Thus, *private* power—in this case, the power of organized capital—was the key element structuring international energy relations under the hegemonic oil regime, suggesting the extent to which interstate relations should not be the privileged object of study in international relations. The shortcomings of neorealist analysis reveal the extent to which a hegemony-counterhegemony framework provides a more useful and nuanced theoretical handle on the interactions in world society.

Notes

1. Aside from the plethora of empirical studies liberally sprinkled throughout the journal, see, for instance, Cowhey and Long (1983); Gowa (1984); Haas (1982, 1983); Haggard and Simmons (1987); Keohane (1982); Krasner (1982); and Stein (1982).

2. There are then two views of hegemony: one about the political and military power among states and the other about domination and subordination in civil society with reliance on consent rather than force. The former usage stresses hegemonic actors such as the great powers, who impose their notions of order on the less powerful as in hegemonic stability theory. The latter usage focuses away from actors and envisions more of a sociopolitical process of leadership by consent.

3. This citation is found in Cox (1977:387; 1981:153). For an elaborate theoretical exposition of his argument, see Cox (1987).

4. See J. Blair's account of the companies' successful evisceration of antitrust prosecution during the Truman and Eisenhower administrations (Blair, 1977:71–76).

5. In 1925, a reluctant Iraqi government signed a seventy-five-year lease with IPC, which promised the Iraqi government the opportunity to

buy 20 percent of the equity of IPC. However, when Iraq later sought to exercise this option, IPC refused to offer any shares for sale, demonstrating how jealously it guarded its control, and blocked attempts by producer governments to enter the industry.

6. Exxon and Mobil together acquired a 23.75 percent stake. The remainder was apportioned 23.75 percent each to BP, Shell, and Compagnie Française Pétrole (CFP). The remaining 5 percent share went to Calouste Gulbenkian personally (Blair, 1977:33).

7. The same problems characterized CFP, the French state-owned oil company, which also tended to operate like any other of the MNOCs.

8. Walter Teagle, the head of Exxon, regularly played poker with President Warren Harding, was a close friend of Calvin Coolidge, advised Herbert Hoover on business matters, and became chairman of the Industry Advisory Board under Roosevelt's New Deal (Sampson, 1979:93). Another example of the revolving door between the U.S. executive branch, the oil industry, commercial banking, and Wall Street corporate law firms was lawyer-lobbyist John McCloy, who represented all seven of the MNOCs and many of the "independents" and was closely linked to the Rockefeller banking interest, Chase-Manhattan bank (Sampson, 1979:254–255). During the Marshall Plan, J. Walter Levy from Mobil Oil and Oscar Brandy from Standard Oil (Indiana) were, respectively, the chief and deputy chief of the Economic Cooperation Administration's oil division. This agency did much to create European markets for Arabian-American Oil Company (ARAMCO) supplies, and Marshall Plan arrangements largely excluded British, Dutch, and French companies (Shaffer, 1983:98–99). Levy later went on to become the chief New York oil consultant of the MNOCs, enjoying great prestige among the members of the "oil establishment."

9. Keohane's argument is that the MNOCs were in support of the proposed agreement because "the government would be achieving for them what they had long sought in world markets through informal collusion and more or less secret agreements" (1984:153). See also Keohane (1984:179).

10. The long-term effect of the tax credits can be clearly seen. In 1974, the United States had a nominal corporate tax rate of 48 percent. That same year the tax liabilities of the nineteen largest U.S. oil companies amounted to a mere 7.6 percent of their before-tax income (Blair, 1977:187). The largest write-off was the foreign tax credit, although super depletion allowances and the recovery of intangible drilling costs were also major tax dodges. In terms of assets, the comparison of the oil industry to other sectors is even more dramatic. In 1965 there was a total of $96.8 billion in assets among the petroleum, automotive, and aerospace industries. The tax burden of $3.2 billion was distributed in the following proportions: the petroleum industry, holding 59.7 percent of these assets, paid only 9.3 percent of these taxes; the automotive sector, holding 31.7 percent of the assets, paid 79.2 percent of the taxes; and the aerospace sector, itself highly favored by the government, paid the remaining 11.5 percent (Blair, 1977:187). These benefits accrued disproportionately to the MNOCs. A more favorable tax regime could hardly be imagined.

11. BP retained 40 percent, Shell 14 percent, and 7 percent each went to Exxon, Mobil, Chevron, Texaco, and Gulf Oil. The remaining 6 percent went to CFP (Keohane, 1984:46).

12. I do not use counterhegemonic in the Gramscian sense of an alternative hegemony that can supplant and replace a weakening existing hege-

mony. A counterhegemonic project rejects the existing hegemonic definitions and asserts an alternative definition, which is used to fight the old
hegemony. It is not necessary that it be strong enough to completely van-
quish the old regime and set itself up as a new hegemony. Thus OPEC did
not aim to supplant the MNOCs completely and run the entire global oil
industry, but rather sought to combat the existing hegemonic definition and
set of rules in the supply end of the industry.

6

Postmodern Political Realism and International Relations Theory's Third Debate

Tony Porter

International relations theory is currently undergoing a transformation comparable to two previous discipline-shaping turning points, the debate between idealism and realism and the debate between behavioralism and traditionalism. This Third Debate involves a rebuilding of the metatheoretical assumptions that had provided the guide to determining what type of theoretical knowledge should be regarded as scientifically acceptable during most of the period since World War II.[1] On one level, the transformation involves the deliberate reincorporation of interpretative approaches from the humanities and a critical reexamination of positivist notions of science that had previously been brought into the discipline from the natural sciences. Yet the transformation could have a far more profound impact on international relations theory than simply adding a renewed interest in the uniquely human activity of meaning-construction to the current focus on behavior as empirical data because it has implications for the epistemology, ontology, methodology, and axiology of the discipline.

This chapter examines one particular aspect of this transformation, the application of postmodernist approaches to international theory. At first glance, postmodernism, whose native territory is literature, art, and architecture, appears to have little relevance for international theory. Yet postmodernist approaches to international theory are worth examining because postmodernism (with its focus on the role of rhetoric in constructing both power relations and bodies of knowledge) may offer insights into the role of meaning construction in the international system itself, and into the current fundamental dissensus regarding the metatheoretical foundations of international relations as a discipline.

What Does the Current Transformation Involve?

The central feature of the current transformation of international theory is a reexamination of the aspiration to a positivist model of science that aimed to imitate the natural sciences. By briefly examining the shortcomings of positivism it is possible to better assess the degree to which postmodernism offers solutions.

The development of international relations theory since World War II exhibits remarkable similarities to developments in other theoretical debates, such as those found within the philosophy of science and comparative politics. This suggests that metatheoretical problems—which were addressed by a mode of thinking shared across disciplines—were more important in shaping the development of international relations theory than were the empirical problems specific to the discipline. This shared mode of thinking about how knowledge is best obtained can be seen as developing in response to common problems that emerged across disciplines in the search for knowledge, and also in response to cultural inclinations related to large-scale social and political challenges.

Positivism as originally developed by Auguste Comte emerged in reaction to metaphysical and essentialist theories, and as such it rejected transcendentally grounded universal laws. As Giddens has noted, Comtean positivism

> seals the rejection of absolutism as characteristic of metaphysical philosophy: the laws that govern the covariance of phenomena always retain a provisional character, since they are induced on the basis of empirical observation, rather than being posited as "absolute essences." (Giddens, 1978:240)

This pragmatic attitude toward theory has been particularly influential in U.S. political science. Bentley (1967), for instance, aimed to ground the study of politics in the group as a mass of activity based on common interests—a grounding he saw as solidly empirical, scientific, and antiutopian. For Bentley, such a grounding could legitimize his version of democracy as action, unbound by the rigidity of institutions.[2]

During the 1950s this pragmatic positivism was influential in international relations theory, as in U.S. political theory in general, in its attempt to respond to the collapse of the League system, and to the statist challenge posed by fascism and communism. In the work of comparativists such as Gabriel Almond, pluralism, pragmatism, and positivism seemed to mesh nicely during the 1950s.[3] The similarity between international theory and comparative politics in their enthusiasm for this solution is easy to overlook because of the tendency of subsequent realists to impose a statist consistency on their theoretical tradition. Yet the realists of the postwar period focused on the individual and society and saw the state as derivative. Herz, Carr, and Niebuhr all stressed the relevance of realism for all aspects of human conduct, and none placed the state at the center of their analyses. Morgenthau stressed the similarity between the U.S. state and the international system. In his view both were the expression of a plurality of competing interest groups (Morgenthau, 1967:164–166).

The subsequent evolution of positivism in international theory is familiar to students of international relations, and its evolution is echoed in other disciplines. During the 1950s and 1960s a generation of theorists attempted to build a quantitative international politics (QIP) based on a solid foundation of statistically significant empirical relationships. By the 1970s, however, doubts and disillusionment had set in as QIP seemed to be having difficulty living up to its promise, or, as J. David Singer put it, to be "snatching defeat from the jaws of victory" (Singer, 1976:167). Three conferences organized by Rosenau to address the problem of cumulation in international theory (Rosenau, 1976) reflected the disillusionment, with most participants stressing the need to move away from atheoretical data-dredging to an emphasis on theory building.[4]

The Third Debate, as with discussions of postpositivism in other disciplines, attempts to overcome positivism's problems by recognizing that social institutions must be brought "back in" at a number of levels. The state has begun to be taken as ontologically primitive, setting the stage for the development of rational choice models in which states are treated as coherent rational actors (Wendt, 1987). Regimes as social institutions are taken seriously despite their incompatibility with positivist epistemology (Kratochwil and Ruggie, 1986). Echoing Thomas Kuhn (1970), theory is seen as embedded in consensual understandings of research communities rather than resulting from the application of universal rules of empirical testing.[5]

Positivism's blindness to the role of social institutions in shaping human actions crippled it theoretically, obscured social constructs that should have been taken as real, and precluded theoretical directions that were not amenable to empirical testing. By presumptuously assuming that it could apprehend universal truths, neglecting its own rootedness in contingent cultural inclinations, and denying the ability of humans to socially reconstruct reality, positivism—at least in the more metatheoretically rigid and unimaginative variants that dominated the social sciences—reached a dead end. It is to postmodernism as an alternative that we will now turn.

Postmodernism and International Theory

Postmodernism is defined as much by its rejection of modernity as by its own internal coherence. The modern project is seen as a cultural construction that attempts to extend one particular mode of thinking—rationality—to all corners of the world, destroying diversity in the name of progress. Rationality is seen as an ideological construction that is a form of power. This power operates by constituting self-disciplined individuals who monitor their own conduct, by ensuring conformity, and by creating boundaries that are used to silence and exclude "others," who are labeled insane, primitive, criminal, terrorist, or the like. Any attempt to read coherence into a phenomenon as diverse as postmodernism inevitably involves simplification. In order to grasp the implications of postmodernist international theory, however, it is useful to draw out some key common features of postmodernism.

Pauline Rosenau (1988) has offered a useful summary of such key features.[6] Postmodernism involves a rejection of method based on reason, of the notion that the mind apprehends an already existing reality, and of the hermeneutic goal of discovering preexisting meaning. As Rosenau put it, "deconstruction involves demystifying a text, tearing it apart to reveal its internal, arbitrary hierarchies, and its presuppositions" (Rosenau, 1988:6). Texts are a creation of the play of signs rather than of the explication of a preexisting logic in the mind of the author. The world is seen as textual, created by the infinite overlapping, interpenetration, and interplay of discourses and texts. Western rational thought is seen as inherently hierarchical, involving the creation of dualisms such as object/subject or right/wrong, and the goal of deconstruction is to subvert these hierarchies.

The notion of a subject, or of "man" as a rational agent, is rejected by postmodernism. The subject is decentered, the "death of the author" is announced, and the notion that history has coherency, that there is a "master narrative," is rejected. Representation in all its forms, including linguistics, politics, science, and art, is rejected as fraudulent, and a focus on the specific, on the local, and on pastiche is advocated. Postmodernism in art and sculpture can be traced in the playful mixture of the detritus of consumer society with artifacts of high culture, in photographs of photographs, and in art breaking out of the museum and entering into daily life (Foster, 1983). It can be seen in the "eclipse of distance" and the "rage against order" that Daniel Bell (1976) perceived in *The Cultural Contradictions of Capitalism.*[7]

Postmodern International Relations Theory

When first encountered, postmodernism appears particularly ill suited to the study of international relations. What could be less relevant to enhancing our understanding of the harsh realities of international conflict?

Indeed some attempts to apply postmodern analyses of texts to international relations are easily dismissed as absurd. For instance, an influential paper by Derrida (1984) given at a conference to encourage literary theorists to engage in "nuclear criticism," argued that because all-out nuclear war has never happened, it is a constructed myth.[8] Therefore, Derrida argued, it is impossible to find any solid foundation on which to argue for or against the accumulation of nuclear weapons. The debate over nuclear weapons is a rhetorical clash. Aside from problems one might have with the ethics of abandoning attempts to ascertain the likelihood of nuclear war, such an argument makes an unsustainable jump from the assertion that projections of scenarios of nuclear war are to some degree constructed, to the assertion that all such projections are completely and equally fabricated.

This chapter argues that such unsustainable jumps are the Achilles heel of much postmodernist political analysis. It would be a mistake to be too hasty in rejecting postmodernism on the basis of such criticisms, however. Two main contributions of postmodernism to our understanding of international relations are worth looking at: (1) the way in which meaning is constructed and manipulated through the use of words and symbols; and (2) the focusing of attention on modernity as a phenomenon.

The Construction of Meaning Through the Manipulation of Symbols

The hyperattentiveness of postmodernism to the way in which meaning is constructed and communicated in symbols can be a source of insight about this aspect of international relations without treating the entire universe as mythic text.

In a world where very few humans experience international relations directly, but rather through newspapers, television, textbooks, movies, and novels, the construction of meaning through the manipulation of words has not received the attention it deserves. Too often, international theorists assume that logical elegance and verisimilitude are qualities sufficient to spread their ideas, overlooking the rhetorical techniques and concrete mechanisms by which ideas are created and disseminated. It is quite likely that Tom Clancy, the author of techno-thrillers such as *Red Storm Rising* and *The Hunt for Red October*, has had far more influence on international relations than has Kenneth Waltz. Former president Ronald Reagan, former vice-president Dan Quayle, numerous U.S. military officers, and a large segment of the U.S. public have expressed their enthusiasm for Clancy's best-selling portrayals of East-West conflict (Der Derian, 1989).

Not only do popular texts have greater influence on international relations than is often recognized, but official documents also have a literary quality and employ textual strategies that are worth analyzing. For instance, McCanles (1984) has pointed out that governments carry on relations through texts such as diplomatic missives, treaties, and the publication of strategies. Klein (1988, 1989) has subjected defense manuals to literary criticism, showing how they manipulate soldiers' perceptions of the enemy, instill discipline, and conceal both the brutality of war and the responsibility for employing weapons of destruction. Deterrence is especially suited to textual analysis because it rests on the communication of threats, rather than the actual employment of force (Luke, 1989).

The importance of the construction of meaning as an object of study in the human sciences is not unique to postmodernism. The *verstehen* tradition in German sociology, and more recent proponents of hermeneutic approaches, which emphasize the importance of studying the interpretations that individuals give to their actions, have some resemblance. Postmodernism differs from these other approaches in its rejection of the notion of coherent individual meaning. The postmodernist focus on the decentered play of signs in texts offers interesting insights into the way in which meaning is created and its links to strategies of domination. As such, it has potential relevance for current analyses of power, which have moved away from the analysis of power as resources to a more relational notion that can involve the manipulation of symbols (Baldwin, 1979).

Deconstruction as a technique to analyze texts to discover internal inconsistencies that reveal hidden assumptions can also be useful. Such hidden assumptions can preclude questioning of the foundations upon which assertions are based. Deconstruction is used to show that all claims are rhetorical and that all foundations of knowledge are arbitrary. A goal is to discover alternative interpretations of texts that recognize a diversity of meanings, and thus subvert the notion that authors can create one legitimate interpretation. Such an approach to reading texts can provide new insights, help avoid the creation of stale academic orthodoxies, and discover clues to metatheoretical contradictions. As an illustration of this, this chapter reviews some postmodern readings of political realist texts that reveal them to be more contradictory than the tradition usually admits.

Solomon, for instance, has argued that Thucydides did not simply record the hard facts of the power politics of his time, but rather engaged in the construction of narrative[9] in order to create meaning and to make universal assertions. Thucydides' observations were not based on direct apprehension of the empirical. As he noted of the speeches he used as sources,

> it was in all cases difficult to carry them word for word in one's memory, so my habit has been to make the speakers say what was in my opinion demanded of them by the various occasions, of course adhering as closely as possible to the general sense of what they really said. (Solomon, 1988:42)

Thucydides' famous observation that the real causes and inevitability of the Peloponnesian War were not the interpretations given by the participants, but "the growth and power of Athens, and the alarm which this inspired in Lacedaemon," was not supported by evidence, but rather based on Thucydides' own interpretation—itself derived from the narrative he constructed as a whole. Similarly, R. B. J. Walker has argued that Machiavelli was committed to the construction of political communities, and that his interest in international relations and war derived from his acceptance of a classical conception of the *polis*, "identified as the location and character of political life within a bounded territorial space" (Walker, 1989:34).

Connolly (1988) has argued that Hobbes used the state of nature not as empirical evidence of the character of humans, but rather as a rhetorical device that served as one aspect of his overall project of advocating political community that was to be achieved through the constitution of self-disciplined individuals who would interact harmoniously by using their God-given faculties of reason. As well, Ashley (1987) has highlighted the commitment of realists such as Morgenthau and Herz to the creation of both a domestic and an international community by their calls for statesmen to build a shared commitment to the norms of diplomacy. These shared realist practices constitute and make possible the state as a bounded territory within which can exist a community based on shared universal values.

Taken together, such accounts of key realist texts undermine the notion that there is a unified tradition upon which present-day realism can draw for legitimacy. Classical realist texts, far from faithfully reporting the objective clash of political powers and from uncovering timeless generalizations about the inevitability of conflict, engage in rhetorical construction of narratives designed to imbue life with meaning. Machiavelli, Hobbes, and Morgenthau, far from cynically accepting the ubiquitous nature of war, are motivated by their commitment to, and belief in, the possibility of constructing human community.

Focusing Attention on Modernity

Postmodernism has defined itself in relationship to modernity, which it regards as a multifaceted cultural, social, and political phenomenon. Modernity can be seen as involving an attitude toward time—more specifically, the view that change is the only constant and that history is progress, involving increasing mastery of nature and perfection of humanity. Modernity can be seen as a master narrative that constitutes the individual as a subject whose actions are disciplined by his or her commitment to universalizing reason.

Postmodernism is characterized by its attempt to step outside of the assumptions of modernism in order to see its violent side, its destruction of nature, its enforcement of uniformity, its suppression of diversity, and its construction of arbitrary constellations of power. Considering the coincidence in time of the modern age and the state-system, surprisingly little attention has been devoted to modernity in international theory. A notable exception is Morse's *Modernization and the Transformation of International Relations* (1976), which seeks to identify a consistent modern trend that started with the creation of the Westphalia system. The Westphalia system represented a rejection of the transcendent Christian community in favor of secular princes whose statesmanship demolished internal barriers to unified domestic markets and preserved these territorial spaces by resisting external threats. For Morse, this classical modern system has changed with industrialization to a system characterized by interdependence and the adoption of coordinated foreign policies centered around "low" rather than "high" politics.

Morse elaborated explicitly, and with historical vision, what a modernist international theory involves. Liberal internationalism (whether in its idealist, functionalist, transnationalist, or regime theory stages) has most often adopted such a vision implicitly, without recognizing its historical specificity. Neither liberal internationalism in general nor Morse in particular adequately recognizes the contingent, reversible, and violent sides of modernity. This is in sharp contrast to recent developments in comparative politics (Apter, 1987).[10] Important trends in comparative politics can be seen as postmodernist (such as found explicitly in Apter [1987]), or as rejecting a utilitarian focus on the individual in favor of a more contingent emphasis on norms and symbols (as found in the neoinstitutionalist view that the state as an institution shapes society).

What is to be gained by stepping outside of the modern framework in order to develop perspective on modernity as a coherent phenomenon? In addition to encouraging more caution toward ahistorical generalizations about international relations, it also offers new insights into the state and its role. Two relationships stand out. First is the relationship between a reasoning, sovereign individual and the constitution of the sovereign state. Second is the role that the image of a violent, uncontrollable, external anarchy plays in constituting a unified, rational, orderly domestic political community.

The Sovereign Individual and the Sovereign State

Viewed as products of modernity, the sovereign individual and the sovereign state can be seen as mutually reinforcing constructs, a relationship captured in the dual meaning of the word "subject." Premodern society involved an overlapping and fragmentation of political authority, legitimized by the ability of those who wielded it to interpret God's word as inscribed in everyday life and sacred texts. Local communities were wrapped in particular dialects and contexts, and higher authorities ruled from outside, directly ordering neither everyday life nor individual consciousness (Connolly, 1984).

With the onset of modernity, a new grounding was needed for both political authority and knowledge. As Connolly put it,

> after God's retreat from the world (he does not disappear altogether) nature becomes a deposit of objects to be understood through humanly constructed categories; words become human instruments of understanding and representation; knowledge is grounded in perception and logic; and agency, purpose, will, and intelligence migrate from a cosmos in which human beings are privileged participants to human beings alone. (Connolly, 1984:3)

Reason replaces revelation as a source of legitimacy. The works of both Hobbes and Rousseau mark this shift. They see reason in nature as the medium through which the light of God is made evident, and see the bringing of human action into convergence with such reason as the mechanism by which both the sovereign individual and the sovereign state are made possible (Connolly, 1984:69).

Max Weber explicitly linked the role of rationality in shaping individual conduct, making bureaucracy possible, and legitimizing the modern state. As Wolin has pointed out, there is a close correspondence between Weber's characterization of science and his characterization of the bureaucratic state (Wolin, 1984:63). Both are legitimized with reference to their method rather than their ends. In Weber the postmodern view—the awareness and fear that the pervasive growth of rationality undermines claims to legitimacy—is evident as well. Meaning in science, individual practice, and politics must come from nonrational sources, whether through the scientist's gift of inspiration and commitment to values based on faith, the Calvinist's asceticism, or the charismatic leader's visions. This contradiction identified by Weber—the inability of rationality to find foundations that are not arbitrary and nonrational—is a central focus of the postmodern approach.

The postmodern sensitivity to the connectedness of rationality, individual sovereignty, state sovereignty, and power offers a source of insight into large-scale historical shifts in the rise and decline, relative power, and degree of unity of states. These are all central questions for international relations theory. The steady erosion of legitimacy of advanced industrial states analyzed by Habermas, Bell, Huntington, and others during the 1970s can be seen as contributed to, in part, by this dynamic.

Anarchy and Order

Postmodernism identifies a relationship between identity and otherness. Identity is constituted by establishing artificial boundaries beyond which otherness is repressed and obscured. For instance, in premodern times madness could be understood as a sign from God, whereas with the constitution of rational individuals it became an incomprehensible illness to be cured. Richard Ashley has gone furthest in applying this postmodern principle to the relationship between international order and domestic anarchy. For Ashley, statesmen use realist discourse as a mechanism of power that differentiates the world into an ahistorical, uncontrollable arena of violence external to the state and an ordered domestic community through which the modern universalizing project can be realized.

As will be indicated below, Ashley's work, while imaginative, suffers from a number of serious problems. Drawing a connection between identity and otherness is not unique to postmodernism. For instance, Volkan (1988) has used Freudian analysis to argue that the creation of enemies is a universal characteristic of a child's psychic development. The notion that rulers encourage xenophobia and war to consolidate their support is common. The postmodern analysis of the sovereignty/anarchy dualism, while needing further development, has a contribution to make in linking this dualism to other features of modernity.

Criticisms of Postmodernism

If postmodernism offers useful insights into international relations theory, it also has fundamental flaws. There are a profusion of criticisms of postmodernism in general and postmodernism in specific fields. Some of these criticisms have centered on the inconsistency of making its own claims, given postmodernism's assertions that all foundations and assumptions are arbitrary. Many critics see the postmodern emphasis on the textual, constructed nature of the world as an unwarranted extension of approaches appropriate for literature to other areas of human practice that are more constrained by an objective reality. This epistemological criticism is joined by criticisms of postmodernism's amoral rejection of any grounds for emancipatory action. Rather than replay these generalized criticisms and debates here, we will focus on the applicability of these criticisms to the use of postmodernist approaches to international theory. The following interrelated weaknesses will be discussed in turn: (1) an intolerance of diversity; (2) an underestimation of material constraints; and (3) an insensitivity to the importance of values and consensus.

Intolerance of Diversity

Although one of postmodernism's most loudly self-proclaimed strengths is its rejection of the modernist repression of difference, postmodern approaches are often exceedingly brutal in their treatment of alternative approaches. There are three reasons for this. First, because of the postmodern view that there is no extratextual referent that can be used as a basis for adjudicating theoretical disputes and that all claims are based on political discursive techniques, postmodern claims themselves must be defended with the use of such techniques. The hubris of the postmodern writer is unconstrained by the modesty and skepticism that is involved in the opposing view that there is an independent reality that, even if knowable, is not yet known. Second, and consonant with the modernist origins against which it is reacting, postmodernism's vitality relies, even more than the faddishness of social sciences in general, on its novelty, on its charting of new territory. This claim to novelty can be based only on a simplification of antecedent theories and discourses. The hubris and the claim to novelty are related to a third factor, which is the adoption of a megahistorical unit, modernity, as a coherent phenomenon to be studied. Giving coherence to such a phenomenon requires doing violence to its diversity. This section illustrates these problems with examples from postmodernist international relations theory, and focuses especially on the work of Richard Ashley, who has been most influential in developing postmodernist international theory.

Ashley clearly has claimed that his work is *not* guilty of the criticisms being made here. He says that it is not his intention

> to hint that in poststructuralism we find a promise of a new and powerful perspective that occupies its own firm ground, that overcomes the limits of other perspectives, and that surpasses them in its ability to answer the questions they readily ask. As we shall see, poststructuralism eschews heroic promises such as these. (Ashley, 1989:259)

In the next paragraph, Ashley initially appears to practice this modesty: "I want only to make plain some of the lines of reasoned argument that poststructuralist discourse, *more than many others,* is disposed to take seriously." Yet he quickly makes the following claim: "poststructuralism expands the agenda of social theory, posing questions that other discourses *must* refuse to ask if they are to affirm their foundations and sustain the limits that define them." Then, within the same paragraph, referring to the question of "historicity"—the poststructuralist notion that the spatial and temporal existence of things is constituted not by essences but by a never-ending play of difference—Ashley says, "It is a question, we shall also find, that modern discourses on international politics, like any discourse participating in the 'regime of modernity,' *simply will not* ask" (Ashley, 1989:259; all emphasis added).

In the space of a page, then, Ashley has taken us through a set of linked, contradictory, rhetorical steps to empower poststructuralism and weaken its opponents: (1) a modest acceptance of its inability to do better than its opponents, (2) an assertion of its relative superiority, (3) an assertion that its opponents are constrained by inherent limitations to their approaches, and (4) an assertion that connotes a willful and deliberate blindness on the part of poststructuralism's opponents. This juxtaposition of a professed acceptance of diversity with a brutal simplification of other approaches runs through Ashley's work. For instance, in referring to modernity on the following page of the chapter, he states that "poststructuralist social theory does not envisage a temporal or spatial field of uniform content having definite boundaries." Yet on a subsequent page he claims that "modern discourse, disciplined by a logocentric disposition, is inclined to comprehend history according to the interpretive model of the *monologue*" (Ashley, 1989:263).

This radical simplification is apparent in Ashley's treatment of international theory. For example, in his analysis of the anarchy *problematique*, he proceeds through what he calls two models of reading of the *problematique*. The first, the "model of the monologue," most explicitly sets out to create a straw target:

> My first reading of theoretical discourse on the anarchy problematique will obey this monological model of interpretation. I shall treat this discourse as a well-bounded text that exhibits a "hard core" unity in its representational claims, and I shall not take seriously its ambiguous, dynamic, and contingent connections to an array of "marginal" themes. (Ashley, 1988:232)

Ashley's goal in this reading is to discover a kind of deep structure, a "totalizing principle from which everything meaningful in this discourse originates."

At first glance, Ashley's second "dialogical" reading appears to recognize diversity:

> According to the model of the dialogue, a discourse or text does not emanate from a unique, autonomous, and rational source. . . . A discourse or text is instead to be comprehended as an "intertext" that penetrates and is penetrated by other texts in the cultural universe within which it moves and takes on meaning. (Ashley, 1988:233)

Yet the second reading, rather than recognizing the nuance and diversity within the realist discourse it targets, instead creates a kind of straw weapon with which to attack it. In this reading he cites nonstate actors as an example of an anomaly for the reliance on the notion of a sovereign being that was revealed by his first reading. He then claims,

> but once nonstate actors are introduced into their discourse and taken seriously, every attempt to represent such a being is immediately undone. It is no longer possible even ideologically to represent a coherent sovereign presence, an identical source of meaning and power. (Ashley, 1988:234)

When the work of real theorists is considered, rather than the caricature drawn by Ashley, the weakness of Ashley's style of theorizing is apparent. Nye and Keohane, for instance, have devoted considerable effort to integrating state and nonstate actors, and concrete criticism of the way in which they do so is more effective than setting up straw battles.

Underestimation of Material Constraints

A sensitivity to the role of text and rhetoric in constituting reality can provide important insights into the functioning of the international system. If extratextual dimensions of human practice are ignored, however, such approaches risk becoming nothing more than interesting stories without relevance for the lives of those billions of people who do not read them. Of the postmodernist international theorists, Ashley has done the most to theorize the constitution of the duality of international anarchy and domestic order. The usefulness of this analysis is undermined by the inflation of the role of theory and theorist, however. Ashley has claimed that

> on the one hand realist power politics is a specific form of political community whose global power and practical autonomy depends, not upon a system of multiple states per se, but upon the simultaneous *empowerment* and practical *delimiting* of the rationalist understandings of community in multiple local settings; on the other hand, realist power politics should be grasped as a community whose normalized practices and rituals of power mobilize global resources, discipline practices, and thereby clear and delimit spaces of domestic politics wherein recognizably capitalist subjects can secure their dominance and the modernist narrative can establish its hegemony. (Ashley, 1987:423)

Ashley thus makes clear that in his view it is realism as a discourse, and not individual realist subjects, that constitute the international system.

Where does this political realism come from? A postmodernist answer would be that it writes itself, that there is no subject, and that it emerges from a decentered play of discourses. This is disingenuous, however, because it would be clear to most people, whatever their stand on the ontological status of the individual, that flesh and blood intellectuals and statesmen are heavily implicated in this activity relative to other humans. This is something that is tacitly acknowledged by those postmodernists who choose to deconstruct specific realists such as Machiavelli, Morgenthau, and Brzezinski.[11]

Ashley's conception of the international system is therefore

extremely elitist, for it rests on the view that statesmen and intellectuals create not only an ideology with a specific, limited effect, but
equally create the state structures, their foreign policies, and the
sense of community and xenophobia that citizens experience.[12] Even
Morgenthau, with his enthusiasm for the aristocratic tradition of
statecraft, was more willing to acknowledge the impact of citizens,
with his stress on the mass character of "nationalistic universalism"
and his acknowledgment of the difficulty statesmen have in obtain-
ing needed popular support.[13]

Insensitivity to the Importance of Values and Consensus

A common feature of postmodernist writing is the characterization
of all values and forms of consensus as artificial constructions that
mask relations of domination. Postmodern writers tend to see themselves as courageous in their willingness to cast off the comfortable
illusion that it is possible to ground knowledge in a solid foundation. In some such interpretations, it is possible to pragmatically
engage in the construction of ideological artifices, whereas in others
such artifices must be relentlessly hunted down and deconstructed.

Ashley's work displays the postmodern characterization of values and consensus. He sees postmodernism and political realists,
whom he approvingly cites, as courageous in the sense noted above.
For instance, in relation to the latter, he says:

> Here theorists and practitioners long ago discovered the void of
> community at the heart of global political life . . . here, there is
> already a well-established tradition of analysis and practice, the
> tradition of political realism itself, whose grasp of the primordial
> emptiness of international politics has allowed it to see the power
> political significance of communitarian conceits in a pluralistic
> world. (Ashley, 1987:413)

For Ashley such discoveries are "unsettling" and "dangerous," posing challenges before which the theorist needs to "gulp."

It is consistent, therefore, that Ashley has applauded Waltz's
emphasis on the last of his three levels of analysis, "man," the state,
and war. Ashley applauds Waltz's *Theory of International Politics*
(1979) because it does not treat "man" as "the originary identity
prior to state and war":

> only by leaving the paradigm of man unproblematic, unspecified,
> and untheorized can the text reserve an ambiguous place at the
> center of its theory—a place to be successively seized by whatever
> figure of man is produced and empowered here and now in the

ceaseless and indeterminate transversal struggles of history.
(Ashley, 1989:298)

Ashley's reading of this text, while picking up on Waltz's personal
commitment to anarchy, ignores the way in which Waltz's structuralism and his use of a rational choice model permeates the text
with modernist foundationalism. In the present context, however,
Ashley's reading of Waltz is more relevant as an example of his
acceptance of ceaseless violence as part of the fabric of history and
life itself, and his suspicion of any claims that "man" can act to end
such violence in any way that does not involve the imposition of further violence by creating relations of power and domination. This
view is echoed by Klein, who has argued that we should "rescue the
centrality of violence from the hands of those managers of security
who, for decades now, offered us little more than an alternative
between different structures of organized peacelessness" (Klein,
1988:314).

Despite postmodernists' tendency to think that they can cast
aside ideological illusions and understand the world amorally, the
approach is based on its own implicit values. In the case of postmodernist international theory, pluralism is privileged over order, dissensus over consensus, and disorder over peace.[14] Rather than
explicitly developing and defending these preferences as values,
however, the attempt is made to treat them as historically given—as
the way things are. Like positivist epistemologies, but with far less
sophistication, such postmodernist approaches rest ultimately on
assertions about ahistorical, ahuman truths, despite their rejection of
the more common positivist notions of truth as corresponding to an
objective reality.

The Relevance of Postmodernism to the Third Debate

As noted at the outset of this chapter, the Third Debate involves
bringing into the discipline interpretative approaches from the
humanities, such as postmodernism. The question remains, however: Does postmodernism help resolve the problems encountered by
positivism in international theory?

As previously noted, postmodernism's focus on the role of
signs, symbols, and texts in constituting relations of domination
helps in understanding an area to which positivism has been blind.
The weaknesses of postmodernism, however, bear an ironic similarity to those of positivism in its inability to adequately theorize the
link between sign and referent. Positivism sees the world as existing

objectively and assumes that images in the human mind can represent this reality through observation. Postmodernism rejects the notion that images have real referents. Images, however, are not consciously constructed by individuals; rather, they are the result of the decentered play of signs. In neither positivism nor postmodernism is there an adequate analysis of the way that humans consciously and actively construct a bridge between referent and sign, between reality and theory.

This failure to adequately theorize the bridge between referent and sign contributes to the tendency of both positivism and postmodernism to oscillate between enormously inflating agency and enormously inflating structure. Not subjecting their metatheoretical foundations to the same epistemology with which they analyze society, lawlike regularities are grounded arbitrarily and rhetorically, rather than with reference to consensual norms that have been constructed by the wider society beyond the academic community. These lawlike regularities are often treated as immutable structures, in apparent contradiction to the emphasis on agency stressed at other times in the approaches.

In the case of positivism, this oscillation is apparent in the differences between the pragmatic pluralism of Bentley and the stifling structural functionalism of the later Talcott Parsons (Binder, 1986). The oscillation can be seen within the work of individual authors, as well as in the relationship celebrating both anarchy and the role of agent of the two superpowers in governing the system. In the case of postmodernism, this can be seen on the one hand in the stress on the decentered play of signs and the belief that it is possible to subvert all hierarchies, and on the other hand in the ubiquity of domination created by reason. To think rationally is to engage in the constitution of power relations. Although postmodernism is *post*-structuralist, it is also post-*structuralist*. The claustrophobia of French structuralism's rigidity has not been opened up to agency, but has rather been transmuted as structure has been decentered and made more flexible—but equally strong. As in pragmatic positivism, power is everywhere and nowhere.

As has been imaginatively demonstrated by Ashley (1987), postmodernism is similar to political realism. He described his Foucaultian approach as "disposed to comprehend all history, including the production of order, in terms of the endless power political clash of multiple wills," treating "the hidden essences, the universal truths, the profound insights into the secret identity that transcends difference . . . or the moral imperatives that women and men are obliged to honor" as a means of reproducing domination.

The resonance with the realist's rejection of abstract ideals and insistence on the ubiquity of power politics is striking. Both postmodernism and political realism see history as dissonance, and order as imposed.

E. H. Carr has argued that "both realism and idealism accepted and incorporated in their philosophies the eighteenth-century belief in progress" (Carr, 1939:65). Yet his description of realism's notion of "progress" is an unusual use of the word because it involves the acceptance of might as right, and what happened as what needed to happen. This passive acceptance of history as it unfolds is not at all similar to the modernist notion of progress as involving human mastery over contingency through the learning and wielding of rational modes of thinking—it is closer to premodernism or postmodernism. Other characteristics of realism that Carr identifies are similarly postmodern: the relativity of thought,[15] the "adjustment of thought to purpose" (i.e., the use of thought as an instrument of power), "the national interest and the universal good" (that universalism is a mask for power politics), and the "critique of the harmony of interests."[16]

Carr recognized the shortcomings of this type of political realism, and as a result advocated a blending of idealist and realist approaches. As he noted, "Most of all, consistent realism breaks down because it fails to provide any ground for meaningful or purposive action" (Carr, 1939:92). For Carr, such action was a fundamental human characteristic that must be oriented by the speculative nature of idealism. As will be indicated below, it is this type of integration that is assisted by a structurationist metatheory.

There is no such integration in postmodernism, however. Postmodernists have put their finger on the same understanding of the self-undermining nature of the Enlightenment tradition that was evident in Weber's concerns about the extension of rationality and bureaucracy, and Durkheim's analysis of the anomie that developed with the growth of organic solidarity. Yet, whereas Weber and Durkheim acknowledged countertendencies, postmodernism sees none. Ironically, for an approach that aims to subvert hierarchical dualisms, the consensual, nondominating potential in modernity is excluded, obscured, and underestimated.

The shortcomings of postmodernism indicate that what is needed in the Third Debate is not simply a new emphasis on interpretative approaches that address the process of meaning construction and its role in establishing power relations. The promise of a reemphasis on meaning construction is in integrating it with an extratextual reality. For this to be successful, such a reality cannot be seen as ahuman, as a mass of action, or as empirically observable covariances. Daily and routine practice offers a promising site for such an integration.

The Need for a Structurationist Metatheory

The emerging body of work that adopts a structurationist or con-structivist approach to international relations offers an important alternative to both positivism and postmodernism in international theory.[17] While an elaboration of these approaches is beyond the scope of the present chapter, common to all those adopting a struc-turationist perspective is the notion that rules can be a medium of action as well as a constraint on action. Structures and agents are mutually constitutive. Agents can learn to manipulate and create rules and structures, but action can have unintended consequences and unconscious habits can constrain action. Yet these constraints are not traced to mysterious deep structure, but rather to the actions of human agents. The advantage of structuration theory in relation-ship to realism's metatheoretical assumptions has already been developed (Wendt, 1987; Dessler, 1989). The advantage of structura-tion theory over postmodernism is important to note here, however. Structuration's emphasis on the constructed nature of society allows it to incorporate postmodernism's insights into the role of symbols and signs in constituting reality. Several key deficiencies of post-modernism are corrected by a structurationist metatheory.

First, agency is acknowledged. Real humans and not just a decentered interplay of signs can be seen as having a role in creating symbols and signs and using them to construct orders. Postmod-ernism's attack on coherent self-identity has been criticized for over-looking the importance of constructing self-identity as a form of resistance for those, such as women and colonized peoples, whose identities are misrepresented or effaced by dominant discourses.[18] Giddens's conception of self-identity is quite different from a post-modern one:

> In the post-traditional order of modernity, and against the back-drop of new forms of mediated experience, self-identity becomes a reflexively organized endeavour. The reflexive project of the self, which consists in the sustaining of coherent, yet continuously revised, biographical narratives, takes place in the context of multiple choice as filtered through abstract systems. (Giddens, 1991:5)

On the one hand, competent agency is likely to avoid the temptation in postmodernism to underestimate the ability of the state to respond to pressures of fragmentation. On the other hand, the structurationist approach is also better able to consider the possibility that postcolonial states can creatively challenge dominant states through discursive struggles at an international level.

Second, with a structurationist metatheory, extratextual reality can be more clearly delimited than is the case with postmodernism. The structurationist emphasis on practices rather than writing requires theorists to establish the links between textual discourses and extratextual change (Giddens, 1987a). Rather than Bentley's mass of action, the notion of mass practices involves a theory of agents who are capable of reflection and construction. The consciously structurable nature of such practices can provide the source of stability lacking in pragmatic pluralism without importing a structure *ex machina*. These practices are a key link with the objective constraints that humans face because it is the discourses that people develop in their everyday struggles to survive and interact with nature that represent the frontier between freedom and necessity. The role of signs in constituting everyday life is a missing link in work such as Ashley's, and a problem that contributes to its elitism.

Third, values can be reintegrated into facts. Kuhn highlighted the role of values in shaping our perceptions of facts but failed to satisfactorily theorize values or how they are agreed upon. Subsequently, Laudan (1984) has suggested ways of reintegrating cognitive values into science so that, rather than acting as an unaccounted-for court of appeal for scientists, they can be assessed with reference to the practice of science. The reintegration of ethical values into the social sciences is equally important. The structurationist emphasis on constructible rules and norms offers a site in which the theorist's own value commitments and the materiality of values can interact.

In contrast to postmodernism, which sees only domination resulting from the manipulation of signs, structurationism recognizes the positive-sum and empowering potential of rule making. Indeed, Giddens has been criticized for inadequate theorization of domination.[19] There is, however, nothing inherent in the structurationist approach that precludes the notion that particular groups can engage in rule making as a mechanism of domination, as Onuf (1989) has shown. This area is one of potentially useful interchange between postmodernism and structurationism. In contrast to postmodernism, which excludes its own interpretation of reality from its characterization of theory as rhetoric, structurationism can be self-conscious about its own assumptions. As such, it is more reflexive[20] and thus it better addresses the Third Debate's focus on reworking metatheoretical assumptions. Structurationism itself can be seen as a set of rules created by human agents to constitute their reality.

Conclusion

International relations is engaged in a process of reexamination of its basic assumptions, a Third Debate that is focused at the level of metatheory. This debate has come about in large part because of dissatisfaction with the inability of positivism to reconcile its pragmatism with its stress on stable lawlike behavior. This Third Debate involves an incorporation of interpretative approaches into the discipline at the level of both metatheory and theory, and has been characterized by a proliferation of paradigms—a new pluralism and relativism regarding what constitutes acceptable knowledge.

This chapter has focused on one particular trend in this new pluralism: postmodernism. Postmodernism offers important insights into the human activity of meaning-construction and its relationship to power politics, but it has important shortcomings that involve its failure to adequately theorize the relationship between sign and referent, between textual and extratextual reality. Ironically, postmodernism and positivism share certain problems, which can be traced to their tendency to ignore the constructed nature of the bridge between sign and referent. Positivism privileges the referent, and postmodernism the sign. Neither sees a need to focus on the struggle of humans to build their interactions with each other and with nature through the standardization of signs, norms, and rules. Such a blindness to this dimension of human creativity leads to difficulty in theorizing those regularities in human conduct that result from rule-using activity. A structurationist metatheory allows us to draw on the postmodern insights about meaning construction and about the relationship between modernity and international relations. It also allows us to relink such analysis with the extratextual world, a world that is alive with contingency and is created by humans for their own fulfillment.

Notes

1. For an elegant portrayal of the Third Debate, see Yosef Lapid (1989).
2. For this interpretation of Bentley, see Binder (1986:7).
3. Binder (1986) gives an excellent account of this period in comparative politics.
4. The malaise is also evident in Vasquez's devastatingly critical

quantitative survey of realist scholarship, in which he concludes that the paradigm "produced only 48 scientifically important findings out of 7,158 realist hypotheses that were tested from 1956 to 1970" (Vasquez, 1983:202).

5. Texts that reflect a recognition and acceptance of the metatheoretical fragmentation of the discipline include Maghroori and Ramberg (1982), Alker and Biersteker (1984), Holsti (1985), Light and Groom (1985), McKinlay and Little (1986), and Ferguson and Mansbach (1988).

6. See also Ihab Hassan (1987), chapter 8, for a succinct presentation. I follow Rosenau and others here in grouping poststructuralism and postmodernism together.

7. On Bell's relation to postmodernism, see Lash (1987).

8. For a criticism using the language of postmodernism, see Solomon (1988).

9. "Narrative meaning is a cognitive process that organizes human experience into temporally meaningful episodes" (Polkinghorne, 1988:1).

10. The abandonment, in the key work centered around the Committee on Comparative Politics of the Social Sciences Research Council, of the optimism of modernization theory, as evident in Binder et al. (1971), marks an important turning point. See also Binder (1986).

11. These three are targeted, respectively, in Walker (1989), Ashley (1989), and Shapiro (1989).

12. Ashley sees realism as a supplement to modernist narrative in general; thus, it is not realism alone that accomplishes this process. The lack of separation between the two is a characteristic ambiguity of Ashley's work. In any case, realism's role is enormous, and the notion of a modernist narrative could also be subject to the same criticisms.

13. Although Morgenthau stressed the ability of statesmen to manipulate the masses (through psychological warfare and propaganda), he also acknowledged an element of conscious choice at the mass level:

> A true political philosophy cannot rely alone upon the inner force of its truths to win the struggle for the minds of men. Rather it must seek to establish a peculiar connection between its truths and the human minds it seeks to influence. That connection is provided by the life experiences and interests which determine the receptiveness of men to political ideas. (Morgenthau, 1967:326)

See also Morgenthau (1967:141).

14. For example, Ashley applauds the anarchy of the international community because it provides the space for antimodernist resistance to domination-producing rationalism:

> How, in particular, might programs of resistance appeal to the community of realist power politics and how might they deploy its ambiguous rituals, not for the sake of tradition, but in order to forestall the further extension of rationalist order, and thereby to maintain the practical space in which alternative projects can be pursued. (Ashley, 1987:428)

15. As Carr put it,

> The realist has thus been enabled to demonstrate that the intellectual theories and ethical standards of utopianism, far from being

the expression of absolute and *a priori* principles, are historically
conditioned, being both products of circumstances and interests
and weapons framed for the furtherance of interests. (Carr,
1939:68)

16. "The doctrine of the harmony of interests thus serves as an inge-
nious moral device invoked, in perfect sincerity, by privileged groups in
order to justify and maintain their dominant position" (Carr, 1939:80). As
noted above, these characteristics of political realism are often insufficiently
acknowledged because of the widespread tendency to reduce it to a set of
looser assumptions of which state-centrism is primary.

17. Such work includes that of Wendt (1987), Wendt and Duvall (1989),
Dessler (1989), and Onuf (1989). For a recent debate, see Hollis and Smith
(1991, 1992) and Wendt (1991, 1992b). Rosenau's 1986 notion of habit-driven
actors is similar to structurationism, although he does not draw on
Giddens's development of the approach as do the other theorists.

18. See, for example, Flax (1990:221), who asks: "without re-membered
selves how can we act? Such questions may be foreclosed within existing
post-modernist discourses, but many feminists insist upon reopening them.
We cannot risk such repression (again)." Similarly, Tiffin (1990:x) has noted
that "while post-modernism has increasingly fetishised 'difference' and 'the
Other,' those 'Othered' by a history of European representation can only
retrieve and reconstitute a post-colonized 'self' against that history wherein
an awareness of 'referential slippage' was inherent in colonial being." See
also Keyman (1993).

19. See, for instance, Thompson (1984), chapter 4, "The Theory of
Structuration."

20. On reflexivity and the Third Debate, see Chapter 2 by Mark
Neufeld.

7

And What About Gender? Feminism and International Relations Theory's Third Debate

SUSAN JUDITH SHIP

> The strength of feminism lies in its ability not to ape the unitary categories and Archimedean points of male theory, philosophy and politics; not to search for the one position from which the truth of all women can be seen, nor the lever that will transform the whole female world, but to abandon the privileges of hierarchies for the multiple connections of the web and the quilt.
>
> —*Chilla Bulbeck* (1988)

Change is astir. The current moment is one of dramatic metamorphosis, not only of events in the real world, but also in our understanding of scientific inquiry, of truth, and of the complexity and indeterminacy of social life. Western scholarship is undergoing a profound shift in the focus of its intellectual activity, redefining its critical function to include not only the requisite task of the regular examination of categories and constructs, but also the self-reflective reeducation of ourselves and our social practices (Malson et al., 1989). Much of feminist scholarship has been at the cutting edge of the movement for emancipatory knowledge and empowering of the researched (see Lather, 1988), given feminism's self-definition as the theory of women's subordination and the active struggles against it.[1] However, many feminists now too are rethinking key metatheoretical presuppositions and questioning the universal validity of core concepts such as patriarchy, the family, and reproduction.

The most important shift within feminist scholarship, found in the reconceptualization of "woman" as a multiple concept and away from that of an undifferentiated notion, has come about in the growing recognition of the diversity of women's experiences (Razamanoglu, 1989). The analysis of race and the insights of post-

colonial studies have chipped away at the conception of woman as a
unitary subject underpinning much of Western feminism (Mohanty,
Russo, and Torres, 1991). The perspectives and experiences of black
women and women of color have challenged the assumption of the
universal applicability of much feminist theorizing, which ultimately is based on the exploration of the experiences of white, Western,
middle-class, heterosexual women (Lorde, 1984; Moraga and
Anzaldua, 1983; hooks, 1983; Hull, Scott, and Smith, 1982; Joseph
and Lewis, 1981; and Dill, 1979). Thus, feminists are coming to reject
totalizing feminisms and are rethinking the validity of the feminist
standpoint position[2] as the basis for theorizing and for action.

Linked to these metatheoretical shifts is the emergence of a new
complexity in feminist thinking about the subjectivity of individual
women (Malson et al., 1989). Renewed usage of the narrative "I" in
recent feminist scholarship is intended to break the subject-object
split that has characterized much of malestream theorizing in order
to distinguish the general from the individual. Another crucial
aspect of this shift in our understanding of women's subjectivity
involves coming to see that women's identity as women cannot be
neatly separated from racial, class, ethnic, linguistic, and national
identities. Thus, identity itself must be seen as multiple, shifting,
and contradictory (see, for example, Alcoff, 1988; Spelman, 1988).
Increasingly, feminist analyses are shifting focus to the exploration
of contradictions and divisions among women, which result from
the multiple social cleavages that differentiate them (Razamanoglu,
1989).

These recent developments have called into question the essential underpinnings of much of feminist theory-making, requiring
more critical scrutiny of presuppositions and of the understanding
of theory itself. Many feminists are now coming to reject an all-
encompassing theory, pointing out that it has served to mask "discourses of elite empowerment, formulating instead an understanding of theory as process, as a constellation of ideas reconfigurated
and reconfiguring within a myriad of practices" (Malson et al.,
1989:12). Totalizing feminism, as theory and as practical politics, has
given way to the "politics of identity and difference" emphasizing
"diversity, particularity, multiple and changing subject positions
and self-representations" (Bannerji, 1991:81). This has led to the
emergence of fragmented and diffused strategies of women's
empowerment, which are more closely linked to the specific needs
and aspirations of particular groups of women.

International relations, too, has been undergoing its own transformation, although the awareness of the relevance of feminist
scholarship and gender analysis has yet to seriously take root in this

particular discipline. The recent wave of critical self-reflection within the discipline spearheaded by a small but growing number of scholars working within diverse theoretical traditions has been hailed in some quarters as a major discipline-transforming debate, with wide-ranging implications, unparalleled by the previous two debates (Lapid, 1989; Holsti, 1985; and Banks, 1985b). Although there is no consensus as to how to characterize this debate, it seems to involve a movement toward theoretical reflexivity, toward the rethinking of the validity of the cherished canons of "science as usual" or positivist-empiricist orthodoxy, and toward a critical scrutiny of the nature of social/political agendas. One of the consequences of this movement has been the challenging of the hegemony of the U.S. brand of state-centric realism with its essentially conservative pro-American value biases and restricted set of concerns. With this move toward enhanced reflexivity, the Third Debate appears to have opened up space for the emergence of international relations theorizing that is both critical and feminist.[3]

However, the Third Debate represents, at best, a limited move in the direction of theoretical reflexivity (see Chapter 2 by Neufeld). While theoretical reflexivity might entail, as Neufeld suggests, "self-awareness about underlying assumptions," little if any attention has been paid to androcentric metatheoretical assumptions in international relations theory. Growing feminist research has highlighted how conceptions of masculinity and femininity (as well as the differential structural locations of classes, or men and women) constitute embedded features of international political and economic processes, which they further serve to sustain (Peterson, 1992; Grant and Newland, 1991; Enloe, 1989; and Yuval-Davis and Anthias, 1989). Yet, academic silence on the nature and role of gender in international relations theorizing and practices continues to be a salient feature of the postpositivist research agenda, whereas feminist scholarship continues to remain at the margins of the discipline.

Male scholars concerned with reflexivity in international relations have largely ignored the relevance of philosophical debates within contemporary feminisms.[4] Longstanding concerns with critical self-reflection within feminist theorizing provide some experience and insights into "both rendering problematic and provisional our most firmly held assumptions, and nevertheless, acting in the world" (Lather, 1991:29). The critical, praxis-oriented feminist empirical research, which concerns itself with the production of emancipatory knowledge and with empowerment, provides a useful starting place for moving critical international relations theorizing in new directions.

This chapter explores the prospects for constructing an international relations project that is both critical and feminist. It argues that the emancipatory potential of such a project is, at best, limited within current forms of theorizing. In fact, it demonstrates the extent to which realism, pluralism, Marxism, and the new international relations theories (postmodernism and critical theory) share unacknowledged androcentric metatheoretical presuppositions, which serve to render invisible the unequal power relations between men and women and the accompanying symbolic discourses that sustain them. The failure to confront the significance of gender in the social construction of knowledge and scientific discourses in the discipline necessarily weakens the "critical" cutting edge of the new critical international relations theories. It furthermore calls into question the emancipatory nature of consequent political projects that do not challenge the interrelated hierarchies of privilege that shape women's diverse experiences of subordination, nor does it integrate their political concerns. In contradistinction, this chapter argues that the challenge facing scholars committed to emancipatory knowledge that is linked to transformative social action is to be found in the construction of a critical feminist international relations perspective, which avoids the pitfalls of replacing "essential man" with "essential woman." In the absence of a commitment to reflexivity, however, it is all too possible that our theoretical and political practices will continue to contribute to structures and discourses of dominance despite our liberating intentions.

Such a project does not represent a call for totalizing theory but rather for historically specific analyses that reveal how different systems of power (gender oppression, racism, class, and neoimperialism) are constituted and intertwined at different points in time to ensure the hegemony of dominant social groups over the state and international institutions. Such a perspective explores the changing relationships among ideas, discourses, institutions, social conditions, and relations, and posits a critique of the prevailing political and social order, thus permitting the development of practical strategies of empowerment. In calling for the forging of closer links between academics and social movements in a collaborative process, critical feminist international relations may fulfill its potential as an empowering political practice whereby research *on* women may become research *for* women.

Metatheoretical Assumptions
About Gender and International Relations

Academic silence on gender in international political and economic processes is rooted in unexamined androcentric metatheoretical assumptions, which underpin all strands of international relations theorization. It is further reinforced, as Fred Halliday (1988) cogently has pointed out, by the virtual absence of women in key decision-making positions in national and international defense, foreign affairs, and economic institutions, as well as other policy-related bodies. This absence of women is coupled with the pervasive ideology that women are not well suited to the demands, pressures, and responsibilities associated with security issues and crisis management. Both the mainstream problem-solving approaches and the critical international relations alternatives continue to theorize as though gender does not matter. Thus, they "invisibilize" gender as a salient variable in their accounts of international processes, marginalize feminist research, and trivialize feminist political issues and concerns. A first step toward the elaboration of a critical feminist international relations project, therefore, entails laying bare the operative androcentric metatheoretical presuppositions about gender in international relations.

The most fundamental androcentric bias in international relations scholarship is evident in the traditional definitions of the legitimate and substantive concerns of the discipline; that is, with "high politics" or military security. These perspectives, deeply ensconced in a preoccupation with the cult of power and destruction, have more recently been echoed in power-oriented analyses of international political economy. These concerns reflect gender differences and inequalities in the material circumstances of men's and women's relations to territories, armies, and armaments. "Men plan wars, they train for them and they conduct them" (As, 1982:355). The strategic version of life has emerged only relatively recently in human history in an attempt to preserve the precarious achievements of the West—its culture, institutions, values, and political economies (Klein, 1988). Much of the literature has been concerned with the outbreak of war in the European theater, principally between the superpowers. The arms trade is viewed by and large from a First World perspective with too many contentious assumptions about the valuable spin-offs from the military to the Third World, downplaying the negative consequences and social implications of militarism (Boulding, 1981). Not surprisingly, far less academic attention has been accorded to articulating a positive politics of peace. Thus, social scientific inquiry is "guided by questions about social life that appear problematic within the experiences characteristic for men, that is, white western bourgeois men" (Harding, 1987:6).

A second and related metatheoretical presupposition shared by all international relations theorization is that only those activities identified by male scholars as worthy of study shape social life in significant ways (Harding, 1987). Thus, international relations as such is seen as relatively unaffected by the activities traditionally undertaken by women. Some feminist researchers have begun to explore how conceptions of gender and the social practices of mothering, human reproduction, sexuality, and marriage inform and shape state practices, interstate relations, and international economic processes. Controlling women's fertility and sexuality has been the object of state manipulation in most societies at varying points in time for purposes of reproducing the labor force, replacing the aging population, and population control, integral to national economic planning and forecasting.

In restricting women's sexuality through marriage and through calls to increased childbearing, women play central roles in ethnic and national processes, such as reproducing the members of ethnic or national groups and in circumscribing their boundaries (Yuval-Davis and Anthias, 1989). State practices, such as ideological mobilization and the use of maternal benefits aimed at women, are and have been implemented in order to increase the membership of specific ethnic and racial groups and, conversely, to restrict the birthrate of specific groups deemed threatening or undesirable. "Calls for a 'White Australia' immigration policy or a Jewish 'return' to Israel are supplemented at times of slack immigration or national crisis with active calls to women to bear children so that no demographic holocaust will take place" (Yuval-Davis and Anthias, 1989:12). Women's role as childbearers has been central to the frequently utilized tactical strategy of the demographic war.

In a related vein, both the mainstream and its radical challengers presume that international political and economic processes are gender neutral (Halliday, 1988). This implies that the different structural locations of groups of men and women in the interstate system and international political economy have no bearing on international relations as such. It also assumes that conceptions of masculinity and femininity do not play important roles in national, state, and international practices, institutions, and discourses. Finally, this conception presumes that international processes have similar effects upon women and men as workers and as citizens.

However, the burgeoning feminist research, still at the margins of the discipline, has questioned these assumptions. Socialist feminists have long drawn attention to the role of women's unpaid domestic and cheap wage labor in the valorization and accumulation of capital, and have shown how women's reproductive and productive activities benefit national and international capital, in addition to individual men (Sokoloff, 1980; Young et al., 1984; Nash and Fernandez-Kelly, 1983). As one feminist succinctly put it, as women, we produce workers for wars, we produce workers for the factories, the mines—for all the dangerous profit-making industries of the world. For without our able-bodied children—past and future workers or society—there wouldn't be a British Empire or Dutch Empire or whatever empire and there wouldn't be any multinational corporations. (Prescod, 1986:12)

Not only do the relative placings of different groups of women and men affect the workings of international politics and economics, but such processes further draw upon conceptions of masculinity and femininity. Feminist peace research has begun to explore the links between sexist socialization practices and ideologies, militarism, the propensity to war, and structural violence (Reardon, 1985; Mansueto, 1983). This research suggests that notions of masculinity, embedded in the socialization of boys into "appropriate gender roles" and in the training of soldiers, encourage militarism and the favoring of aggressive foreign policy initiatives involving the use of force, if not recourse to war (Reardon, 1985). The masculine role of the male-warrior has been isolated as a central metaphor in the conceptualization and practice of politics in the West, as symbolized by the Barracks Community, which rendered synonymous community, military capacity, civic personality, citizenship, and masculinity, providing the ideological justification for excluding women as women until very recently (Harstock, 1984).[5] Thus, male hegemony over symbol and meaning systems is crucial to the understanding of the origins of Western state formation and its evolution. In extending this idea, Peterson (1989a) links conceptions of gender, class, and race with the unequal structural locations of different groups of men and women.

Conceptions of gender were, furthermore, essential to the symbolic discourses legitimating the colonization of Third World peoples.

Ladylike behavior was the mainstay of imperialist civilization. Like sanitation and Christianity, feminine respectability was meant to convince both the colonizing and the colonized peoples that foreign conquest was right and necessary. Ladylike behaviour would also have an uplifting effect on colonized men: it would encourage them to act according to those Victorian standards of "manliness" thought crucial for colonial order. Part of the empire-building masculinity was protection of the respectable [read: white, Western, and bourgeois] lady. She stood for the civilizing mission which, in turn, justified the colonization of benighted peoples. (Enloe, 1989:48)

Western notions of appropriate gender roles for women and capitalist penetration of Third World subsistence economies combined to further illustrate the gender-differentiated impact of these processes on women. Colonial administrators imposed Western notions of appropriate gender roles, which interacted with preexisting forms of gender stratification and reinforced them to the detriment of the bulk of Third World women. In precolonial Africa, for example, women tended to play important roles in food production in subsistence economies, and their control over food supplies gave them substantial power. The colonial seizure of communal lands, in some cases traditionally controlled by women, turned these lands over to men in the form of private property (Bulbeck, 1988). Men were generally recruited into cash crop farming and wage labor, whereas women were left to meet the subsistence needs of their families (Robertson and Berger, 1986). Furthermore, gender differences in education also entailed preparing men for paid labor and women for unpaid domestic work. Thus, most African women, apart from those who became part of the small African petty-bourgeoisie, have been marginalized into the traditional but now socially undervalued activities of African women: subsistence production and child care. The processes of Westernization and capitalist penetration of African societies have had contradictory and often detrimental consequences for women (Sen and Grown, 1987).

Furthermore, the Women in Development (WID) projects, designed as a response to arrest the rapidly deteriorating situation of the poorest female producers and reproducers in Third World countries, have failed, all too often, to significantly alter the plight of these women (Maguire, 1984). WID ideology rests upon the assumption that peasant women's deteriorating position is a result of their marginal integration into the development process and advocates the expansion of political, economic, and social opportunities for women beyond their traditional roles (World Bank, 1979:22). However, WID projects aim to ameliorate peasant women's situations within the confines of the status quo rather than confronting the existing structural gender and class inequalities.

The impact of war on men and women also reveals gender-specific consequences. Men in most countries of the world generally have been recruited into combat roles, although this is now beginning to change. Women, more often than not, have been the victims of war, rather than its perpetrators (As, 1982). Women and their children constitute 80 percent of the roughly 15 million refugees, most of whom are scattered about the Third World, more than half of them in Africa alone (Allmen et al., 1989). "Rape, abduction, sexual harassment, physical evidence and 'sexual favours' in return for documents and/or relief goods remains a distressing reality for many refugee women" (Ptolemy, 1989:22).

But women not only have been victims of war, they also have engaged as combatants in military activities. Nevertheless, women's participation in wars of national liberation usually reveals similar patters of gender subordination. More often than not, they perform the tasks most closely associated with "women's work," such as cooking, sewing, and taking care of the wounded (Karol, 1970). As the Cuban and Nicaraguan national liberation experiences reveal, men control the national liberation movements and then assume control over the state (Peterson, 1989b).

The occlusion of unequal gender power relations and the silencing of women's voices are further reinforced by positivism-empiricism or the prevailing conception of science as the search for order and regularity. The quest for regularity takes socially constructed inequalities of power as givens rather than something to be problematized. Furthermore, positivism-empiricism rests upon the assumption that its impersonal rationalist epistemology is gender neutral. Rather, science as usual, or the positivist-empiricist version of instrumental reason itself, is rooted in a Western male ontology; with none other than essential man constituting the rational, unitary, and transcendental "subject of enlightenment" (Hawkesworth, 1989). This methodology serves to render women's socially distinct experiences invisible and to silence their voices (Stanley and Wise, 1983). Given positivism-empiricism's inability to inquire into the social construction of meaning and symbol systems embedded in social categories and constructs, it cannot confront its gendered presuppositions, which equate human behavior with masculine behavior or mankind with humanity.

Androcentric biases are further evidenced in the assumption held by international relations scholars who advocate alternative epistemological and methodological projects to positivism-empiricism—that feminist work in epistemology has little to offer critical international relations theory. Some feminists have argued for the abandonment of the strictly impersonal rationalist epistemologies and are exploring alternative conceptions of epistemology that broaden the notion of the critical function of knowledge by including, in addition to reason, empathy, connectedness, personal accountability, and the subjecting of knowledge claims to dialogue (Collins, 1989).[6]

A final androcentric bias is operative in the assumption that female-identified values and women's political concerns do not and should not play important roles in restructuring international economic and political processes.[7] Yet despite the gains women have made in the last decade,

> United Nations statistics put the current status of women into stark
> perspective. While they represent 50% of the world population and
> 1/3 of the official labour force, they account for nearly 2/3 of all
> working hours, receive 1/10th of world income and own less than
> 1% of world property. (Duley and Diduk, 1986:48)

A cross-nation study by Newland of women's participation in
national politics revealed that roughly 5 percent of all women
accede to key positions of power (Newland, 1975). This study
showed a global pattern of hierarchical stratification in which
women are found at the lower rungs of the political pyramid, which
has been the case as well with women's participation in international organizations such as the World Bank and the various UN agencies (Enloe, 1989). While the Third Debate as a whole has not yet
seriously addressed the differing political projects, values, and
visions of the good life embedded in different paradigms, the failure
to acknowledge feminism as a paradigm or confront gender subordination as an object for political change undermines the credibility
of epistemological and political projects that call themselves "emancipatory."

Gender and the Third Debate

The central question, then, is whether dominant forms of theorization open up space for theorizing gender. Whitworth (1989) has suggested three criteria for assessing the extent to which such a project
is possible. Such a theory must allow for the explanation of the
social construction of ideas—of gender itself. Second, such a theory
must be able to account for the empirical variability and historically
changing nature of gender as a product of the struggles of actors and
changing material conditions. Third, such a theory must permit us
to talk about the power relations and inequalities between men and
women. Although the theories in current usage, whether they are
mainstream or radical, cannot fulfill these three criteria, Robert
Cox's neo-Marxist Gramscian approach remains the most fruitful
theoretical perspective for the development of critical feminist international relations.

Realism and Gender

Realism constitutes the predominant and hegemonic tradition in
international relations theory. "There is little in this tradition that
could provide space for theorizing about gender" (Whitworth,

1989:267). The dominant form of structural realism, with its positivist-empiricist orientation, is fundamentally incapable of theorizing meaning, let alone gender.[8] However, the now marginalized classical realism, "although it makes no explicit reference to gender, recognizes that meaning is socially constructed, contingent and historically variable" (Whitworth, 1989:267). Thus, it would at least *appear* to open up space for feminist theorizing.

However, both realism's embedded concept of human nature and its ontological commitments to states and statesmen preclude any real possibility of opening up space for a critical feminist international relations project. Realism's static concept of humans as self-interested egoists does not permit an understanding of human nature as changing or as being socially constructed. Furthermore, the concept of human nature that underpins the image of actors, in realism's vision of the international system, generally "resembles the rational man in economic market models: autonomous, atomistic, self-interested and self-helping, formally equal though differences in power are acknowledged" (Peterson, 1989a:2). Such a view of human nature, rather than being universal, is more closely associated with the characteristic behavior of white, Western, bourgeois men and attendant conceptions of masculinity. Fear and distrust are the prominent emotions, given the insecure and uncertain nature of the anarchic international realm, rendering the female-identified regard for the other as problematic and inappropriate (Peterson, 1989a). This model correlates rational self-interested calculation with morality and emotion with immorality, such that moral action in the anarchic self-help international realm requires, as Peterson (1989a) remarks, the unachievable triumph of reason over passion; the masculine-identified over the female-identified.

In contrast, an alternative female-identified model of human nature views the self rather as connected, interdependent, and interrelated. Associated with maternal thinking and an ethic of care, individuals are not viewed as equal, but rather unique; each with his or her special needs. Passion, knowledge, and prudence complement each other in this view of human nature. This model's view of "highly personalized relationships are at the same time, congruent with the international system of the medieval era" (Peterson, 1989a:3). Therefore, the realist concept of an eternal, universal, and gender-neutral human nature reveals itself to be none other than "Homo economicus," a historically rooted, antisocial, gendered, class-based, white, Western concept. The realist approach precludes analysis of the historical and cultural variability of gender.

Furthermore, the realist concept of the state as a unitary, rational actor and as ontologically privileged takes the state itself as given, rather than socially constructed. The failure to problematize the structural origins of the state and symbolic discourses that surround it ultimately means that realists also take as given the unequal power relations between men and those between men and women, which are constitutive of its formation. It has been pointed out that in Western social formations, "the transition from kin-based to citizenship-based political societies institutionalized gender hierarchy as well as racial and class hierarchies" (Peterson, 1989b:12).

The historical experience of women in Western states until recently has been one of virtual exclusion from the public domain. The "invisibilization" of women is further reinforced through realism's commitment to the state as public but insulated and disconnected from civil society and domestic politics. The state/domestic society dichotomy replicates the public/private split characteristic of post–seventeenth-century Western social, political, and economic evolution. In this dichotomy, politics, economics, and culture were viewed as the public world of men—that is, white, upper-class men—whereas women were relegated to the private but apolitical world of the family and personal relations. The dichotomizing of public and domestic spheres characteristic of realist theorizing ultimately means that realism is silent as to the complex series of functions that the state performs in organizing and upholding interconnected hierarchies of race, class, and gender privilege. It is also silent as to how inequalities of social power inform and shape political power at the level of the state and at the level of the international system. Thus, the realist concept of the state renders invisible the unequal gender relations resulting from the virtually exclusive male monopoly over state power.

Gender and Liberal Pluralism

Liberal pluralist perspectives would appear, at first glance, to offer more fertile ground for theorizing about gender insofar as they have sought to enlarge the scope of international relations theory beyond realism's limited preoccupation with the security dilemma and rigid state-centric focus. Nevertheless, these perspectives (whether reflected in Robert Keohane's neorealist liberal institutionalist regime approach, or in John Burton's World Society Model, or the more radical World Order Models Project) provide limited space for theorizing about gender.

The regime perspective, in contrast to realism's very pessimistic view, focuses on the possibilities for cooperation among self-interested actors in the anarchic sphere of international politics.

Adherents to this view, such as Robert Keohane (1984), contend that international cooperation exists and can be promoted by strengthening the normative frameworks or regimes around which actors' expectations converge through their institutionalization. More recently, Keohane (1989) has called for an alliance between neoliberal institutionalism and feminism to further this theoretical-political project. A novel gesture in such a gender-blind and gender-biased discipline, this enterprise must be treated with extreme reserve. Such an alliance is inherently problematic and reveals all of the deficiencies of the "add women and stir" perspective that dominated early feminist scholarship's approach to redressing women's invisibility (Harding, 1987).

Regime theory appears to offer an epistemology that views meaning as socially constituted, given its theoretical emphasis on the normative and ideational framework underlying international behavior. However, this framework fails to deliver on its epistemological promise because, in fact, it does not account for the way in which such norms are constructed by social actors. In not problematizing how norms are constructed, regime analyses fail to inquire into how power relations and inequalities of power may affect the institutionalization and legitimation of certain norms and courses of action to the detriment of others. As such, it can not provide an adequate framework for the analysis of the social construction of meaning in general. Therefore, as regime analysis also cannot explain how gender is socially constructed, a partnership between feminism and neoliberal institutionalism is, at best, highly problematic, and at worst, it implies a subtle maneuver to incorporate counterhegemonic discourse into its institutionalist political project.

Keohane does not offer a clear account of the nature of such a partnership, principally with respect to how norms and expectations of the future would be decided and whose would prevail (Peterson, 1989a, 1989b). The inability to clarify how such norms would be established is related to the limits of the regime framework. This leaves open the strong possibility that problems in need of explanation and political action will continue to be defined within the terms set by white, Western, bourgeois male liberal institutionalists concerned with managing the so-called decline of U.S. hegemony, as demonstrated by Keohane's suggestion that these two social forces should "act collectively in areas of world politics in which humans seek to cope with collective problems such as those arising from ecological and economic interdependence" (Keohane, 1989:246). Furthermore, this focus offers no guarantees that gender-specific issues such as violence against women or the deteriorating capacities of the majority of Third World female producers to feed their families, generally invisible in the mainstream agendas of pressing international problems, will become political priorities for sustained collective action.

More importantly, the extent to which regime analyses can provide the basis for an emancipatory political project that speaks to the aspirations of all women is severely limited. Regime perspectives take structural inequalities in the international political economy and interstate system as given and seek to work within these parameters. As a consequence, power inequalities among actors that arise from structural inequalities in social power at the national and international levels remain outside the scope of the regime analytic framework. Thus, regime analysis cannot explain the inequalities of power among men, between men and women, and among women or how these may differentially affect capacities to influence and shape the direction of international cooperation. Its piecemeal approach to the issue of area cooperation ultimately means that the regime perspective is most compatible with a liberal feminism that does not seek to alter the underlying sexual division of labor or the class and racial hierarchies that shape the multiple forms of women's subordination.

Burton's World Society Model, although more radical in its analysis of the origins of conflict and in its political project than neoliberal institutionalism, opens up little space for theorizing gender. In Burton's view, violence and conflict are essentially subjective phenomena arising from the failure to satisfy basic human needs. His cobweb model of international relations posits that a world society approach aimed at satisfying basic human needs, conceived of as universal and discoverable through the objective precision of social science inquiry, would promote positive peace, harmony, and global cooperation.

However, an appeal to the objectivity of social science in establishing basic universal human needs denies the fact that science itself cannot neatly be separated from the subjective understandings and values of social scientists. Feminist criticisms of scientific inquiry have documented the variable ways in which masculinist ontologies and meanings are embedded in the conceptual edifice of science as knowledge-producing activity. Gender-blindness in much of social science research means that insufficient attention has been accorded to the special needs of women, as they vary by race, class, and their state's place in the international political economy. For example, the absence of war, viewed as a necessary and sufficient condition of individual security, constitutes the realist concept of international security. This concept of security rarely, if ever, has been broadened to include the multiple forms of violence against women as women and reveals an androcentric bias. Thus, under the rubric of human needs, Burton's model may very well serve to render women's gender-specific needs invisible.

Despite Burton's emphasis on the subjectivity of actors, his conception is not without problems. He offers us a static and ahistorical conception, which cannot grasp how subjective understandings of human needs change with changing social conditions and the struggles of actors. Burton's assumption that the causes of conflict are essentially subjective, rooted in the perceptions of individual actors, although useful in drawing attention to the subjective dimensions of conflict, cannot account for their material and structural bases, which are rooted in inequalities of power (Whitworth, 1989). This further weakens the ability of this framework to come to grips with the changing, unequal power relations between men and women. As Whitworth (1989) so cogently has pointed out, this perspective suffers from the limits inherent in the liberal feminist approach to development (WID); it brings women into international relations without confronting the structural dimensions of women's subordination.

In bridging the gap between liberal pluralist models of international processes and critical international relations theories, the World Order Models Project (Falk, 1975) appears to open up significant space for theorizing gender, given its broad set of concerns for social justice, equitable redistribution of material resources, application of human rights, ecological balance, and peace. Despite this approach's sensitivity to the values, preferences, perspectives, and priorities of the Third World and the Eastern Bloc actors, "the conflict of interest between men and women resulting from women's oppression has been virtually ignored" (Reardon, 1985:74). Not surprisingly, women's preferences have yet to be incorporated into the data collection for the planning and pursuit of a preferred world (Reardon, 1985). The exclusion of women's issues and a gender analysis in the World Order Models Project working papers and conferences, in part, has resulted from the absence of female participants working on substantive feminist issues (Reardon, 1985).

Even as a pioneer of this model, Falk, in his more recent work on authoritarianism, has ignored its gender-specific impact on women, and, as a direct consequence of not exploring the links between sexism and militarism, his proposals for demilitarization initiatives do not include eliminating sexist practices (Reardon, 1985). Thus, the failure to confront gender subordination as an integral dimension of international life remains a specific failing of the World Order Models Project.

Gender and Marxism

Marxism, long marginalized from the mainstream[9] in international relations (unlike liberal pluralist and realist perspectives), has always addressed the "woman question," albeit in a partial and limited way. Within classical Marxism, the gender subordination of women is viewed as derivative of social class oppression; that is, as a result of the unequal social relations of production engendered by capitalism and the rise of private property. Therefore, the social relations of production are said to constitute the material basis for women's subordination in the family, in the household, and within social processes as a whole rather than the relations between men and women per se. The organization of the family and the subordinate position of women within it are determined by capitalist social relations and are seen as a consequence of the structural separation of production from the household, allowing men to enter the sphere of wage labor or social production and relegating women to nonremunerated privatized domestic labor in the household (Molyneux, 1984). For classical Marxism, women's subordination results from dual determinations: from social class divisions based on private property and their exclusion from wage labor. According to this analysis, then, only a proletarian socialist revolution can liberate women.

However, not only have Marx's tools of analysis come under severe criticism for being sex-blind and gender-blind, but real socialism thus far has yet to eliminate the gender subordination of women. This suggests that the flaws are not simply a question of praxis, but are inherent in its theory of women's subordination. For example, Marx's analysis of women in paid work assumes that the conditions of exploitation are the same for male and female wage labor. However, gender shapes the differential insertion of women into the labor market and is the cause of their superexploitation. Women are concentrated in low-paying jobs, in nonunionized sectors of the economy, and in the reserve labor supply. Gender biases also plague Marx's analysis of women's domestic work. Marx never acknowledged "women's economic contribution to capital in the form of unpaid domestic labor" (Sokoloff, 1980:114). Similarly, in conceiving of women's role in the family strictly as a consumer of her husband's wages rather than a producer of surplus value, Marx ignored the economic contribution of wives to their families, which also served to benefit individual men.

Whereas the early Marxist feminists[10] attempted to come to grips with some of the deficiencies in classical Marxism's position on women by focusing on women's special relationship to capital, and integrating the role of unpaid domestic labor in the valorization of capital, the functionalist and reductionist thrust of this type of theoretical explanation has come under sustained criticism (Barrett, 1985). Although the historical materialist method has enabled Marxist feminists to account for the diversity of women's experiences as they are differentiated by social class and a nation's place in the international political economy, Marxist feminists have as yet to integrate a theoretical understanding of how "race" and ethnicity differentiate women's relations to production and reproduction, as well as divide them politically (Carby, 1982; Davis, 1981; hooks, 1986; Amina, 1984; Bhavnani and Coulson, 1984).

The essential dilemma, however, remains. Marxism-feminism cannot explain why women rather than men undertake domestic activities, why men as opposed to women should have been freed to engage in wage labor, nor, finally, why women are ghettoized in certain low-paying gender-typed occupations. It cannot do so because the shared focus of analysis is on women's roles in social production and in the social reproduction of capital exclusively, rather than power relations between men and women emanating from the unequal sexual division of labor and social discourses sustaining women's subordination. Marx was concerned with explaining the dynamics of the economic division of labor and not the sexual division of labor. Those areas of human reproduction or the social activities that pertain to the reproduction and care of people in the context of the family, marriage, and filiation, are viewed as women's work and lie outside the scope of this analytic framework. The sexual division of labor in the family is seen as natural and biologically based, and the reproduction and care of human beings is viewed as outside the scope of social production.

As a consequence of the failure to confront the social construction of gender roles and discourses that sustain women's suitability for domestic work, women in socialist countries, like their counterparts in liberal capitalist democracies, continue to bear the exclusive burdens of child care and domestic work, whether they are engaged in wage labor or not. Women workers are faced with a double shift. Furthermore, the literature on the socialist experiences in the Eastern Bloc and the Third World indicate that women continue to occupy subordinate roles in the economy, polity, society, and family, irrespective of the differences in levels of economic development (Molyneux, 1984; Croll, 1981a, 1981b). Women's subordination, then, cannot be explained solely in terms of the demands of the production system or those of a determinate mode of production.

Gender and Critical International Relations

Critical international relations theories, critical theory, and post-modernism (see Chapter 2 by Neufeld; see also Renagger and Hoffman, 1992) appear to offer the most fertile ground for a feminist international relations project. Yet for all their initial promise, they have remained very much science as usual. The relative newness of the postpositivist international relations projects makes it very difficult to assess the effects on actual research and the development of new theoretical perspectives (Peterson, 1989a, 1989b), but a number of disturbing trends raise questions about the viability of a critical feminist international relations project within the ambit of these perspectives.

For all their emphasis on the critical function of theory, much of the new theoretical enterprises, like the metatheoretical debates themselves, have been conspicuous in their virtual silence on the role and place of gender within their intellectual endeavors. Thus, critical theories and postmodernist approaches (see, for example, Der Derian and Shapiro, 1989), as is the case with their mainstream counterparts, fail to confront the multiple ways in which gendered presuppositions inform and shape epistemological, ontological, and axiological assumptions underpinning theory, methodology, international practices, and political projects. Whereas some of the post-modernist and deconstructionist literature outside of the discipline has included gender in its catalog of hierarchical dualisms at the core of Western discourses that oppress people and silence their voices, this has not been the case within the international relations literature per se.[11] In its failure to adequately deconstruct the West, malestream postmodernist international relations theory denies the inequalities of power between different groups of men and women that shape how dominant discourses and symbolic representations are imposed, in addition to assuming that men and women have shared equally in the benefits of Western imperialism.

In addition to masculinist biases, some of the theorizing continues to be further articulated from white Western bourgeois perspectives, such as is the case with Richard Ashley's dialectical competence model, which attempts to synthesize the insights of critical theory and realism (Ashley, 1984). Despite efforts to open up space for marginalized persons, much of the new international relations postmodernism appears to reinforce class-privileged, Eurocentric, white male discourse. The inability to address gendered, class, and Eurocentered biases necessarily weakens the critical self-reflexive thrust of these projects, leaving intact the interrelated hierarchies of privilege, which may serve to reinforce them in the real world. This possibility is further strengthened in the light of the problematic treatment of meaning construction in the new critical international relations literature.

Scholarly attention in the discipline is now beginning to shift attention onto the construction of meaning as a social practice (Wendt, 1987), and rightly so, given that this key dimension lies outside the scope of positivism-empiricism and has been minimized by much of the radical structuralist Marxist perspectives. How people, particularly women, perceive themselves with regard to the structures of race, class, and gender is essential to an understanding of consciousness and effective political action. With the exception of Robert Cox's transnational historical materialism, much of the new work in the discipline treats language, social discourses, the politics of identity, and meaning construction as sites of political struggle and activity in isolation from social conditions and social relations. This approach, of the world as text, deflects attention away from the power relations that permit certain social discourses to be heard and maintained. "Groups unequal in power are also unequal in their resources to implement their perspectives outside their particular groups insofar as they lack control over the apparatuses of society that sustain ideological hegemony" (Collins, 1989:749). Although Cox, in his theoretical perspective, articulates the links between social relations of domination, control over production, social institutions, and ideas in ways that are empirically relevant for political action, he too, does not give sufficient weight to the intersection of hierarchies of privilege, gender, race, and class within his schema. However, Cox's theoretical perspective remains the most fruitful line of theorizing for those committed to emancipatory knowledge.

Much of this critical international relations literature is aimed at empowerment, but the links between theory and praxis remain problematic. The antifoundationalist and relativist positions of postmodernist thinkers, when pushed to their logical conclusion, ultimately deny the basis for political action by oppressed groups, masking a suspicious inherent conservatism and elitism. If the postmodernist thinkers outside the discipline provide any clues, the extreme antifoundationalist and relativist position of Jean Baudrillard, for example, ultimately denies the basis for political action by oppressed groups. Thus, it can be argued, they mask an inherent conservatism and elitism. Others, such as Felix Guattari and Gilles Deleuze, move toward a new but rather vague form of radical politics. At the same time, Jean François Lyotard refurbishes old liberal politics with new labels (Best and Kellner, 1991). Therefore, in totality, postmodernism provides no uniform direction for a critical feminist understanding of global politics. The new criti-

148   *Susan Judith Ship*

cal international relations theories, like their predecessors, such as the Frankfurt School, remain confined to the "magic circle of academic institutions" (Mies, 1983) and reproduce yet again the structural separation between theory and the practical politics of engaged struggle. The academic institutionalization of feminism within such a perspective and mode of knowledge production contains the inherent danger of its deradicalization, as theory and as political practice.

Conclusion: Toward a Critical Feminist International Relations Project

Deconstruction of the dominant forms of theorization in international relations—both the mainstream and the critical alternatives—reveals that these prevailing systems of conceptualization and methods for representing and understanding social reality are biased because "they invalidate women's experiences and promote the values and interests of the men that created them" (Jaggar, 1983:371). As a corrective to essential man, much of the early feminist scholarship in the social sciences substituted essential woman in its place.

In international relations, this approach has dominated much of the feminist work on women and peace and remains highly problematic. Sarah Ruddick (1983) has questioned whether the equating of women with peace and men with war, men with the role of the protector and women as the protected, does not, in fact, reinforce gender stereotypes. Such essentialist stereotyping denies the fact that "women all over the world have and do participate in the war industry as prostitutes, wives, widows, social workers, nurses, defense workers or even mothers of soldiers" (Bulbeck, 1988:97). Identifying women with peace and a pacifist stance has not necessarily been endorsed by women in the Third World, many of whom have actively participated in national liberation struggles, and such a perspective would serve to exclude these Third World women from the category "women," viewed as such. Furthermore, it has been convincingly argued that feminist explanations as to how women's identities are socially constructed during wartime draw exclusively on the experiences of white Western women, and constitute a narrow and contentious base from which to make generalizations about women and war (Bulbeck, 1988). Thus, feminist theorizing that replaces generic man with generic woman privileges the experiences of white, Western, middle-class, heterosexual women, and thereby denies the diversity of women's experiences and the contradictions among women that arise from the multiple cleavages that divide them.

A critical feminist international relations project, then, builds upon a common opposition to gender oppression but also confronts the contradictions and complexities of power relations among women "involving the intersection of gender, class, race and imperialism, where white women may simultaneously be privileged and oppressed" (Stasiulis, 1990:283). The self-reflexive and critical edge of such theorizing must necessarily go beyond merely uncovering hidden male-centered biases camouflaged by the impersonal language of malestream social science. It must also "uncover and reject the generalizing impersonal when used by white middle class feminists to speak for all women" (Hess and Marx Ferree, 1987:12). The inclusion of a methodological postulate such as "conscious partiality" (Mies, 1983), involving self-conscious reflection on the significance of gender, race, class, and imperialism in constructing social science discourses, constitutes a useful corrective. Conscious partiality also involves the deliberate inclusion of gender, race, class, and imperialism in theorizing and research design.

The development of critical feminist international relations, then, takes as its starting point the awareness that "woman" as a social category is only meaningful "in reference to a fusion of adjectives which symbolize particular historical trajectories, material circumstances and cultural experiences and that our gender is constituted and represented differently according to our differential locations within the global relations of power" (Brah, 1991:59–60). Our insertion into these global relations of power is realized through a complex web of economic, political, and ideological processes. As Brah has pointed out, we do not simply exist in these processes as women but as differentiated categories such as white middle-class women, working-class women, black women, refugee or immigrant women, and Third World women, in which each description refers to a specific and particular social condition.

Broadening the scope of feminism to include the struggle against all forms of oppression is essential to developing critical feminist international relations theory because, for most women, specific oppression as women is inextricably linked to problems of imperialism, ethnicity, nationality, racism, and social class (Sen and Grown, 1987). Thus, it becomes important to focus on how different but intersecting systems of power, such as gender oppression, racism, class, and neoimperialism, are historically and socially constituted at a given moment in time, enabling dominant social groups to construct or sustain their hegemony at the levels of the state and international institutions. This involves "determin[ing] the structural locations of different groups of men and women in concrete and historically specific social relations and link[ing] these to accompanying discourses of denigration, subordination and exploitation" (Stasiulis, 1990:290).

This perspective, then, explores the changing relationships among ideas, language, social discourses, social conditions, and social relations, in order to open up space for articulating practical strategies of empowerment of particularly disadvantaged groups of women. It allows us to evaluate the degree to which both a given set of institutional arrangements and alternate emancipatory political projects, aimed at transforming single issues (the state, the interstate system, and/or the international political economy), empower women, or rather different categories of women. Women's empowerment may be understood to involve the radical transformation of power:

> to gain control over their lives and their bodies, to obtain the right
> to make choices in their own lives, to gain access and control over
> material and non-material resources and to gain the right to define
> the kinds of societies [national and international] they want.
> (Maguire, 1984:2)

Therefore, as feminism constitutes the political expression of the concerns and interests of women from different regions, classes, nationalities, or ethnic and racial groups, a critical feminist international relations project recognizes that feminism cannot be monolithic in its goals, issues, and strategies (Sen and Grown, 1987). Gender subordination, although universal, cannot be grounded in a rigid conception of universality: "there is and must be a diversity of feminisms, responsive to the different needs and concerns of different women and defined by them for themselves" (Sen and Grown, 1987:19).

As an empowering political practice, feminists must develop research "which is both a way of understanding women's subordination and of bringing change" (Currie and Kazi, 1987:93) so that research *on* women may become research *for* women. This type of research becomes possible when personal awareness and consciousness-raising, the hallmarks of the radical feminist political project, become linked to the social—to the process not only of individual change, but to social change in the active struggle to dismantle oppressive systems of power. Theory and research must become a collaborative process between academics and those actively engaged in political struggles to ensure that research is conducted in the interests of women rather than simply being research about women.

Notes

1. There is considerable disagreement among the different strands of feminism over where to situate the locus of women's subordination. See, for example, Caroline Razamanoglu (1989).

2. Marlee Kline (1989) has shown how the feminist standpoint position, elaborated by Nancy Harstock (1983), fails to account for the experiences of women of color.

3. The critical international relations project is one in which theory performs the functions of criticizing the boundaries of human understanding, outlining the potentialities for change, and sketching the possibilities for increasing human autonomy. See Hoffman (1987).

4. R. B. J. Walker (1992) and Robert Keohane (1989) are notable exceptions.

5. In *Inessential Woman*, Elizabeth Spelman (1988) shows that the theory and practice of Western statist politics differentiate between white women and women of color. This is not explored in Harstock's (1984) analysis.

6. See also Jagger's (1983) chapter on feminist epistemologies.

7. Robert Keohane is a notable exception. He has argued for the joining of liberal institutionalism with feminism. See Keohane (1989).

8. Kenneth Waltz (1979) is the best example of this trend.

9. The Marxist tradition in international relations broadly groups together the Marxist and neo-Marxist theories of imperialism, the internationalization of capital, *dependencia*, underdevelopment, and Wallerstein's World Systems perspectives. Its set of concerns include the study of imperialism, the dynamics and demise of the international capitalist economy, the structural dependency of Third World political economies, movements of national liberation, and the prospects for socialism. Both the tools of analysis and political projects are seen by the mainstream of the discipline as incompatible with or irrelevant to international relations' traditional concerns. See, for example, Holsti (1985).

10. See Sokoloff (1980) for an extensive discussion of the evolution of Marxist feminist and socialist feminist theories of women's subordination.

11. Feminist postmodernist international relations is, of course, the exception, although its account of gender is problematic.

8

Problematizing the State in International Relations Theory

E. Fuat Keyman

This chapter discusses the concept of the state in international relations theory. Its intention, however, is not to provide a comprehensive overview of the question, but rather to focus on two specific issues. The first concerns what we will argue to be the untheorized nature of the state in international relations, leading to what Halliday has termed a theoretical "impasse" integral to the recent transformation of theory in the field. Stemming from this, the second issue addressed in this chapter is the proposed solution to the impasse.[1]

A potential resolution to this impasse has been offered in the recent rediscovery of the state by social theorists, which has given rise to the state-centric model of international society. It has been suggested that the incorporation into international relations theory of this model would help overcome its impasse insofar as it provides a number of useful insights for a better conceptualization of the state. It will be argued here, however, that the call for such incorporation is an attempt to construct an agency *problematique* and that its contribution to international relations theory, although important and serious, should be critically assessed. More specifically, it is suggested that although the state-centric model argues correctly that theorizing international relations cannot be tackled without an adequate account of the state, this cannot be done without fully understanding the state in relation to society.

The interrelationship between the two constructs of state and society must be understood in both theoretical and empirical terms. In other words, it is not "either the state or society" but "both the state and society" as theoretical objects of inquiry that should be employed in the process of theorizing international relations. The either/or logic leads to a false dichotomy between the state and society, as in the case of the state-centric model. However, the "both/and" logic makes it possible to think of the state and society in relational terms without reducing one to the other. Consequently, the both/and logic brings about a conception of the state not only as a complex institutional ensemble with its own spatial and temporal specificity, but also as a site where condensation of political forces takes place (Jessop, 1990:341–342). The state constitutes not only "the sovereign place within which the highest internal laws and policies are enacted and from which strategies toward external states and nonstate peoples proceed," but also "the site of the most fundamental division between inside and outside, us and them, domestic and foreign, the sphere of citizen entitlements and that of strategic responses" (Connolly, 1991:201). In this sense, the both/and logic enables one to take into consideration not only the geopolitical dimension of international relations, but also the economic and discursive/cultural practices integral to the process of the constitution and reproduction of world orders, states, and societies.

The State and International Relations Theory

There is little doubt that one of the most problematic concepts in the study of international relations has been the state. The concept itself has always been regarded as the key to understanding the operation of the international system, its structure, and its fundamental characteristics.[2] The realist paradigm assumes in an a priori fashion that the international system cannot exist without the state, insofar as states and interactions among them constitute the system itself. Such an assumption, of course, stresses the unity of the state and the concomitant development of a state system, and suggests that the state is the basic unit of analysis in the study of international relations. In the realist paradigm,

> the state is viewed as the "essential actor" whose interests, power, decisions, practices, and interactions with other states define and exhaust the scope and content of international politics as an autonomous sphere . . . there is no political life absent of states, prior to states, or independent of states. Political interests that are not reducible to state interests enter the international political realm only insofar as they are mediated by state interests. (Ashley, 1983:470)

This does not mean that the state, or more precisely its conceptualization, has been the primary concern of international relations theory. As Walker has correctly pointed out,

> to speak of the state itself, however, is to confront a number of difficulties. For although the state has long been the central category of international political theory, its precise nature has remained rather enigmatic. The worst caricatures of it are well known: the billiard ball or black box operating within a determinist mechanical system; the proliferating categories of early decision-making theory; the identification of politics with the more or less formal institutions of government. At the other extreme, there are finely detailed analyses of the foreign-policy making processes of individual states in which the state, as state, is dissolved in particularities. Even apart from these extremes, it would be difficult to argue that international political theory possesses anything like an adequate account of the nature of the state. (Walker, 1984:531–532)

In other words, instead of taking the state as an object of theoretical inquiry, international relations theory has uncritically tended to conceive of it as the main actor, as an ontological entity, or as an observable given institutional entity.

The consequences of this tendency are clear. The concept of the state, for example, has been used interchangeably with nation, power, and sovereignty in realist scholarship (Ferguson and Mansbach, 1988:7). As a result, the realist paradigm tends to reduce the state to the decisionmaking process whereby the only objective is to maintain nation-interest, defined as "the struggle for national power" (Morgenthau, 1967:2–3). In this sense, the decisionmaking process is considered to be independent of domestic society, thereby defining the autonomy of the political sphere characterized by state action and power.

The autonomy from domestic politics accorded the state by realism, as well as the struggle for national power (its primary ahistorical function), makes the state an unproblematic entity exempted from scientific (falsificationist) or any other kind of critical inquiry (Ashley, 1984:238). The state is viewed as a decisionmaking subject, "an external object, an untheorized fact, an ahistorical entity" (George, 1989:99). Viewed in this manner, the state represents "an unproblematic unity, an entity whose existence, boundaries, identifying structures, constituencies, legitimations, interests and capacities to make self-regarding decisions can be treated as given" (Ashley, 1984:238).

In this context the state does not need to be theorized, because it speaks for itself—just as the facts do in positivism. This untheorized nature, however, has created a problem for international relations theory (Halliday, 1987a; Higgott, 1988; Giddens, 1984; Caporosa, 1989). Ferguson and Mansbach have asserted that the concept of the state became an "obstacle to international relations theory" (Ferguson and Mansbach, 1989:2). Likewise, Krasner, who once argued that the state should become a major concern of scholarly discourse, admitted that his attempt to think of the state as an analytical construct failed because he did not problematize state–civil society relations (Krasner, 1989:189).

A partial answer to this problem of the state seemed at first to be answered by work in historical sociology. Halliday has observed that as the state was becoming problematized in international relations theory "the comparable trend within sociology [was] . . . to re-examine the state and to reassert its centrality in historical and contemporary contexts" (Halliday, 1987a:217). Social theorists, such as Skocpol, Evans, Giddens, and Mann, were proposing new ways to develop a theory of the state.[3] Common to their proposals were the assumptions that a proper theory of the state should be historically defined, that is, placed in a historical process that is both national and international in nature. In other words, a proper analysis of the emergence, development, role, and functions of the nation-state would necessarily entail taking into account the international dimension of state behavior, state power, and state action.

At an epistemological level, central to such analysis is the rejection of structuralist and instrumentalist understandings of the state that conceive of state action as a manifestation of societal patterns of conflictual relations between social collective actors.[4] In so doing, it reintroduces the category of "agency," by which the state as an institutional agent is theorized through a historical analysis of interactions between structures and agencies. This project finds its expression in, among others, Theda Skocpol's call for "bringing the state back in" (Skocpol, 1985). Skocpol's aim is to explain the potential autonomy of the state by means of historical sociology, and in so doing implies the construction of a state-centric model that permits the reading of social and global relations within the context of the structure-agency dialectic. If the debate on the state has reached an impasse, as Halliday has suggested, one way to overcome this problem might be to integrate into international relations theory new developments in the theory of the state, to study them, and in so doing to theorize the state in an adequate way. It is this proposed solution to the problem of the state in international relations theory that will be discussed critically in what follows.

The Agency *Problematique* and the Theory of the State

The state-centric model, advanced by Theda Skocpol, Michael Mann, and Anthony Giddens,[5] is founded upon three basic theoretical propositions derived from a critique of the society-centric model as a "reductionist" theory of the state.[6] First, in regard to the ontological structure of the state, it is suggested that the state should be viewed as a potentially autonomous institutional agent with its own life and history. This suggestion has two implications. On the one hand, it creates a similarity between realism and the state-centric model with respect to the potential autonomy accorded to the state. On the other hand, it implies that the society-centric theories of the state fail to recognize the specificity of the state insofar as they have concentrated their attention almost exclusively on the societal determinants of state action, neglecting, as a result, the distinct institutional features of the state.

Second, the state-centric model insists that the theory of the state should take geopolitics seriously. State-centric analyses argue that society-centric theories of the state have tended to ignore the international dimension, leaving them unable to explore all the sources of state power. It is also on this point that realism and the state-centric model converge. Indeed, as Linklater has argued, the state-centric model derives its critique from the realist assertion that geopolitics is the primary point of reference in international relations theory (Linklater, 1986:303–307).

Third, in its conceptualization of the state as an institutional agent, the state-centric model claims to have reintroduced the category of agency into the domain of social theory as well as into international relations theory. The reintroduction of agency rescues social theory from its subordination to the structuralist and functionalist orthodoxies that have constituted the epistemological basis of the society-centric theories of the state. This rescue, the state-centric model contends, can provide a solution to the ongoing sociological question: How do social agents make history, but not in the manner of their own choosing? With respect to international relations theory, this rescue involves a nonfunctionalist theorization of the state (Halliday, 1987a:210–217).

This state-centric model marks a contribution to international relations theory. It should be noted, however, that the model and the agency *problematique* it develops, although escaping functionalism and arguing for the necessity of a recognition of the specificity of the state, eventually constructs an institutionally essentialist theory of the state. Essentialism refers to a mode of analysis in which one category is elevated to privileged status—that is, is used as an entry into history—thus becoming the principal point of reference by which social relations and their reproduction are read off.[7] In the state-centric model, the concept of the state as a potentially autonomous agent functions precisely as an essentialist theoretical construct. It becomes the privileged entry into the history of the emergence, development, and reproduction of modern societies. As a consequence, the model tends to be just as reductionist as the society-centric theories of the state that it aims to criticize. With respect to international relations theory, this means that the state-centric model offers only a partial solution to the problem of the state, which in turn weakens the validity of the assertion that it is through the incorporation of this model that international relations theory's impasse can be overcome.

Bringing the State Back In: The State-Centric Model

Theda Skocpol has characterized her work as a call to "bring the state back in," thereby making it possible to move beyond highly speculative theoretical debates concerning the autonomy of the state. Her intention is to convince the reader that state theory has to be developed from a particular vantage point, one that is historical and comparative. Her conclusion is that the state has to be conceived of as an institution, a social actor, and a set of bureaucratic apparatuses. State policy and structure should not be derived from social structures, but should be considered in their internal specificity, which stems from their historical and spatial dimensions.

If states should be regarded as distinctive structures with their own histories as well as in terms of the complex global circumstances that provide the context for state action, how should the state itself be conceptualized? Probably one of the most striking features of the conception of the state as a distinct organization with its own specific history is that it very clearly bears the mark of Max Weber (within the context of the potential autonomy of the state and state power), and of the historian Otto Hintze (within the context of the significance of the interstate system to the study of the state).

The idea that it is important to relate the state both to its national social formation and to the context of global conditions and pressures, according to Skocpol, involves an emphasis placed upon "the territorial basis of the state" (Skocpol, 1985). Herein lies the significance of Weber for Skocpol's approach to the state. Weber conceptualizes the state as an organization that claims a monopoly of power and coercion in a given territory (Weber, 1948:77–78). This means that states, especially national states, always function in relation to other territories and are always concerned with their own boundaries with other states. This has led Skocpol to propose that the geopolitical framework of state action preexisted capitalism and allowed the state to act as an independent actor. It is the territoriality of state action that makes the state operate outside and above civil society, that makes it clear that it preceded capitalist development, and that gives the state its own history.

Skocpol also follows Hintze by asserting that the structure of the state cannot be properly analyzed without taking into account the international dimension of state action. Hintze has argued that there are two phenomena that determine the real organization of the state. First, there is the structure of social classes, and second, there is the external ordering of states—their position relative to each other, and their overall position in the world. Struggles among social classes at home and conflict among nations abroad have a dramatic impact on the organization and power of states. The "shape" of a state—its size, external configuration, military structure, ethnic relations, and labor composition, among other things—is deeply rooted in the history of external events and conditions (Held, 1984:68). It is from Hintze's argument that Skocpol has extrapolated the idea that the state constitutes a "dual anchorage" between socioeconomic structures and an international system of states. States may be affected by capitalist development, but this does not mean that they are the products of that development: "Indeed, just as capitalist development has spurred transformation of states and the international state system, so have these 'acted back' upon the course of capital accumulation within nations and on a world scale" (Skocpol, 1980:110).

According to Skocpol, in recognizing the internal specificity of the state, one can see that "the state is fundamentally Janus-faced, with an intrinsically dual anchorage in class-divided socio-economic structures and an international system of states" (Skocpol, 1979:32). Furthermore,

> the international state system as a transnational structure of military competition was not originally created by capitalism. Throughout modern world history, it represents an analytically autonomous level of transnational reality—interdependent in its structure and dynamics with world capitalism, but not reducible to it. (Skocpol, 1979:22)

That is to say, the international state system antedated the rise of capitalism, providing a historical space where the state could gain potential autonomy vis-à-vis the social formation to which it belonged.

The recognition of the historical specificity of the state allows Skocpol to criticize the systemic understanding of international relations with reference to world-systems theory. World-systems theory argues that since the sixteenth century the world capitalist system has characterized international relations and that the interstate system can only establish the political superstructure of that system. Following Hintze's dual anchorage thesis, Skocpol has raised a crucial question: Does the interstate system constitute a political superstructure or a distinct historical reality?

In this respect, world-systems theory can be said to fail to appreciate the independent efficacy of the state by reducing the state to the system. In contrast, Skocpol's approach to the state incorporates a conception of history that is not unilinear but consists of a number of processes, interdependent but not reducible to one another. Thus, the Janus-faced characterization of the state allows Skocpol to stress the importance of the recognition of the specificity of the state.

The recognition of the specificity of the state also allows Skocpol both to analyze state policy and structure through a historical-comparative sociological optic and to construct the theory of the state as the basis of the state-centric model. Thus, the state refers to a set of administrative, policing, and military organizations headed, and more or less well coordinated by, an executive authority. Nevertheless, the administrative and coercive organizations are the basis of state power. Skocpol has suggested that such a conception illuminates the ways the capacities of state organizations create state power; the ways state policies are formulated in relation to the interests of social and political groups and the existing global circumstances; and finally, how state personnel create their own modus operandi and formulate policies through which the state regulates internal security and competes with other states.[8] Consequently, bringing the state back in avoids an abstract theory of the state and allows for the study of how the state shapes and reshapes social and politico-economic relations in a given society.

The Incorporation of "Bringing the State Back In" into International Relations Theory: Halliday's Contribution

According to Fred Halliday, international relations theory has reached an impasse due to the fact that it has never attempted to conceptualize the state—nor has it tried to go further than the description of the state that presupposes that the state refers to a national territorial totality.

Thus the "state" (e.g., Britain, Russia, America, etc.) comprises in conceptual form what is denoted visually on a map—the country as a whole and all that is within it: territory, government, people, society. There could be no better summary of this view than that of Northedge in the introductory chapter to his *International Political System: A State*, in the sense used in this book, is a territorial association of people recognized for purposes of law and diplomacy as a legally equal member of the system of states. It is in reality a means of organizing people for the purpose of their participation in the international system. (Halliday, 1987a:217)

Contrary to the a priori assumption that the state constitutes a national-territory totality, there exists in the realm of sociology an alternative approach to the state, which, by drawing on Max Weber and Otto Hintze, defines it as "a specific set of coercive and administrative institutions, distinct from the broader political, social and national context in which it finds itself" (Halliday, 1987a:218). The latter definition of the state, Halliday has suggested, saves the state from being "a troublesome abstraction" and establishes a proper means by which to come to terms with "real states" in all their complexity. Moreover, it helps to explicate the way in which states gain sovereignty, control their own territory, and create a mode of representation of their peoples. Finally, and more importantly, it appears to be more able to generate questions about "the effectiveness of the international dimension."

Halliday has argued in this context that conceptualizing the state as a set of coercive and administrative institutions enables one to pose questions such as why and how participation in the international realm strengthens or weakens states; why and under what circumstances it permits states to gain autonomy and act independently vis-à-vis the social formations they govern; and under what conditions states become less or more responsive to, and representative of, their social formations precisely because of their international role.

The least that can be said, therefore, is that an alternative conceptualization of the state permits analytical questions and avenues of research markedly different from the totality approach. In the first place this alternative definition of the state opens up a set of conceptual distinctions that are often confused and conflated in literature on international relations, but which need to be separated out if the state-society relationship is to be more clearly identified. (Halliday, 1987a:219)

At this point, it becomes clear that Halliday's intention is in fact to introduce a *problematique* into international relations theory based on the conception of the state as an institutional agent consisting of a set of coercive and administrative institutions and focusing on the state-society relationship. It is a *problematique,* Halliday has asserted, that is able to contribute to the development of international relations theory because it opens up a set of conceptual distinctions that are of significance in understanding state structure and state action and that permits new analytical questions and avenues of research.

There are at least three distinctions upon which Halliday's assertion rests. The first is a distinction between state and society. He has argued that the state constitutes an ensemble of coercive and administrative apparatuses and that the access of social groups to them varies according to the power, wealth, and political skills of these groups. The second distinction is that between the state and government. Contrary to conventional international political discourse that sees the state and government as identical entities, the new *problematique* with its institutional conception of the state separates "the ensemble of administrative apparatuses" from "the executive personnel formally in position of supreme control" in order to refute the assumption that the state represents society as a whole, and also to show that in certain circumstances elements within the state may resist or actively oppose the policies of government (Halliday, 1987a:219). The third distinction is that between state and nation. The term nation-state, as it is used in the conventional international political discourse, refers to a national and territorial entity based on an assumption of ethnic homogeneity and political representativeness. According to Halliday, this does not apply empirically to the structure of international relations. Within the structure of international relations, states with different political regimes may have different modes of representation. As well, there exists ethnic diversity and there may be a gap between a mode of international conduct and national interest (Halliday, 1987a:220). The distinction between state and nation therefore permits the question of how far the national state represents the nation.

In addition to these distinctions, the *problematique* that Halliday has developed consists of four research avenues, which are fundamental to an accurate understanding of the modern state. The first concerns the origin of the state. Here Halliday draws on Charles Tilly's text, *The Formation of National States in Western Europe* (1975), and argues that the origin of the modern nation-state lies in coercion and extraction, "both against the populations subjected to states and against rivals" (Halliday, 1987a:220). The state therefore should be referred to as an "instrument of subjugation" or as a "protection racket." Halliday's argument implies that the conventional understanding of the state as a national territorial entity understates the subjugation of the state in its origin and overstates its representational function, although the meaning of representation has changed over time.[9]

The second research avenue is related to the importance of the world-historical context in shaping the internal organization of the state. Here Halliday affirms the central argument of *Bringing the State Back In* (Evans, Rueschemeyer, and Skocpol, 1985) that geopolitics provides the context and formative influence for states, and adds that this is true not only for postcolonial states, but also for European states.

The third avenue of research is to show how states are formative of societies. By this Halliday means the ideological and organizational functions of states—functions having to do with the formation of national consciousness, of national ideologies, and of national economies (Halliday, 1987a:221).

The fourth avenue concerns the question of state capacities, especially those that are central to the state's own internal composition and relation to society. As the agenda of *Bringing the State Back In* has suggested, an explanation for state capacities requires comparative and historical investigations through which one could explicate how states govern and administer their own populations and territories, impose control on societal relations, and produce effects in the constitution of those relations. Such investigations, according to Halliday, not only help to go beyond the concept of sovereignty that presupposes that the state assumes a monopoly of power and legitimacy in its own territorial formation, but also demonstrate the significance of the international dimension for state capacities.

Having outlined the basic distinctions and the central research avenues that his *problematique* emphasizes, Halliday concludes that they provide useful insights for the conception of the state as a set of coercive and administrative institutions. At the same time, they show the ways the state as an analytical and theoretical construct can affect, and also contribute to, international relations theory. They do so by pointing out the quality of the structure of the state as a domestic as well as an international agent.

Although useful for the analytical questions it raises and research avenues it develops, Halliday's *problematique* does not do more than integrate into international relations theory the state-centric model constructed by Skocpol. Furthermore, such integration is not realized by Halliday through a critical examination of the state-centric model. Instead Halliday has taken *Bringing the State Back In*, made use of the concept of the state developed by it, and introduced that concept and its analytical and methodological characteristics to international relations theory. However, this integration leaves unaddressed two concepts also not addressed thoroughly by Skocpol's state-centric model: the concept of state power (the relationship of state and power), and that of modern society (the main features of the process of the constitution of modern societal affairs). Even though Halliday's *problematique* is devoted to exploring analytical and methodological categories in such a way as to construct a theory of the state for international relations, it dismisses or disregards the concept of power that has always been so central to any understanding of the state. The second concept is also crucial if the construction of the state-centric model is not to be made at the expense of societal relations and their historical forms.

Neither Skocpol nor Halliday has provided deep and extensive explanations of these concepts. Nevertheless, there have been attempts within historical sociology to construct a theory of the state on the basis of these two concepts, which have centered around the institutional conception of the state as a potentially autonomous agent. They equally place a special emphasis on both the international dimension and on geopolitics to conceptualize state autonomy. As in the case of *Bringing the State Back In* and Halliday's *problematique*, it can be argued that they should be considered historical-sociological contributions to international relations theory, which constitutes at the level of epistemology an agency *problematique*.[10] Michael Mann's "Autonomous Power of the State" (1984) and Anthony Giddens's *The Nation-State and Violence* (1987b) will be examined as illustrative of these attempts.

The Autonomous Power of the State

In what sense can the state be considered to have a distinct identity? It is this question that led Michael Mann to undertake the task of exploring the links between states, societies, and geopolitics with the intention of seeking the sources of state autonomy. Although his conception of the state appears to be identical to that of *Bringing the State Back In*, Mann has followed a different research avenue, searching for the sources of state autonomy on the basis of the concept of power, and employing a historical and spatial understanding of society. Mann's attempt to analyze the sources of state autonomy broadens and deepens the boundaries of the state-centric model by integrating into it a historical-spatial analysis of power. The concept of power provides Mann with an analytical and theoretical device by which to sustain the state/society separation as the basis of the state-centric model.

Mann has argued from the outset that the general tendency in contemporary political discourse has been to assume that the state acts in a society as a national and territorial entity (Mann, 1986:2). For Mann, this tendency, which results from a "unitary" understanding of national social formations, should be considered methodologically and historically untenable precisely because state, culture, and economy almost never coincide historically. At the heart of Mann's statement lies the argument that societies do not constitute unitary and organic entities. Once society is conceived of as an unproblematic, unitary entity, it becomes impossible to recognize the specificity of the state because the totality-based conception of society results in either the equation of the nation-state and society or the dissolution of the state into economy or culture. State, economy, and culture have their own histories, their own conditions of existence. None of them can be the basic unit of society; they only constitute different networks of society.

As had Skocpol and Halliday, Mann has conceptualized the international system as consisting of a number of processes. Yet he has added to the agency *problematique* an element lacking with Skocpol and Halliday, that is, the epistemological basis of such a conceptualization. A nonunitary conception of society allows Mann both to analyze the interstate system in its historical and spatial specificity and to argue for its irreducibility to other processes.

Mann has extrapolated from this nonunitary understanding of society a methodological proposition that "societies are constituted of multiple overlapping and intersecting socio-spatial networks of power" defining institutional means of attaining human goals. These networks are defined as ideological, economic, military, and political power relations constituting sociospatial and organizational means of social control of people, materials, and territories (Mann, 1986:2–3). The organizational and sociospatial model of power, therefore, illuminates not only the way in which networks of social interaction operate in a given society and historical context, but also how organizational and institutional means are used to attain power.

The political power network derives from the utility of centralized, institutionalized, and territorialized regulation of many aspects of social relations. It consists of regulations and means of coercion centrally administered and territorially bounded, which, Mann had suggested, constitute state power (Mann, 1986:27). Moreover, the exercise of power brings about the state's distinctive contribution to

social life insofar as political relations concern one particular area—
the "center," or the state. Political power, for this reason, is located
at the center and exercised outward. In addition, political organization of the state is not delimited by the national sphere, but has an
international dimension as well. As Mann has put it:

> Domestically, the state is territorially centralized and territorially
> bounded. States can thus attain greater autonomous power when
> social life generates emergent possibilities for enhanced coopera-
> tion and exploitation of a centralized form over a confined territori-
> al area. It depends predominantly upon techniques of authoritative
> power, because it is centralized, though not as much so as military
> organization. . . . But states' territorial boundaries—in a world
> never yet dominated by a single state—also give rise to an area of
> regulated inter-state relations. . . . Clearly, geopolitical organization
> is very different from the other power organizations mentioned so
> far. It is indeed normally ignored by sociological theory. But it is an
> essential part of social life and it is not reducible to the "internal"
> power configurations of its component states. (Mann, 1986:27)

There are three ways, Mann has argued, in which the state
appropriates its power. They are identified as the "necessity of the
state," the "multiplicity" of its functions, and its "territorial centrality" (Mann, 1984:195–201). For Mann, the necessity of the state is a
historical fact. Simple historical observation shows that throughout
history no complex civilized societies existed without a center of
binding rule-making authority whose function is to implement rules
and regulations necessary to create order and social cohesion. In
addition, throughout history, complex societies have existed—and
still do exist—in a multistate civilization, which makes necessary the
creation of certain rules of conduct, especially with regard to the
protection of life and property, and requires the establishment and
maintenance of a monopolistic organization that has been the
province of the state. For this reason "necessity," claims Mann, is
"the mother of state power."

The second way in which the state appropriates power depends
upon the multiplicity of state functions: from the maintenance of
internal order, military defense, and aggression, to the maintenance
of infrastructures and economic distribution (which has both domestic and international dimensions). Mann has suggested that such
functions lead the state to be involved in a multiplicity of relations
with collective actors, which requires it to perform multiple maneu-
vers—and it is its maneuvering ability that constitutes "the birth-
place of state power."

The third basis for state power derives from the territorial centrality of the state. The reason Mann has attributed significance to

the territorially centralized nature of the state is twofold. On the one hand, it provides a theoretical basis for Mann to criticize the society-centric understanding of the relative autonomy of the state vis-à-vis social classes and groups. On the other hand, it allows Mann to conceptualize state autonomy and state power within the context of geopolitics.

Consequently, Mann has suggested that together the necessity, multiplicity, and territorial centrality of the state account for its autonomous power. By these means, the state possesses an independence from civil society and behaves as an actor with a will to power. Mann's suggestion, then, involves: (1) a critique of the society-centric model that derives state autonomy from "the means of power used in all social relations"; (2) the modification of the state-centric model by elaborating the way in which the state acquires a potential autonomy; and (3) the explanation of state power in terms of its sociospatial and organizational nature.

The Nation-State and Modernity

Anthony Giddens, in his book *The Nation-State and Violence* (1987b), has provided an institutional understanding of the state (founded on the theory of modernity), that, according to him, is also a precondition for an analysis of "power." Central to Giddens's view of modernity is his interpretation of history as a nonevolutionary process involving a number of "discontinuities." Modernity is a "discontinuist interpretation of modern history," which emphasizes the contrast between traditional and modern social formations as well as divergences and ruptures within the modernizing process (Giddens, 1987b:31).

Giddens shares with Mann the view that any theoretical position that reduces the components of society to a single factor has to be rejected. The modern world, Giddens has suggested, has been shaped through the intersection of capitalism, industrialism, and the nation-state system. Each component, although interrelated, has its own dynamics and history:

> There are four institutional clusterings associated with modernity: heightened surveillance, capitalistic enterprise, industrial production and the consolidation of centralized control of the means of violence. None is wholly reducible to any of the others. (Giddens, 1987b:5)

Giddens has proposed that each component of modernity con-

stitutes "an institutional clustering" that refers to both organizational and institutional dimensions of a location. A location has an institutional characteristic containing certain practices that have the
greatest time-space extension within social totalities. It acquires an
organizational capacity as it possesses an ability to use reflexively
knowledge about the conditions of system reproduction "to influence, shape or modify that system reproduction" (Giddens,
1987b:12). The nation-state is, for example, an institutional clustering
whose actions involve both an expression of its time-space extension
and its ability to produce effects in the process of the reproduction
of the system as a whole.

To account for both the specificity and the relational nature of
the institutional clusterings of modern society, Giddens has made
two crucial theoretical distinctions. The first concerns the sources of
power and the second the concept of history. Like Mann, Giddens
has considered the institutional clusterings to be both "configurations of power" and forms of domination. Power, however, is
defined as a "transformative capacity": "the capability to intervene
in a given set of events so as in some way to alter them" (Giddens,
1987b:7). To be a social agent is to have power, that is, to have a
transformative capacity. The transformative capacity derives from
the resources that agents employ in the course of their activities.
Such resources are both "allocative" and "authoritative." Allocative
resources refer to "dominion over material facilities, including material goods and the natural forces that may be harnessed in their production." Authoritative resources, on the other hand, concern "the
means of dominion over the activities of human beings themselves"
(Giddens, 1987b:168).

Giddens has suggested that these resources have to be distinguished because giving primacy to the former, which classical social
theory and Marxist discourse tend to do, creates a reductionist
image of society. Reductionism occurs when state power is deduced
from actions of agents based on allocative resources, which
inevitably ignores the fact that state power stems to a large extent
from the authoritative resources. Taking the allocative resources as
the prime mover for modernity implies overestimating the role of
capitalism and industrialization in the process of shaping modern
society. Such estimates necessarily fail to recognize the importance
of interactions between competing sovereign nation-states in that
process. For this reason, Giddens has argued that it is important to
explore the reciprocal interactions between allocative and authoritative resources, and among the three institutional clusterings of the
modern world, making none the prime mover of history.

As for the concept of history, Giddens has pointed out the significance of distinguishing industrialization from capitalism. For Giddens, industrialization refers to a process of controlling or dominating the natural world, whereas capitalism constitutes a specific mode of production. This distinction led Giddens to suggest that "the emergence of modern capitalism [as a specific mode of production] does not represent the high point of a progressive scheme of social development, but rather the coming of a type of society radically different from all prior forms of social order" (Giddens, 1987b:31–32). This society is a capitalist society that has a nation-state that indicates its sovereign character. Recognizing that modern society is a capitalist society that is also a nation-state thus allows Giddens both to emphasize the discontinuous character of history and to elevate the nation-state to the forefront of the analysis of modernity.

Having established the basic parameters of his understanding of modernity—the discontinuous interpretation of history, institutional power configurations, and the nation-state as an institutional cluster—Giddens has concentrated his attention on the question of the nation-state. Jessop has summarized accurately the principle features of Giddens's account of the nation-state in the following way:

> For Giddens the rise of the modern state is associated with (a) a centralized legal order, (b) centralized administration, (c) a centrally organized taxation system, articulated with a rational monetary system, (d) major innovations in military organization reflected in the international state system and the separation of external military force from internal policing, (e) the development of the modern nation in conjunction with the nation-state, (f) the development of communication, information, and surveillance possibilities, (g) internal pacification through the disciplinary society, and (h) the development of democracy in the sense of a pluralistic polyarchy and citizenship rights—as the reciprocal of the enhanced surveillance and the ideology of the general interest involved in the modern state. (Jessop, 1986:216)

Among the above-listed features, (a), (b), and (c) refer to the territorial centrality of the nation-state and illuminate why a capitalist society is also a nation-state. Feature (d) indicates the significance of the international context for the development of the nation-state system; and (e), (f), (g), and (h) concern the effective techniques that the nation-state employs in its involvement in the process of reproduction of its own national and territorially organized social formation. Thus, Giddens shares Skocpol and Mann's view of the state. By the state, Giddens means an impersonal and sovereign political order capable of administering and controlling a given territory. The state constitutes a sovereign political order with the capability of having sufficient primacy over social classes and collectivities on the one hand, and of possessing sufficient power to monitor societal affairs through its surveillance techniques.[11]

This power of the state—here Giddens also agrees with Skocpol and Mann—stems to a large extent from the international dimension of state action. For Giddens, both the global consolidation of industrial capitalism and the global ascendency of the nation-state are processes that are intertwined but not reducible to each other. It would be a mistake to conflate them, as world-systems theory has done. Each component has to be analyzed separately.

That said, Giddens has made two propositions as to how to think of the interstate system. The first is that nation-states exist only in systemic relations with other nation-states. This means that international relations is coequal with the origins of nation-states. The second is that the internal administrative coordination of nation-states depends upon "reflexively monitored conditions of an international nature" (Giddens, 1987b:4). This proposition is important for Giddens to establish a link between domestic politics and international politics. Giddens establishes such a link both by placing a special emphasis on the ability of the state to influence domestic policy and by locating the nation-state as well as the interstate system in an institutional conception of modernity. This is where Giddens's contribution to the state-centric model lies.

Conclusion: Bringing (Civil) Society Back In

The foregoing discussion of the state-centric model implies (1) the rediscovery of the state through the critique of the society-centric model, (2) the attribution of a separate and independent space to the state, and (3) the significance of both domestic and international dimensions to the autonomy of state action. At an epistemological level, these claims amount to (4) the reintroduction of the category of agency and the construction of an agency *problematique.* In what follows, these four central aspects of the model are critically assessed. It is argued that each aspect, although an important contribution to international relations theory, reveals what can be called "the institutionalist essentialist nature" of the state-centric model. Such essentialism, it is shown, results from the failure to recognize the relational character of the state–civil society distinction, and the accordance of "primacy" to agency over structure.

The Rediscovery of the State

The state-centric model's attempt to reintroduce the state to contemporary social theory involves:

1. considering the state to be a potentially autonomous actor;
2. analyzing the state through a historically grounded comparative method;
3. regarding internal organizational factors and international relations (the inter-state system) as codeterminants of state action;
4. viewing society as an intersection of a number of power networks in which the primary one is the political power exercised by the state; and
5. locating the question of the state within a comprehensive account of modernity.

It is on the basis of these elements that the state-centric model can be said to have provided useful epistemological and analytical categories for the study of states. Although its rediscovery of the state must therefore be welcomed, the fact that such rediscovery gives rise to the construction of a distinct statist mode of reasoning reveals the essentialist nature of the model in a number of ways.

In constructing their own statist mode of reasoning, Skocpol, Halliday, Mann, and Giddens make two crucial assertions. The first is that the state-centric model, as opposed to the society-centric model, adequately explains the process of reproduction and the role of the state within it. However, in doing so, the model hardly touches on the connection between capitalist structuring and restructuring of the economic and the nation-state (the political). Although the model argues that the institutional development of modern societies happens to be capitalist and that the nation-state is a state articulated with capitalism, it does not attempt to explore and account for how such an articulation has occurred in these societies.[12] Instead, the model focuses on the state and its impact on the development of capitalism as a mode of production. Thus, Skocpol has suggested that the state, under certain circumstances, shapes and reshapes social relations.[13] Mann, while recognizing the irreducible character of power networks, has accorded primacy to the political power network. Likewise, Giddens has regarded the nation-state not only as a major institution, but also as the defining and integrating institution of modern societies. Hence, at the level of methodology, the political becomes the primary concern at the expense of the economic, which results in the emergence of the problem of political reductionism in the state-centric model.

Political struggles are not reducible to economic factors. Nevertheless, they cannot exist alone in the absence of economic practices (among others). This means that political struggles are always articulated with economic factors and discursive practices within a society, which can be understood only as historically changing through a complex interrelationship with the state. For this reason, if the state and its power are to be examined adequately, society has to be taken into account insofar as it constitutes a context for structural limitations on state capacities. Focusing on the operation of the political, or on political struggles in and of themselves without due reference to the historical and social context in which they are initiated, inevitably reduces the complex character of the process of reproduction to state capacities.

For instance, Giddens correctly has defined modern societies as capitalist societies but has not given enough consideration to the role of the state in the expanded reproduction of capitalism. Mann has pointed out the importance of the infrastructural power sources of the modern state for its autonomous power, but has failed to see the connection between the state and the expanded reproduction of capitalism. When the economy is taken into account, it is considered a situation in which the political is primary. Of course, to criticize the state-centric model for ignoring the welfare dimension of the nation-state does not mean to give primacy to the question of the expanded reproduction of capitalism. What it means is to stress the significance of linking capitalism and the nation-state at the level of both the national and the international. More importantly, it means to think of society in relational terms. As such, society is not an expressive or structural totality (as in the case of the society-centric model), nor is it an economic/cultural sphere whose condition of existence is shaped and reshaped by the state (as in the case of the state-centric model), but rather it is a relational totality whose mode of operation is codetermined by an articulation of political, economic, and cultural/discursive practices. Contrary to the state-centric model, thinking of society as a relational totality allows for an understanding of modern societies as capitalist societies with a nation-state, as Giddens correctly has suggested, without taking a reductionist stance.

The second assertion concerns the definition of the state. Skocpol has defined the state as an institutional actor that has its own life and history. In the course of its construction, this definition has three basic assumptions: (1) that the state contains a true essence, a homogeneous structure; (2) that the state acquires the capacity to act; and (3) that state managers, or in Giddens's terminology the governing class, are able to form the state's policy and therefore constitute the personification of the state's capacities and powers. Two suggestions follow from these assumptions: that political power should be regarded as independent organizational power specific to the state, and that it is the state that secures the process of reproduction. That is to say, it is possible and proper to read the constitution of social and political-economic relations and their reproduction via an analysis of the state. These two suggestions together not only reinforce the problem of political reductionism, but also render the model an institutionally essentialist one.

Viewed within the context of the definition of the state as an institutional agency, state managers, or the governing class, are referred to as "historical subjects" able to constitute their own realm of existence. They also appear to act independently in their implementation of state policies. This means that the bureaucratic structures and administrative arrangements exist independently of class contradictions, political controversies, and ideological struggles. Such structures and arrangements are considered to have been constituted by a set of rules and procedures. However, the implication of such a consideration is to take the state as an unproblematic given, or, in other words, to reduce it to one of its multiple determinations—in particular, the institutional organization of the state. By ignoring the importance of social classes, struggles initiated by social movements against the existing order that the state tries to secure, and the concrete ramifications of the expanded reproduction of capital, the state-centric model's attempt to specify the functioning of the political with its institutional definition again becomes subject to political reductionism.

The problem of reductionism gives rise to the emergence in the state-centric model of institutional essentialism, as the state is used to account for the process of reproduction. As has been noted, one of the principal aims of the state-centric model is to provide a reading of the functioning of social formations through its concept of the state as an institutional agency. At the level of epistemology, its aim to do so implies the call for a return to agency, or a reintroduction of agency in the structure/agency dialectic. However, the resolution of the structure/agency problem is based on the primacy of the agent (the state) over the structure, which is as essentialist as the structuralist *problematique*. As implied in its title, the state-centric model takes the state as the center of its mode of operation, makes it a privileged category by according political power primacy over the other forms of power, and then employs it to read social relations without giving any consideration to constraining factors other than political and military ones.

Here the point is not that the theory of the state cannot constitute a way of accounting for the process of reproduction. Rather, it is that the model becomes essentialist when such a theory is postulated as "the way" of doing so. The problem of essentialism, combined with political reductionism, inevitably prevents the state-centric model from recognizing the impact of structural limitations, apart from geopolitics, on state policies—limitations that are of significance in the constitution of modern society as a capitalist society. To argue that state policies should be regarded as a site of multiple determinations and structural limitations is not necessarily to affirm the structuralist understanding of modern society and international relations. Instead it reaffirms, on the one hand, the utility of truly considering the state within the context of the structure/agency problem (Wendt, 1992a); on the other hand, it reaffirms the view of the state not only as a potentially autonomous institutional agency, but also as a "site" where condensation of political forces takes place. However, in order to view the state in this manner, it is necessary to embed the state in society as a relational totality, rather than drawing a false distinction between the state and society (Jessop, 1990:287–288).

The Independent Spatial Organization of the State

Given the fact that in recent years the problem of the state–civil society distinction has been revitalized within the realm of political sociology, the state-centric model's designation of the state as a separate and independent space appears to be important. However, it proves unsatisfactory due precisely to the fact that it is not only purely analytical but it also derives from a false dichotomy drawn between the state and society. This prevents the model from problematizing the relationship between the state and civil society.

The state–civil society distinction can be said to have been rediscovered in the realm of political sociology in general, and of European politics and social theory in particular. In the course of its rediscovery, as John Keane has observed correctly, three particular points of reference emerged in which the usefulness of the distinction was examined (Keane, 1988:4). These points of reference are the analytical relevance of the distinction, its normative significance, and its political potential. In Civil Society and the State, Keane has suggested that each point of reference also constitutes a distinct object of inquiry. The analytical distinction between the state and civil society involves a specific aim, which is to examine the origins, development, and transformation of particular institutions. It therefore attempts to

> selectively identify key institutions and actors, examine their complex patterns of interaction and attempt to reach some conclusions—based on theoretical distinctions, empirical research and informed judgements—concerning their origins, in that it is concerned only with constructing an explanatory understanding of complex socio-political realities. (Keane, 1988:14)

The normative usage of the distinction, on the contrary, concerns the preservation of democracy, and it has two complementary normative functions—a precautionary function and an advocacy function. It is used to show the possible undesirable consequences of the separation of the state and civil society as in the analysis of both the totalitarian and the authoritarian political regimes. According to Keane, this "precautionary function" does not lead to the rejection of the distinction, but instead "it supplements its advocacy function which consists in normative efforts to highlight the need for (greater) pluralism in the distribution of social and political power" (Keane, 1988:28). This normative usage therefore aims to promote critical understanding. On the other hand, the political usage of the distinction, although associated with the normative usage, presents a unique approach, given its focus on the political implications of the distinction and its historical time. It is intended to problematize the historical context in which the distinction has been revitalized. This historical context is often characterized as a late capitalist, postmodern condition articulated with the crisis of the welfare state, the rise of social movements, the emergence of neoconservatism, and the crisis and restructuring of international capitalism.

Of these usages of the state–civil society distinction, the one with which the state-centric model is concerned is the analytical one. It seeks to shed light on the analytical relevance of the distinction by focusing exclusively on the state. It is true that the distinction between the state and civil society has an analytical relevance for the theory of the state. However, it is equally true that its relevance to the problem of civil society is more complex than it suggests. The state-centric model underestimates the complexity inherent in civil society by ignoring the dynamic and relational character of it, which arises from its spatial organization based on class and nonclass political struggles and calculations. If society is to be regarded as a formation that is historically emergent, nonunitary, and constituted, then categories that have been developed to analyze the constitution of such a formation have to be political as much as they are analytic.

Keane has described the complex character of civil society in the following way:

> The rise and maturation of capitalism has not been synonymous with the universal influence of commodity production and exchange, the irreversible destruction of "community life", the general spread of class materialism and possessive individualism, or the growth of class conflict as the central social conflict. At one time or another, modern civil societies have comprised not only capitalist economies but an eclectic variety of non-economic organizations. Modern civil societies have comprised a constellation of juxtaposed and changing elements that resist reduction to a common denominator, or essential core or generative first principle. They have included capitalist economies and households: social movements and voluntary public spheres (churches, organizations of professionals and independent communications media and cultural institutions); political parties, electoral associations and other "gatekeepers" of the state-civil society division; as well as "disciplinary" institutions such as schools, hospitals, asylums and prisons. (Keane, 1988:9–20)

Keane's description of civil society indicates the importance of political calculations insofar as it emphasizes both the organizational principles of civil society and political struggles embedded within these principles. Two points are worth emphasizing here. First, to recognize the complexity inherent in the organization of civil society means also to employ a more complex definition of politics than the state-centric model provides. As we have seen, Skocpol, Halliday, Mann, and, to a large extent, Giddens tend to associate political power with state power, to consider politics in terms of the conventional definition of civil society, and to conceive of class power as an economic power. However, politics contains struggles over structures of meaning as well as over the process of construction of collective identities, both class and nonclass. Neither of these is reducible to economic phenomena. Political struggle in this sense is not only economic or political (state power), but also ideological and discursive. To reduce political (class or nonclass) struggles to economic phenomena in order to determine the location of the state is to deny the significance of the discursive and ideological character of those struggles, which, in fact, constitute the very complexity of civil society as a relational totality (Keyman and Jenson, 1990; Cohen and Arato, 1992).

Second, that the relationship between power and politics is crucial to the problematization of the state–civil society distinction requires a relational and a nonmonolithic conception of power. The state-centric model, however, fails to provide one. As we have pointed out, Mann and Giddens explicitly have stated that society is constituted by networks of power relations. It is, without doubt, important to conceive of modern society in terms of power relations. But it is equally important to take into account the question of the resistance to power to understand both the relational character of power and the dynamic nature of the state–civil society relationship. Neither Mann nor Giddens has provided an account of the resistance to power, and, as a result, their conception of power becomes one-sided: the power of the state to regulate and control civil societal affairs.

Thus, by employing only the analytical usage of the state–civil society distinction, the state-centric model not only ignores the relational character of that distinction, but also makes use of it by regarding the former as the determinant of the latter. Civil society is subordinated to the state, its historicity is completely neglected, and more importantly it is not integrated into the process of theorizing state action and state power. Consequently, the state becomes the essence of the analysis of modern societies, functions as a historical idealization of those societies, and also creates its own history by acting as an independent spatial organization.

The Significance of Both Domestic and International Dimensions of State Action

Perhaps the most important contribution of the state-centric model to the development of the theory of the state is its focus on the international dimension of state action. The international dimension is crucial for two reasons. First, the existence of international relations was integral to the process of the very constitution of the modern state as the nation-state. It is argued by the state-centric model that both Marxist and liberal discourses fail to comprehend that the state is a nation-state. The former, by concerning itself almost exclusively with the role of the state in the process of the reproduction of capitalist social relations, fails to situate its national focus. The latter, when the national focus is investigated at all, defines it in historical and cultural terms.[14] Consequently, both discourses fail to recognize the institutional basis of the nation-state system (the international context) that makes central the territoriality of the state.

Second, the international dimension gives the nation-state specificity. The formation of the nation-state has its own history and institutional organization, which cannot be reduced to the emergence of the capitalist mode of production, although its development is obviously connected with the spread of capitalism. Thus, the state-centric model asserts that the nation-state system predates capitalism and constitutes what can be called the geopolitical transnational reality, which marks the international dimension of state action— one of the primary sources of the autonomous power of the nation- state.

By recognizing the significance of the geopolitical transnational reality, Skocpol has argued that the nation-state is an organization for itself and represents an analytically autonomous level of transna- tional reality—independent in its structure and dynamics from world capitalism, but not reducible to it. Halliday follows Skocpol's argument in his suggestion that a theory of the state constructed through the recognition of its historical and spatial specificity is needed if international relations theory is to be advanced. In the same vein, Giddens has suggested that the nation-state system is a primary set of processes in which the world geopolitical order enjoys ontological parity. Mann appears to agree with Giddens that the nation-state's relation to capitalism is "contingent"; there is nothing in the capitalist mode of production that requires a multi- state system. Thus, the nation-state cannot be treated as a single unity. It represents a duality insofar as its domestic life is separable from its geopolitics. And it is its geopolitics that reproduces and even increases its autonomy and its autonomous power.

Of course, the state-centric model's attempt to place a special emphasis on the reciprocal relation of constitution between nation- states and the contemporary world system is important for the study of the state and of international relations. As for the latter, it illumi- nates why it is necessary to conceptualize the state rather than take it as a given ontological reality. The reciprocity between the nation- state as the state of a modern-capitalist society and the constitution of international relations marks the coming into existence of discon- tinuity in the course of historical developments of societies as well as international relations. It also demonstrates why it is important to consider the latter as a set of geopolitical, economic, and social processes that affect the constitution of national social formations.

In this sense, the state-centric model can be said to provide a reading of international relations based on the concept of the nation- state as an institutional sociospatial organization. In doing so, it takes as its unit of analysis a national social formation; deals with it in a nonstructuralist manner; and concentrates its attention on the structure, capacities, power, and policies of the state in that forma- tion. Thus it offers an account of international relations by defining it as an inter-(nation)-state system.

However, the structure of international relations is so complex that it cannot be reduced to interstate relations. It is important indeed to take seriously the question of how to conceptualize the state in order to advance our understanding of international relations. This should not lead one to read off its functioning with reference only to the interactions between nation-states. For instance, the construction of the post–World War II world order cannot be said to have been simply geopolitical, and therefore based on the primacy of the interstate system. Such construction had as its economic basis a specific regime of accumulation, Fordism, and functioned as a compromise of embedded liberalism. This meant the regulation of specific industrialization policies, namely Keynesianism and welfare states in national markets (especially within the context of European societies), and liberal internationalism in the world economy. Such regulation, however, cannot be reduced to the interstate system, nor can it be seen as secondary to geopolitics.

Likewise, the ideological forms and discursive practices that play a significant role in the process of the construction and reproduction of the world order cannot be said to have been created only by nation-states. International organizations were also integral to the reproduction of that order under U.S. hegemonic leadership. It is through and within these organizations that the basic ideologies and discursive norms of the world order were produced and presented as universal (Cox, 1981:238–241). In other words, even though geopolitics constitutes one of the defining features of global relations, it cannot be used as the foundation for those relations.

Although it is necessary to think of the state as a theoretical construct that should not be simply derived from structural determinants, this should not lead one to take the state as the basic unit of analysis or the center of an analysis of those relations. But the state-centric model does so, and as a result it ignores the importance of global economic relations and ideological/discursive practices for the analysis not only of geopolitics but also of the international dimension of state action. The state-centric model's attempt to incorporate the international dimension into the theory of the state, which undoubtedly constitutes the model's most important contribution to contemporary political discourse, therefore becomes subject to the problem of reductionism.

Thus, going back to Halliday's proposal that a theory of the state is necessary in order to overcome the impasse that international relations theory has reached, it can be concluded here that it would be a mistake to do so by incorporating the state-centric model, which operates with a statist image of international relations and an essentialist conception of the state. If it is to be used to overcome an impasse, what is at stake is not international relations theory, but the realist paradigm and the impasse it has reached. Indeed, the significance of the state-centric model and its agency *problematique* to international relations theory lies in its contribution to realism, that is, in its ability to provide a thorough historical and theoretical account of the state and the interstate system.

Finally, the foregoing critical examination of the state-centric model indicates that the process of theorizing and studying the state(s) should be embedded in an understanding of society as a relational totality. This enables one to analyze state-society interactions without reducing one to the other, and without falling into false dichotomies, while recognizing the specificity and centrality of the state without privileging it.

Notes

1. This solution has been proposed first by Halliday (1987b), and followed by Jarvis (1989) and Linklater (1986, 1990). The need for taking the rediscovery of the state seriously has also been expressed by Higgott (1988) and Rosenberg (1990).

2. This argument has been made within the context of the general perception of international relations theory as being dominated by the realist paradigm. See Walker (1984, 1989), Higgott (1988), and Ashley (1989).

3. See Skocpol (1979); Evans, Rueschemeyer, and Skocpol (1985); Giddens (1987b); and Mann (1984, 1986).

4. For a detailed discussion of these theories, see Carnoy (1984) and Jessop (1982).

5. Each of these authors provides a distinctive critique of theories of the state. Despite differences, however, all three can be said to offer a state-centric alternative that aims at elevating the concept of the state to the center of contemporary political discourse. The state-centric model also involves corporatist and neoinstitutionalist theories of the state. For a detailed discussion and critique of these theories, see McLennan (1989) and Therborn (1986).

6. The society-centric model involves all theories of the state, whether liberal or Marxist. Yet, the structuralist theories of the state, especially the one developed by Poulantzas, constitute the basic target of the state-centric model.

7. For the concept of essentialism, see Derrida (1978), and Laclau and Mouffe (1985). In international relations theory, the concept was used by Ashley (1989) and Walker (1989) to characterize the realist paradigm.

8. This point has also been made by Held (1984).

9. Here Halliday's targets are realism in both its traditional and contemporary forms: structural realism and modified structural realism and Marxist political discourse in world-systems theory and structuralism, especially the Poulantzasian version of the theory of the state.

10. Likewise, Jarvis (1989), Rosenberg (1990), and Linklater (1986, 1990) have thought of Mann and Giddens as integral to the agency *problematique* (based on a historical sociological account of states, societies, and geopolitics).

11. This conception of the state appears to be one based on the

Weberian idea of the state complemented by the conception of disciplinary society developed by Foucault (1977).

12. The post–World War II world order had a specific economic basis, which was also one of the defining features of U.S. hegemony. The compromise of embedded liberalism, or the Fordist regime of accumulation and its extension, were the concepts with which such basis was identified. Nowhere in the state-centric model is attention paid to the economic foundation of the interstate system in that order. For a detailed account of post–World War II world order, see Lipietz (1987), Gilpin (1987), and Boyer (1990).

13. It should be pointed out here that Skocpol's account of the ability of the state to reshape social relations involves considering the state-economy relations. Her analysis of the New Deal exemplifies this. However, her analysis privileges the state over the economic, in that the latter is read off by the former.

14. This critique of the Marxist and liberal discourses has been made explicitly by Mann and Giddens. For them, the institutional conception of nation also makes it clear that the territorial dimension constitutes one of the defining features of the state and its sovereign power. For details, see Mann (1986) and Giddens (1987a, 1987b).

Bibliography

Adorno, T. W. (1973) *Negative Dialectics.* New York: Seabury Press.

Alcoff, L. (1988) "Cultural Feminism Versus Post-Structuralism: The Identity Crisis in Feminist Theory," *Signs* 13:3.

Alker, H., and T. Biersteker (1984) "The Dialectics of World Order: Notes for Some Future Archaeologist of International Savoir Faire," *International Studies Quarterly* 28:2 (June).

Allmen, E., O. Cass, I. Kaprielian, H. Moussa, and L. Ricciutelli. (1989) "Editorial," *Canadian Women's Studies* (Special Issue on Refugee Women) 10:1.

Amina, M. (1984) "Black Women, the Economic Crisis and the British State," *Feminist Review* 17.

Apter, D. E. (1987) *Rethinking Development: Modernization, Dependency, and Postmodern Politics.* Newbury Park, Calif.: Sage.

As, B. (1982) "A Materialist View of Men's and Women's Attitudes to War," *Women's Studies International Forum* 5:3/4.

Ashley, R. K. (1981) "Political Realism and Human Interests," *International Studies Quarterly* 25:2 (June).

Ashley, R. K. (1983) "Three Modes of Economism," *International Studies Quarterly* 27:4.

Ashley, R. K. (1984) "The Poverty of Neo-Realism," *International Organization* 38:2 (Spring).

Ashley, R. K. (1987) "The Geopolitics of Geopolitical Space: Toward a Critical Social Theory of International Politics," *Alternatives* 12.

Ashley, R. K. (1988) "Untying the Sovereign State: A Double Reading of the Anarchy Problematique," *Millennium* 13.

Ashley, R. K. (1989) "Living on the Borderlines: Man, Poststructuralism and War," in J. Der Derian and M. Shapiro, eds., *International/Intertextual Relations.* Lexington, Mass.: Lexington Books.

Ashley, R. K., and R. B. J. Walker (1990) "Reading Dissidence/Writing the Discipline: Crisis and the Question of Sovereignty in International Studies," *International Studies Quarterly* 34:3.

Baldwin, D. A. (1979) "Power Analysis and World Politics: New Trends Versus Old Tendencies," *World Politics* 31:2.

Banks, M. (1985a) "The Inter-Paradigm Debate," in M. Light & A. J. R. Groom, eds., *International Relations: A Handbook of Current Theory.* London: Pinter.

Banks, M. (1985b) "Where Are We Now?" *Review of International Studies* 11.

Bannerji, H. (1991) "But Who Speaks for Us?" in H. Bannerji, L. Carty, K. Delhi, S. Heald, and K. McKenna, eds., *Unsettling Relations: The University as a Site of Feminist Struggles.* Toronto: Women's Press.

Barfield, C., Jr. (1990) "Commetary," in J. Bhagwati and H. T. Patrick, eds., *Aggressive Unilateralism: America's 301 Trade Policy and the World Trading System.* Ann Arbor: The University of Michigan Press.

Barrett, M. (1985) *Women's Oppression Today: Problems in Marxist Feminist Analysis.* London: Verso.

Baucus, Max (1989) "A New Trade Strategy: The Case for Bilateral Trade Agreements," *Cornell International Law Journal* 22:1 (Winter).

Bell, D. (1976) *The Cultural Contradictions of Capitalism.* New York: Basic Books.

Bello, J. H., and A. F. Holmer (1990) "The Heart of the 1988 Trade Act: A Legislative History of the Amendments to Section 301," in J. Bhagwati and H. T. Patrick, eds., *Aggressive Unilateralism: America's 301 Trade Policy and the World Trading System.* Ann Arbor: The University of Michigan Press.

Ben-Dor, G. (1983) *State and Conflict in the Middle East.* New York: Praeger.

Ben-Dor, G., and D. Dewitt, eds. (1987) *Conflict Management in the Middle East.* Lexington, Mass.: Lexington Books.

Bentley, A. F. (1967) *The Process of Government.* Cambridge, Mass.: Belknap.

Bernstein, R. (1985) *Beyond Objectivism and Relativism: Science, Hermeneutics, and Praxis.* Philadelphia: University of Pennsylvania Press.

Best, S., and D. Kellner (1991) *Post-Modern Theory: Critical Interrogations.* New York: Guilford Press.

Bhagwati, J. (1988) *Protectionism.* Cambridge, Mass.: MIT Press.

Bhagwati, J. (1990) "Aggressive Unilateralism: An Overview," in J. Bhagwati and H. T. Patrick, eds., *Aggressive Unilateralism: America's 301 Trade Policy and the World Trading System.* Ann Arbor: The University of Michigan Press.

Bhagwati, J. N., and D. A. Irwin (1987) "The Return of Reciprocitarians— U.S. Trade Policy Today," *The World Economy* 10:2 (June).

Bhavnani, K.-K., and M. Coulson (1984) "Transforming Socialist-Feminism: The Challenge of Racism," *Feminist Review* 23.

Biersteker, T. J. (1989) "Critical Reflections on Post-Positivism in International Relations," *International Studies Quarterly* 33:3.

Binder, L., J. S. Coleman, J. LaPalombara, L. W. Pye, S. Verba, and M. Wiener (1971) *Crises and Sequences in Political Development.* Princeton, N.J.: Princeton University Press.

Binder, L. (1986) "The Natural History of Development Theory," *Comparative Studies of Society and History* 7.

Blair, J. (1977) *The Control of Oil.* New York: Vintage.

Boulding, E. (1981) "Perspectives of Women Researchers on Disarmament, National Security and World Order," *Women's Studies International Quarterly* 4:1.

Boyer, R. (1990) *The Regulation School: A Critical Introduction.* New York: Columbia University Press.

Brah, A. (1991) "Difference, Diversity, Differentiation," *International Review of Sociology* 2.

Bulbeck, C. (1988) *One World Women's Movement*. London: Pluto Press.

Buzan, B. (1987) *An Introduction to Strategic Studies: Military Technology and International Relations*. London: Macmillan.

Caporosa, J. A., ed. (1989) *The Elusive State*. London: Sage Publications.

Carby, H. (1982) "White Woman Listen! Black Feminism and the Boundaries of Sisterhood," *Empire Strikes Back: Race and Racism in 70s Britain*. London: Hutchinson.

Carnoy, M. (1984) *The State and Political Theory*. Princeton, N.J.: Princeton University Press.

Carr, E. H. (1939) *The Twenty Years' Crisis*. London: Macmillan.

Chalmers, A. F. (1982) *What Is This Thing Called Science?* 2nd ed. St. Lucia, Queensland: University of Queensland Press.

Cohen, J. L., and A. Arato (1992) *Civil Society and Political Theory*. Cambridge, Mass.: MIT Press.

Collins, P. (1989) "The Social Construction of Black Feminist Thought," *Signs* 14:4.

Connolly, W. E. (1974) "Theoretical Self-Consciousness," in W. Connolly and G. Gordon, eds., *Social Structure and Political Theory*. London: D.C. Heath.

Connolly, W. E. (1984) "Introduction: Legitimacy and Modernity," in W. Connolly, ed., *Legitimacy and the State*. New York: New York University Press.

Connolly, W. E. (1988) *Political Theory and Modernity*. Oxford: Basil Blackwell Ltd.

Connolly, W. E. (1991) *Identity/Difference: Democratic Negotiations of Political Paradox*. Ithaca, N.Y.: Cornell University Press.

Connor, W. (1978) "A Nation Is a Notion, Is a State, Is an Ethnic Group, Is a . . . ," *Ethnic and Racial Studies* 1:4 (October).

Cooper, R. N. (1968) *The Economics of Interdependence*. New York: McGraw-Hill.

Cowhey, P., and E. Long (1983) "Testing Theories of Regime Change: Hegemonic Decline or Surplus Capacity?" *International Organization* 37:2 (Spring).

Cox, R. W. (1977) "Labour and Hegemony," *International Organization* 31:3 (Summer).

Cox, R. W. (1981) "Social Forces, States and World Orders: Beyond International Relations Theory," *Millennium* 10:2.

Cox, R. W. (1982) "Production and Hegemony: Toward a Political Economy of World Order," in H. K. Jacobsen and D. Sidjanski, eds., *The Emerging International Economic Order: Dynamic Processes, Constraints and Opportunities*. Beverly Hills: Sage Publications.

Cox, R. W. (1983) "Gramsci, Hegemony, and International Relations: An Essay in Method," *Millennium* 12:2.

Cox, R. W. (1986) "Social Forces, States and World Order: Beyond International Relations Theory," in R. Keohane, ed., *Neorealism and Its Critics*. New York: Columbia University Press.

Cox, R. W. (1987) *Production, Power and World Order: Social Forces in the Making of History*. New York: Columbia University Press.

Cox, R. W. (1992) "Multilateralism and World Order," *Review of International Studies* 18:2 (April).

Croll, E. (1981a) "Women in Rural Production and Reproduction in the Soviet Union, China, Cuba and Tanzania: Case Studies," *Signs* 7:2.

Croll, E. (1981b) "Women in Rural Production and Reproduction in the Soviet Union, China, Cuba and Tanzania: Socialist Development Experiences," *Signs* 7:2.

Currie, D., and H. Kazi (1987) "Academic Feminism and the Process of De-Radicalization: Re-Examinining the Issues," *Feminist Review* 26.

Czempiel, E.-O., and J. N. Rosenau, eds. (1989) *Global Problems and Theoretical Challenges*. Lexington, Mass.: Lexington Books.

Davis, A. (1981) *Women, Race and Class*. New York: Vintage.

Der Derian, J. (1989) "Spy Versus Spy: The Intertextual Power of International Intrigue," in J. Der Derian and M. J. Shapiro, eds., *International/Intertextual Relations*. Lexington, Mass.: Lexington Books.

Der Derian, J., and M. J. Shapiro, eds. (1989) *International/Intertextual Relations*. Lexington, Mass.: Lexington Books.

deReuck, A. (1984) "The Logic of Conflict: Its Origins, Development and Resolution," in M. Banks, ed., *Conflicts in World Society*. Brighton, Sussex: Harvester.

Derrida, J. (1978) *Writing and Difference*. Chicago: University of Chicago Press.

Derrida, J. (1984) "No Apocalypse, Not Now (Full Speed Ahead, Seven Missiles, Seven Missives)," *Diacritics* (Summer).

Dessler, D. (1989) "What's at Stake in the Agent-Structure Debate?" *International Organization* 43:3.

Dill, B. T. (1979) "The Dialectics of Black Womanhood," *Signs* 4:3 (Spring).

Drake, W. J., and K. Nicolaïdis (1992) "Ideas, Interests, and Institutionalization: 'Trade in Services' and the Uruguay Round," *International Organization* 46:1 (Winter).

Duley, M. I., and S. Diduk (1986) "Women, Colonialism and Development," in M. I. Duley and M. I. Edwards, eds., *The Cross-Cultural Study of Women*. New York: The Feminist Press.

Dullforce, W. (1989) "U.S. Unveils Plan to Liberalise Trade in Services," *Financial Times* (October).

Dullforce, W. (1990) "EC Commits Itself to Liberalising Trade in Services," *Financial Times* (December).

Easton, D. (1971) "The New Revolution in Political Science," in D. Easton, ed., *The Political System: An Inquiry into the State of Political Science*, 2nd ed. New York: Alfred A. Knopf.

Enloe, C. (1989) *Bananas, Beaches and Bases: Making Feminist Sense of International Politics*. London: Pandora Press.

Evans, P. B., D. Rueschemeyer, and T. Skocpol, eds. (1985) *Bringing the State Back In*. New York: Cambridge University Press.

Falk, R. (1975) *A Study of Future Worlds*. New York: Free Press.

Farouk-Sluglett, M., and P. Sluglett (1990) "Iraq Since 1986: The Strengthening of Saddam," *Middle East Report* 167 (November–December).

Feketekuty, G. (1990) "U.S. Policy on 301 and Super 301," in J. Bhagwati and H. T. Patrick, eds., *Aggressive Unilateralism: America's 301 Trade Policy and the World Trading System*. Ann Arbor: The University of Michigan Press.

Ferguson, Y. H., and R. W. Mansbach (1988) *The Elusive Quest: Theory and International Politics*. Columbia: University of South Carolina Press.

Ferguson, Y. H., and R. W. Mansbach (1989) *The State, Conceptual Chaos, and the Future of International Relations Theory*. Boulder, Colo.: Lynne Rienner Publishers.

Feyerabend, P. (1975) *Against Method*. New York: New Left Books.

Flax, J. (1990) *Thinking Fragments: Psychoanalysis, Feminism, and Postmodernism in the Contemporary West*. Berkeley: University of California Press.

Foster, H., ed. (1983) *The Anti-Aesthetic: Essays on Postmodern Culture*. Port Townsend, Wash.: Bay Press.

Foucault, M. (1977) *Discipline and Punish: The Birth of Prison*. London: Allen Lane.

Fraser, N., and L. Nicholson (1988) "Social Criticism Without Philosophy: An Encounter Between Feminism and Postmodernism," *Theory, Culture and Society* 5.

Frei, D. (1985) "Empathy in Conflict Management," *International Journal: Managing Conflict* (Autumn).

Gadamer, H. G. (1988) *Truth and Method*. New York: Crossroad.

Galtung, J. (1964) "A Structural Theory of Aggression," *Journal of Peace Research* 1.

George, J. (1989) "International Relations and the Search for Thinking Space: Another View of the Third Debate," *International Studies Quarterly* 33:3.

George, J., and D. Campbell (1990) "Patterns of Dissent and the Celebration of Difference: Critical Social Theory and International Relations," *International Studies Quarterly* 34:3 (September).

Giddens, A. (1978) "Positivism and Its Critics," in T. Bottomore and R. Nisbet, eds., *A History of Sociological Analysis*. New York: Basic Books.

Giddens, A. (1984) *The Constitution of Society*. Berkeley: University of California Press.

Giddens, A. (1987a) "Structuralism, Post-Structuralism and the Production of Culture," in A. Giddens and J. H. Turner, eds., *Social Theory Today*. Cambridge, UK: Polity Press.

Giddens, A. (1987b) *The Nation-State and Violence*. Berkeley: University of California Press.

Giddens, A. (1991) *Modernity and Self-Identity: Self and Society in the Late Modern Age*. Stanford, Calif.: Stanford University Press.

Gill, S. (1991) *American Hegemony and the Trilateral Commission*. Cambridge: Cambridge University Press.

Gill, S., and D. Law (1988) *The Global Political Economy: Perspectives, Problems and Policies*. Baltimore, Md.: The Johns Hopkins University Press.

Gilpin, R. (1987) *The Political Economy of International Relations*. Princeton, N.J.: Princeton University Press.

Gowa, J. (1984) "Hegemons, IOs, and Markets," *International Organization* 38:4 (Autumn).

Grant, R., and K. Newland, eds. (1991) *Gender and International Relations*. Bloomington: Indiana University Press.

Haas, E. (1982) "Words Can Hurt You; or, Who Said What to Whom About Regimes," *International Organization* 36:2 (Spring).

Haas, E. (1983) "Regime Decay: Conflict Management and International Organizations, 1945–1981," *International Organization* 37:2 (Spring).

Habermas, J. (1971) *Knowledge and Human Interests*. Boston: Beacon Press.

Habermas, J. (1984) *The Theory of Communicative Action*, trans., T. McCarthy, trans. Boston: Beacon Press.

Haggard, S., and B. Simmons (1987) "Theories of International Regimes," *International Organization* 41:3 (Summer).

Halliday, F. (1987a) "State and Society in International Relations: A Second Agenda," *Millennium* 16:2.

Halliday, F. (1987b) "Vigilantism in International Relations: Kubalkova, Cruickshank and Marxist Theory," *Review of International Studies* 13.

Halliday, F. (1988) "Hidden from International Relations: Women and the International Arena," *Millennium* 17:3 (Winter).

Harding, S. (1987) "Introduction: Is There a Feminist Method?" in S. Harding, ed., *Feminism and Methodology: Social Science Issues.* Bloomington: Indiana University Press.

Harstock, N. (1983) "The Feminist Standpoint: Developing the Ground for a Specifically Feminist Historical Materialism," in S. Harding and M. B. Hintikka, eds., *Discovering Reality.* Dordrecht, Holland: Reidel.

Harstock, N. (1984) "The Barracks Community in Western Political Thought: Prolegomena to a Feminist Critique of War and Politics," in J. Stiegm, ed., *Women's Views of the Public World of Men.* New York: Transnational Publishers.

Harstock, N. (1987) "Rethinking Modernism: Minority Versus Majority Theories," *Cultural Critique* 7.

Hassan, I. (1987) *The Postmodern Turn: Essays in Postmodern Theory and Culture.* Columbus: Ohio State University Press.

Hawkesworth. M. (1989) "Knower, Knowing, Known: Feminist Theory and Claims of Truth," *Signs* 14:3.

Held, D. (1984) *The Idea of the Modern State.* London: Open University Press.

Hess, B., and M. Marx Ferree (1987) "Introduction," *Analyzing Gender: A Handbook of Social Science Research.* Newbury Park, Calif.: Sage.

Higgott, R. A. (1988) *New Directions in International Relations: Australian Perspectives.* Canberra: The Australian National University Press.

Hoffman, M. (1987) "Critical Theory and the Inter-Paradigm Debate," *Millennium* 16:2.

Hollis, M., and S. Smith (1991) "Beware of Gurus: Structure and Action in International Relations," *Review of International Studies* 17:4 (October).

Hollis, M., and S. Smith (1992) "Structure and Action: Further Comment," *Review of International Studies* 18:2 (April).

Holsti, J. K. (1985) *The Dividing Discipline: Hegemony and Diversity in International Theory.* Boston: Allen & Unwin.

Holsti, J. K. (1989) "Mirror, Mirror on the Wall, Which Are the Fairest Theories of All?" *International Studies Quarterly* 33:3.

Hooglund, E. (1991) "The Other Face of War," *The Middle East Report* 170.

hooks, b. (1983) *Feminist Theory from Margin to Center.* Boston: Beacon Press.

hooks, b. (1986) "Sisterhood: Political Solidarity Between Women," *Feminist Review* 23.

Hull, G., P. Bell Scott, and B. Smith, eds. (1982) *All the Women Are White, All the Blacks Are Men but Some of Us Are Brave.* New York: The Feminist Press.

Huntzinger, J. (1987) *Introduction aux relations internationales.* Paris: Editions du Seuil.

Ikenberry, G. J. (1992) "A World Economy Restored: Expert Consensus and the Anglo-American Postwar Settlement," *International Organization* 46:1 (Winter).

Inside U.S. Trade. (various issues, 1989–1991) Washington, DC: Inside Washington Publishers.

Jaggar, A. (1983) *Feminist Politics and Human Nature.* Totowa, N.J.: Rowman and Allenheld.

Jarvis, A. (1989) "Societies, States, and Geopolitics," *Review of International Studies* 15.

Jessop, B. (1982) *The Capitalist State.* London: Macmillan.

Jessop, B. (1986) "Review of *The Nation-State and Violence*," *Capital and Class* 29.

Jessop, B. (1990) *State Theory: Putting Capitalist States in Their Place.* University Park: The Pennsylvania State University Press.

Joseph, G., and J. Lewis (1981) *Common Differences: Conflicts in Black and White Feminist Perspectives.* New York: Anchor Books.

Karol, K. S. (1970) *Guerrillas in Power: The Course of the Cuban Revolution.* New York: Hill and Wang.

Keane, J. (1988) *Civil Society and the State.* London: Verso.

Keenes, E. (1989) "Paradigms of International Relations: Bringing Politics Back In," *International Journal* 44.

Keenes, E., G. Legare, and J.-F. Rioux. (1987) "The Reconstruction of Neo-Realism From Counter-Hegemonic Discourse," *Occasional Papers* 14. Ottawa: Department of Political Science, Carleton University.

Keohane, R. O. (1982) "The Demand for International Regimes," *International Organization* 36:2 (Spring).

Keohane, R. O. (1984) *After Hegemony: Cooperation and Discord in the World Political Economy.* Princeton, N.J.: Princeton University Press.

Keohane, R. O. (1986) "Theory of World Politics: Structural Realism and Beyond," in R. Keohane, ed., *Neorealism and Its Critics.* New York: Columbia University Press.

Keohane, R. O. (1989) "International Relations Theory: Contributions of a Feminist Standpoint," *Millennium* 18:2.

Keohane, R. O., and J. S. Nye, Jr. (1977) *Power and Interdependence.* Boston: Little Brown.

Keyman, E. F. (1993) "The Working of Power in Representation: The Problem of the Other and the Politics of Cultural Difference in International Political Economy," Paper presented at the Annual Meeting of the International Studies Association, Acapulco, Mexico, March.

Keyman, E. F., and J. Jenson (1990) "Must We Be All Postmodern?" *Studies in Political Economy* 31.

Khan, F. (1988) "Ethnopolitics: The Kurdish Factor in the Iraq-Iran War," *Middle East Focus* 10:4 (Summer).

Klein, B. S. (1988) "After Strategy: The Search for Post-Modern Politics of Peace," *Alternatives* 13.

Klein, B. S. (1989) "The Textual Strategies of the Military: Or Have You Read Any Good Defense Manuals Lately," in J. Der Derian and M. J. Shapiro, eds., *International/Intertextual Relations.* Lexington, Mass.: Lexington Books.

Kline, M. (1989) "Women's Oppression and Racism: A Critique of the Feminist Standpoint," in J. Vorst et al., eds., *Race, Class, Gender: Bonds and Barriers.* Toronto: The Society for Socialist Studies/Between the Lines.

Knorr, K., and J. Rosenau, eds. (1969) *Contending Approaches to International Politics*. Princeton, N.J.: Princeton University Press.

Korany, B., ed. (1987) *Analyse des relations internationales: Approches, concepts et données*. Montréal: Gaëtan Morin.

Krasner, S. (1982) "Regimes and the Limits of Realism: Regimes as Autonomous Variables," *International Organization* 36:3 (Spring).

Krasner, S. (1984) "Approaches to the State: Alternative Conceptions and Historical Dynamics," *Comparative Politics* 16:2 (January).

Krasner, S. (1989) "Sovereignty: An Institutional Perspective," in J. A. Caporasa, ed., *The Elusive State*. London: Sage Publications.

Kratochwil, F., and J. G. Ruggie (1986) "International Organization: A State of the Art or an Art of the State," *International Organization* 40:4 (Autumn).

Kuhn, T. (1970) *The Structure of Scientific Revolutions*, 2nd ed. Chicago: University of Chicago Press.

Laclau, E., and Mouffe, C. (1985) *Hegemony and Socialist Strategy*. London: Verso.

Lakatos, I., and A. Musgrave, eds. (1970) *Criticism and the Growth of Knowledge*. Cambridge: Cambridge University Press.

Lapid, Y. (1989) "The Third Debate: On the Prospects of International Theory in a Post-Positivist Era," *International Studies Quarterly* 33:3 (September).

Lash, S. (1987) "Modernity or Modernism?: Weber and Contemporary Social Theory," in S. Lash and S. Whimster, eds., *Max Weber: Rationality and Modernity*. London: Allen & Unwin.

Lather, P. (1988) "Feminist Perspectives on Empowering Research Methodologies," *Women's Studies International Forum* 11:6.

Lather, P. (1991) *Getting Smart: Feminist Research and Pedagogy with/in the Postmodern*. New York: Routledge.

Laudan, L. (1984) *Science and Values*. Berkeley: University of California Press.

Light, M., and A. J. R. Groom, eds. (1985) *International Relations: A Handbook of Current Theory*. London: Pinter.

Linklater, A. (1986) "Realism, Marxism, and Critical International Theory," *Review of International Studies* 12.

Linklater, A. (1990) *Beyond Realism and Marxism: Critical Theory and International Relations*. London: Macmillan.

Lipietz, A. (1987) *Mirages and Miracles*. London: Verso.

Lorde, A. (1984) *Sister Outside*. New York: Crossing Press.

Luke, T. W. (1989) "What's Wrong with Deterrence? A Semiotic Interpretation of National Security Policy," in J. Der Derian and M. J. Shapiro, eds., *International/Intertextual Relations*. Lexington, Mass.: Lexington Books.

Maghroori, R., and B. Ramberg, eds. (1982) *Globalism Versus Realism: International Relations' Third Debate*. Boulder, Colo.: Westview.

Maguire, P. (1984) *Women in Development: An Alternative Analysis*. Amherst: University of Massachusetts Press.

Malson, M., J. F. O'Barr, S. Westphal-Wihl, and M. Wyer, eds. (1989) *Feminist Theory in Practice and Process*. Chicago: University of Chicago Press.

Mann, M. (1984) "Autonomous Power of the State," *Archives européennes de sociologie* 25.

Mann, M. (1986) *The Sources of Social Power.* Cambridge: Cambridge University Press.

Mansueto, C. (1983) "Take the Toys Away from the Boys: Competition and the Nuclear Arms Race," in D. Thompson, ed., *Over Our Dead Bodies: Women Against the Bomb.* London: Virago.

McCanles, M. (1984) "Machiavelli and the Paradoxes of Deterrence," *Diacritics* (Summer).

McKinlay, R. D., and R. Little (1986) *Global Problems and World Order.* Madison: University of Wisconsin Press.

McLennan, G. (1989) *Marxism, Pluralism and Beyond.* Cambridge, UK: Polity Press.

Mead, W. R. (1992) "Bushism, Found," *Harper's Magazine* (September).

Mies, M. (1983) "Towards a Methodology for Feminist Research," in G. Bowles and R. Duelli Klein, eds., *Theories of Women's Studies.* London: Routledge and Keagan Paul.

Milner, H. (1990) "The Political Economy of U.S. Trade Policy: A Study in the Super 301 Provision," in J. Bhagwati and H. T. Patrick, eds., *Aggressive Unilateralism: America's 301 Trade Policy and the World Trading System.* Ann Arbor: The University of Michigan Press.

Mohanty, C., A. Russo, and L. Torres, eds. (1991) *Third World Women and the Politics of Feminism.* Bloomington: Indiana University Press.

Molyneux, M. (1984) "Women in Socialist Societies: Problems of Theory and Practice," in K. Young, C. Wolkowitz, and R. McCullagh, eds., *Of Marriage and the Market: Women's Subordination Internationally and Its Lessons.* London: Routledge and Keagan Paul.

Moraga, C., and G. Anzaldua, eds. (1983) *This Bridge Called My Back: Writings by Radical Women of Color.* New York: Kitchen Table Press.

Morgenthau, H. J. (1967) *Politics Among Nations,* 4th ed. New York: Alfred A. Knopf.

Morgenthau, H. J. (1973) *Politics Among Nations,* 5th ed. New York: Alfred A. Knopf.

Morse, E. L. (1976) *Modernization and the Transformation of International Relations.* New York: The Free Press.

Nash, J., and M. Fernandez-Kelly, eds. (1983) *Women, Men and the International Division of Labor.* Albany: State University of New York Press.

Newland, K. (1975) "Women in Politics: A Global Review," *WorldWatch* (December).

Nielsson, G. P. (1985) "States and Nation Groups: A Global Taxonomy," in E. A. Tiryakian and R. Rogowski, eds., *New Nationalisms of the Developed West.* Boston: Allen.

Olson, W., and N. Onuf (1985) "The Growth of a Discipline Reviewed," in S. Smith, ed., *International Relations: British and American Perspectives.* Oxford: Basic Blackwell.

Onuf, N. G. (1989) *World of Our Making: Rules and Rule in Social Theory and International Relations.* Columbia: University of South Carolina Press.

Peterson, V. S. (1989a) "Sex and the Sovereign State: What's at Stake in Taking Feminism Seriously," unpublished paper (December).

Peterson, V. S. (1989b) "Clarification and Contestation: A Conference on 'Women, the State and War': What Difference Does Gender Make?" unpublished paper.

Peterson, V. S., ed. (1992) *Gendered States: Feminist (Re)Visions of International Relations Theory*. Boulder, Colo.: Lynne Rienner Publishers.

Polkinghorne, D. E. (1988) *Narrative Knowing and the Human Sciences*. Albany: State University of New York.

"Policing Thoughts," (1992) *The Economist* (August 22).

Popper, K. (1970) "Normal Science and Its Dangers," in I. Lakatos and A. Musgrave, eds., *Criticism and the Growth of Knowledge*. Cambridge: Cambridge University Press.

Prescod, M. (1986) *Bringing It All Back Home*. London: Falling Wall Press.

Prowse, M. (1991) "Americans Know Not GATT—and Care Even Less," *Financial Times of London* (May 14).

Ptolemy, K. (1989) "First International Consultation on Refugee Women: Geneva, November 1988," *Canadian Women's Studies* 10:1.

Razamanoglu, C. (1989) *Feminism and the Contradiction of Oppression*. London: Routledge and Keagan Paul.

Reardon, B. (1985) *Sexism and the War System*. New York: Teacher's College Press.

Rennager, N., and M. Hoffman (1992) "Modernity, Postmodernism and International Relations," in J. Doherty, E. Graham, and M. Malek, eds., *Postmodernism and the Social Sciences*. London: Macmillan.

Robertson, C., and I. Berger, eds. (1986) *Women and Class in Africa*. New York: Africa Publishing, Holmes and Meier.

Rorty, R. (1979) *Philosophy and the Mirror of Nature*. Princeton, N.J.: Princeton University Press.

Rorty, R. (1982) *Consequences of Pragmatism*. Brighton: Harvester Press.

Rosenau, J. N., ed. (1976) *In Search of Global Patterns*. New York: Free Press.

Rosenau, J. N. (1982) "Order and Disorder in the Study of World Politics," in R. Maghroori and B. Ramberg, eds., *Globalism Versus Realism: International Relations' Third Debate*. Boulder, Colo.: Westview Press.

Rosenau, J. N. (1986) "Before Cooperation: Hegemons, Regimes, and Habit-Driven Actors in World Politics," *International Organization* 40:4 (Autumn).

Rosenau, J. N. (1990) *Turbulence in World Politics: A Theory of Change and Continuity*. Princeton, N.J.: Princeton University Press.

Rosenau, P. (1988) "Post-Structural, Post-Modern Political Science: Toward Global Paradigm Change?" Paper prepared for the International Political Science Association's Fourteenth World Congress, Washington, D.C.

Rosenau, P. (1990) "Once Again into the Fray: International Relations Confronts the Humanities," *Millennium* 19:1 (Spring).

Rosenberg, J. (1990) "A Non-Realist Theory of Sovereignty," *Millennium* 19:2.

Ruddick, S. (1983) "Pacifying the Forces: Drafting Women in the Interests of Peace," *Signs* 8:3.

Said, E. W. (1979) *Orientalism*. New York: Vintage Books.

Said, E. W. (1991) "The Intellectuals and the War," *Middle East Report* 171 (July–August).

Sampson, A. (1979) *The Seven Sisters*. New York: Bantam Books.

Sen, G., and K. Grown (1987) *Development, Crises and Alternate Visions*. New York: Monthly Review Press.

Shaffer, E. (1983) *Canada's Oil and the American Empire*. Edmonton: Hurtig Publishers.

Shapiro, M. J. (1989) "Representing World Politics: The Sport/War

Intertext," in J. Der Derian and M. Shapiro, eds., *International/ Intertextual Relations*. Lexington, Mass.: Lexington Books.

Singer, J. D. (1976) "Tribal Sins on the QIP Reservation," in J. N. Rosenau, ed., *In Search of Global Patterns*. New York: Free Press.

Sivard, R. L. (1988) *World Military and Social Expenditures*. Washington, D.C.: World Arms Control and Disarmament Agency.

Sjolander, C. T. (1993) "Unilateralism and Multilateralism: The United States and the Negotiation of the GATS," *International Journal* 48 (Winter).

Skocpol, T. (1979) *States and Social Revolutions*. Cambridge: Cambridge University Press.

Skocpol, T. (1980) "Political Reponse to Capitalist Crisis: Neo-Marxist Theories of the State and the Case of the New Deal," *Politics and Society* 10:2.

Skocpol, T. (1985) "Bringing the State Back In: Strategies of Analysis in Current Research," in P. B. Evans, D. Rueschemeyer, and T. Skocpol, eds., *Bringing the State Back In*. New York: Cambridge University Press.

Smith, S. (1987) "Paradigm Dominance in International Relations: The Development of International Relations as a Social Science," *Millennium* 16:2.

Sokoloff, N. (1980) *Between Money and Love: The Dialectics of Women's Home and Market Work*. New York: Praeger.

Solomon, J. F. (1988) *Discourse and Reference in the Nuclear Age*. Norman: University of Oklahoma Press.

Spelman, E. (1988) *Inessential Woman: Problems of Exclusion in Feminist Thought*. Boston: Beacon Press.

Stanley, L., and S. Wise (1983) *Breaking Out: Feminist Consciousness and Feminist Research*. London: Routledge and Keagan Paul.

Stasiulis, D. (1990) "Theorizing Connections: Gender, Race, Ethnicity and Class," in P. Li, ed., *Race and Ethnic Relations in Canada*. Toronto: Oxford University Press.

Stein, A. (1982) "Coordination and Collaboration: Regimes in an Anarchic World," *International Organization* 36:2 (Spring).

Stork, J., and A. M. Lesch (1990) "Background to the Crisis: Why War?" *Middle East Report* 167 (November–December).

(The) Strategic Survey (various issues, 1978–1989). Stockholm: The International Institute for Strategic Studies.

Taylor, C. (1979) *Hegel and Modern Society*. Cambridge: Cambridge University Press.

Taylor, C. (1985) *Philosophy and the Human Sciences*. Cambridge: Cambridge University Press.

Therborn, G. (1986) "Neo-Marxist, Pluralist, Corporatist, Statist Theories and the Welfare State," in A. Kazancigil, ed., *The State in Global Perspective*. Paris: UNESCO Publications.

Thompson, J. B. (1984) *Studies in the Theory of Ideology*. Cambridge, UK: Polity Press.

Tiffin, H. (1990) "Introduction," in I. Adam and H. Tiffin, eds., *Past the Last Post: Theorizing Post-Colonialism and Post-Modernism*. Calgary: University of Calgary Press.

Tilly, C. (1975) *The Formation of National States in Western Europe*. Princeton, N.J.: Princeton University Press.

UNCTAD (1989) *Trade and Development Report, 1989*. New York: United Nations.

UNCTAD (1991) *Trade and Development Report, 1991.* New York: United Nations.

UN Statistical Yearbook. (1980, 1981, 1985, 1989). New York: United Nations Publishing Office.

Vasquez, J. A. (1983) *The Power of Power Politics: A Critique.* New Brunswick, N.J.: Rutgers University Press.

Viotti, P., and M. Kauppi, eds. (1987) *International Relations Theory: Realism, Pluralism, Globalism.* New York: Macmillan.

Volkan, V. D. (1988) *The Need to Have Enemies and Allies.* New York: Jason Aronson.

Walker, R. B. J. (1984) "The Territorial State and the Theme of Gulliver," *International Journal* 39:3.

Walker, R. B. J. (1987) "Realism, Change, and International Political Theory," *International Studies Quarterly* 31:1.

Walker, R. B. J. (1989) "*The Prince* and 'The Pauper': Tradition, Modernity, and Practice in the Theory of International Relations," in J. Der Derian and M. J. Shapiro, eds., *International/Intertextual Relations.* Lexington, Mass.: Lexington Books.

Walker, R. B. J. (1992) "Gender and Critique in the Theory of International Relations," in V. S. Peterson, ed., *Gendered States: Feminist (Re)Visions of International Relations Theory.* Boulder, Colo.: Lynne Rienner Publishers.

Waltz, K. N. (1979) *Theory of International Politics.* Reading, Mass.: Addison-Wesley.

Weber, M. (1948) in H. M. Gerthy, ed., *From Max Weber: Essays in Sociology.* London: Macmillan.

Wendt, A. (1987) "The Agent-Structure Problem in International Affairs Theory," *International Organization* 41:3 (Summer).

Wendt, A. (1991) "Bridging the Theory/Metatheory Gap in International Relations," *Review of International Studies* 17:4 (October).

Wendt, A. (1992a) "Anarchy Is What States Make of It," *International Organization* 46.

Wendt, A. (1992b) "Levels of Analysis vs. Agents and Structures, Part III," *Review of International Studies* 18:2 (April).

Wendt, A., and R. Duvall (1989) "Institutions and International Order," in E.-O. Czempiel and J. N. Rosenau, eds., *Global Problems and Theoretical Challenges.* Lexington, Mass.: Lexington Books.

West, C. (1989) *The American Evasion of Philosophy: A Genealogy of Pragmatism.* Madison: The University of Wisconsin Press.

Whitworth, S. (1989) "Gender in the Inter-Paradigm Debate," *Millennium* 18:2.

Winham, G. (1986) *International Trade and the Tokyo Round Negotiation.* Princeton, N.J.: Princeton University Press.

Winham, G. (1992) *The Evolution of International Trade Agreements.* Toronto: University of Toronto Press.

Wolin, S. S. (1984) "Max Weber: Legitimation, Method, and Politics of Theory," in W. Connolly, ed., *Legitimacy and the State.* New York: New York University Press.

World Bank (1979) *Recognizing the "Invisible" Woman in Development: The World Bank Experience.* Washington, D.C.: World Bank.

Young, K., C. Wolkowitz, and R. McCullagh, eds. (1984) *Of Marriage and the Market: Women's Subordination Internationally and Its Lessons.* London: Routledge and Keagan Paul.

Yuval-Davis, N., and F. Anthias, eds. (1989) *Woman-Nation-State.* London: Macmillan.

Index

About the Contributors

Wayne S. Cox is a lecturer at the Department of Political Studies, Queen's University, Kingston, Ontario.

E. Fuat Keyman is a postdoctoral fellow at the Department of Political Science, Wellesley College, Wellesley, Massachusetts.

Gregg J. Legare is a researcher with Environment Canada.

Mark Neufeld is a member of the Department of Political Science, Trent University, Peterborough, Ontario.

Tony Porter is a member of the Department of Political Science, McMaster University, Hamilton, Ontario.

Susan Judith Ship is a lecturer at the Department of Political Science, University of Ottawa, Ottawa, Ontario.

Claire Turenne Sjolander is a member of the Department of Political Science, University of Ottawa, Ottawa, Ontario.

About the Book

The metatheoretical debates between positivists and postpositivists that characterized the development of IR theory during the 1980s left at least one major question unanswered: What does postpositivist scholarship look like? This book offers an answer to that question, proceeding from the premise that the metatheoretical debates have reached an impasse, and suggesting that scholarship motivated by theoretical reflexivity provides a base on which alternative, more useful, understandings of international relations can be developed.

Sharing a common critical perspective on the traditional development of IR theory, each of the chapters seriously questions the state-centric realist and the positivist assumptions that have guided so much of the scholarship in the field. The authors trace the evolution of the various IR debates, elaborate on the meaning of theoretical reflexivity, consider applications of the approach to important contemporary issues (international trade, the Gulf wars, the global energy regime), and examine the contributions to reflexivity of other contemporary theoretical traditions.